Hey Ranger!

Hang on and paddle harder! (Bureau of Land Management/Photo by LuVerne Grussing)

Hey Ranger!

True Tales of Humor & Misadventure from America's National Parks

Jim Burnett

TAYLOR TRADE PUBLISHING
Dallas • Lanham • Boulder • New York • Toronto • Oxford

First Taylor Trade Publishing edition 2005

This Taylor Trade Publishing paperback edition of *Hey Ranger!* is an original publication. It is published by arrangement with the author.

Published by Taylor Trade Publishing
An imprint of The Rowman & Littlefield Publishing Group, Inc.
4501 Forbes Boulevard, Suite 200
Lanham, MD 20706

Distributed by NATIONAL BOOK NETWORK

Library of Congress Cataloging-in-Publication Data

Burnett, Jim.
Hey Ranger! : true tales of humor and misadventure from America's national parks / Jim Burnett.— 1st Taylor Trade ed.
p. cm.
Includes bibliographical references and index.
ISBN 1-58979-191-6 (pbk. : alk. paper)
1. National parks and reserves—United States—Anecdotes. 2. Outdoor life—United States—Anecdotes. 3. Accidents—United States—Anecdotes. 4. National parks and reserves—United States—Humor. 5. Outdoor life—United States—Humor. 6. Burnett, Jim—Anecdotes. 7. Park rangers—United States—Biography—Anecdotes. 8. United States—Description and travel—Anecdotes. I. Title.
E160.B77 2005
333.78'3'0973—dc22

2004021056

™ The paper used in this publication meets the minimum requirements of American National Standard for Information Sciences—Permanence of Paper for Printed Library Materials, ANSI/NISO Z39.48-1992.

Manufactured in the United States of America.

Contents

Foreword: Rangers to the Rescue

During an early spring trip to Shenandoah National Park, my sons and I got caught in an unexpected snowstorm. Over the last few years, we have been hiking portions of the Appalachian Trail, and this particular weekend we had chosen to hike into Shenandoah in Virginia. By the time we reached Skyline Drive and were to catch a ride back to our car (18 miles away), snow had closed the road, leaving us stranded.

Fortunately, National Park Service rangers found us and drove us through the snow back to our car. We were only three of who knows how many people who were rescued that day, and it was only one day out of 365. What struck me most about this experience is that no matter what the "normal" job of these rangers—providing education, clearing trails, enforcing the law—both of them stopped what they were doing to help us.

The staff of the Park Service is truly outstanding. Nearly all rangers are Jacks and Jills of many trades and can be counted on to fill in as needed. The public considers the Park Service one of the most admired federal agencies, and its staff has an esprit de corps that is referenced by management experts.

Millions of visitors tour the national parks each year, and many of them report that these once-in-a-lifetime visits are made even more memorable by interaction with a ranger. Although many of the visitor-ranger encounters shared here by Jim are memorable for other reasons, most visitors report that the campfire stories, historic tours, and wildlife hikes led by rangers were unforgettable experiences.

This past summer, my family and I had a chance to tour 12 national parks. It was a trip of a lifetime. And along with the spectacular, awe-inspiring vistas at Grand Canyon and the magnificent cliff dwellings at Mesa Verde, the most memorable experiences involved park rangers, such as the Grand Canyon ranger who brought the exploration of the Colorado River to life with historical detail and vivid imagery of John Wesley Powell's arduous adventure scores of years before. But an alarming trend is emerging in our national parks and was evident in 11 of the 12 parks we visited. All but one of those parks were reducing the number of seasonal or full-time Park Service staff because of insufficient annual funding.

Regrettably, the national parks have suffered from budget parsimony for years. Meager operating budget increases have been eaten up by inflation, Homeland Security expenses, and other mandated, but unfunded, programs. Consequently, the budget available to many individual park superintendents for daily park operations has declined significantly, and across the system, national parks operate, on average, with only two-thirds of the needed funding. The impact of this shortfall on the experiences of visitors and the condition of the parks is unmistakable.

It shouldn't be this way. America's national parks are among our most treasured places and rangers play a vital role in safeguarding these integral parts of America's heritage. Not only do they keep us out of trouble when we venture off the trails or hike in a snowstorm, but park rangers breathe life into the history preserved in our National Park System. For more information or to help encourage Congress and the administration to protect the national parks and the park rangers who celebrate and preserve these great places, please see the listing of organizations such as the National Parks Conservation Association in the appendix at the end of this book.

I hope you enjoy reading Jim's stories as much as I did and that his words instill in you a new appreciation for the nation's park rangers and the landscapes, historic sites, and cultural treasures they work to protect every day.

Tom Kiernan
President, National Parks Conservation Association

Introduction

America's national parks include a remarkable variety of sights and experiences, from tiny Thaddeus Kosciuszko National Memorial in Pennsylvania (.02 acres) to the 13.2 million-acre Wrangell-St. Elias National Park and Preserve in Alaska. People from all over the world made about 270 million visits last year to parks from Acadia to Zion and to more than 380 other sites in our national park system. While the majority of those visits provided plenty of fun and years of great memories, it is inevitable that bringing that many people into close contact with Mother Nature (and with each other) will also result in some unforgettable and occasionally humorous misadventures.

During a thirty-year career as a National Park Service Ranger, I had the opportunity to live and work in parks all across the country and to encounter literally thousands of park visitors in an amazing variety of situations. My fellow rangers and I were often greeted by the phrase "Hey, ranger," but the way that those two little words are spoken can convey a world of different meanings. Depending upon the circumstances, they might mean, "Hi, how're you doing?" "Help, come quick!" or sometimes, "Oops, I sure didn't expect to see *you* here!" Frequently, the term heralded the reporting of momentous or even bizarre events—and some of those situations are what this book is all about.

Two other comments have been heard many times by virtually anyone who has worked in a park: "I always wanted to be a ranger" and "I sure wish I had your job!" I always took those words as a compliment and I am really glad that I had the opportunity, but like any other career, rangering does have its moments. Included in the following chapters are a few behind-the-scenes glimpses at some unusual aspects of life as a ranger—and as one of those unsung heroes, a ranger's spouse.

Most of the events described in this book are taken directly from my own experiences during three decades of life in the parks. A few others, which are based on official reports or accounts from fellow rangers, were simply too good to leave out. Although many of the following stories are based on some degree of misfortune or ineptitude on the part of park visitors (or sometimes even myself), the tone of the book is intended to be light, so I have included only those events that had at least a relatively happy ending. It's not my intention to poke too much fun at anyone, so where appropriate, the names have been changed or eliminated to protect the innocent (or the guilty, as the case may be).

I've grouped these tales into sections, based on the park where the situation took place. At the beginning of each section, I'll introduce the area involved to help set the stage and make it easier for you to visualize the action as the stories unfold. Outdoor adventures are a little bit like buying real estate—they're all about location, location, location—and none of these episodes is likely to have occurred in your neighborhood!

For those of you who don't have firsthand experience with the federal bureaucracy, one more piece of information will help you understand some terminology. The National Park Service manages hundreds of sites with an almost dizzying array of names, including national parks, monuments, historical parks, historic sites, memorials, recreation areas, rivers, seashores, preserves, and more. Just to keep life simple, throughout the book I'll refer to all of these areas simply as "parks."

As you read some of these accounts, you may think, "No, that couldn't have really happened!" Believe me, it really did. For many current-day visitors to national parks the "great outdoors" is an alien environment, and most of what they know about dealing with the natural world comes from a TV program or magazine article. The expression, "I know just enough to be dangerous" applies in a big way to some people who decide to try a canoe trip, climb a mountain, spend a night in a campground, or even just take a short hike on a nature trail.

I've also concluded that a few park visitors take their goal to "get away from it all" a little too seriously and simply leave their brains at home when they go on vacation. As a result, they end up doing things that they would never dream of attempting in their native habitat, whether that happens to be a big city, suburbia, or a small town. Sometimes this situation is compounded when people try to cram too much fun into too little time, resulting in a trip that might more accurately be called "wreck-reation" than recreation.

Finally, a quote from novelist Will Henry sums up the root cause of some people's misadventures: "The Lord pours in the brains of some with teaspoons, and still gets his arm joggled even so."

Now, I know that none of my readers fall into any of the above categories, so I trust you will enjoy these stories with a clear conscience. However, just to help ensure that one of your trips won't show up in a sequel to this book or on the evening news, I'll share a few tips in the final chapter, "Don't be a Victim of Your Vacation." I hope they'll help make your next visit to a park a memorable one for all the right reasons, so whenever you have a chance to say, "Hey, ranger!" the only thing you'll need to add is, "Have a great day!"

Setting the Stage: Lake Mead National Recreation Area

In the early 1930s, the government was looking for a site to construct a dam on the Colorado River for purposes of controlling flooding, generating electricity, and providing a reliable source of water for the desert Southwest. They found an ideal site about an hour's drive southeast of Las Vegas, at a point where the Colorado is confined in a deep, narrow canyon. When work on the massive Hoover Dam was completed in 1936, more than a hundred miles of the Colorado River disappeared under one of the largest artificially created bodies of water in the world, now known as Lake Mead.

The Bureau of Reclamation still operates the dam, which over the years has been called both Boulder Dam and Hoover Dam. That agency recognized that this huge body of water in the middle of the desert would be a magnet for recreational use, so they entered into an agreement with the National Park Service (NPS) to manage public use of the lake and the surrounding shoreline. A second dam was constructed in the late 1940s about 70 miles downstream on the Colorado, impounding Lake Mohave. The NPS also assumed responsibility for recreational use in that area, and in 1964 Congress established Lake Mead National Recreation Area, which includes both Lake Mead and Lake Mohave.

As the name implies, a "national recreation area" differs from a "national park" primarily in its focus on active recreation, such as boating, fishing, and water skiing, as opposed to a greater emphasis on preserving the natural scene. Recreation areas also tend to provide more development, such as paved boat ramps and large marinas, and some may allow activities such as hunting, which are not permitted in national parks.

Lake Mead National Recreation Area is an enormous area, and this size and the distance between ranger stations make for some real challenges for the park staff. The park includes about 1.5 million acres, and Lake Mead alone has 550 miles of shoreline and covers 233 square miles. One source states that the lake is 115 miles in length, which works out to a long boat ride! The trip by road from one place in this park to another can be even longer, which means that in case of an emergency, it can take quite a while for help to arrive. It's also a busy place, with more than 7.5 million visits a year.

This is serious desert country, with lots of rugged, rocky canyons, bare mountains and not a lot of greenery, except along the lakeshore itself. The desert has its own unique form of beauty, and if you're lucky enough to visit during a rare wet spring, the wildflower display is spectacular. When it comes to appreciating the desert landscape, most people either love it or hate it—this is a land of extremes in many ways.

Most of the following stories occurred at or near Willow Beach, a developed area located near the upper end of Lake Mohave and 13 miles downstream from Hoover Dam at a wide spot in Black Canyon. That canyon continues downstream from Willow Beach for about another 11 miles, where the terrain suddenly widens out into a real lake in much more open country.

The result in the vicinity of Willow Beach is something of a hybrid between a lake and the original Colorado River, and many of the locals still refer to it as "the river" rather than a lake. The canyon walls confine the water to a fairly narrow width, ranging anywhere from several hundred yards at wide spots like Willow Beach to some stretches where the "lake" is less than one hundred feet wide. Black Canyon is appropriately named, and in places the bare, rocky walls run almost straight up for hundreds of feet. Depending upon the weather and time of day, the canyon can be strikingly beautiful or downright menacing.

At the time I was assigned there, Willow Beach was often a busy place and included a ranger station, a large NPS campground, a picnic area, housing for two rangers and two maintenance employees, a boat ramp, and a privately-operated resort with a motel, restaurant, store, sizeable marina, and other facilities. The boat ramp and the resort are still there, somewhat scaled down, but the campground and most of the park-operated facilities have been removed because they were located in areas at serious risk from flash flooding.

A real surprise for first-time visitors to Willow Beach is the cold water in the river. Year-round, the water varies little from a temperature of 52°. That's chilly anytime, but dramatically so when the surrounding air temperature is 120° or more (measured in the shade!) How can that be, you ask? A lot of visitors did just that, and some still wouldn't believe me when I told them how cold the water was, until they dipped a toe or finger into the river.

Hoover Dam is 726 feet high, so the water in Lake Mead impounded behind the dam is several hundred feet deep. This may be the desert, but far below the surface the water stays cold year-round. The water discharged through the dam and into the river, while not taken from the bottom of the lake, is still quite chilly and remains so for about the first 18 miles or so of river below the dam. This clear, cold water makes this part of Lake Mohave ideal habitat for rainbow trout, and Willow Beach has long been known in fishing circles as a good spot to catch some "big ones."

This cold water made a big difference in the kind of visitors we got at Willow Beach. Since the contrast between the air and water temperatures made it uncomfortable or even dangerous for people to be in the water very long, that part of the river was closed to water skiing and swimming. The narrow, twisting canyon also was simply not safe for water skiing. As a result, visitors who were interested in those activities went to other locations in the recreation area. Willow Beach tended to attract both family groups and an older crowd who came primarily to fish, camp, or just take it easy. As you'll see in the next few chapters, older doesn't always mean wiser, and this little desert oasis was certainly not without its share of adventures.

For more information about Lake Mead National Recreation Area, see the park's website at www.nps.gov/lame, write to the park at 601 Nevada Way, Boulder City, NV 89005, or phone 702-293-8907.

2

The Snakes Aren't Always in the Grass

In the previous chapter, I talked about the cold water that exists all year in the upper end of Lake Mohave. In case you missed that discourse, all you really need to know at this point is that the water temperature in the narrow canyon downstream from Hoover Dam stays very close to 52° year-round. That cold water led to some interesting adventures, one of which involved a rattlesnake.

You may recall from a long-ago biology class that snakes are cold-blooded, which contrary to popular belief does not refer to their attitude, as in "cold-blooded killers," but instead to the fact that, unlike mammals, they can't regulate their body temperature. This is why they become inactive in cold weather, and you often see snakes out in the open sunning themselves on a cool day. This fact, combined with that cold water in the river below Hoover Dam, creates the potential for some unusual situations.

Lake Mead *is* in the desert, and we had our fair share of rattlesnakes. Occasionally, snakes would end up in the cold water, perhaps in the process of trying to swim to the other side. Yes, rattlesnakes and their cousins like water moccasins can swim, a cheering thought you can keep in mind on your next dip in the creek or tubing expedition down your favorite river. You may know why the chicken crossed the road, but I have absolutely no idea why the snake crossed the river—or at least tried to.

Because the cold water in the Colorado River below Hoover Dam quickly affected their metabolism, these snakes would usually fall into a stupor during their swim and end up floating on top of the water. To a casual observer, it appeared that these critters had gone to that great desert in the sky, or wherever it is snakes go for their final destination.

One afternoon two fishermen happened to come upon such a slumbering serpent and made one of those infamous decisions known as an assumption. ("Assumption" is a term that traces its origins to the root word "assume," which meant **A**ctions **S**eldom **S**upported **U**nder **M**eticulous **E**xamination.)

Assuming that the snake was dead, the fishermen decided to take it home, apparently intending to use its various component parts to make belt buckles, hat bands, necklaces, and other works of folk art that appeal to a certain segment of the population. After spotting the seemingly dead snake floating in the water, they fished the hapless reptile out with a boat paddle and tossed it into the bottom of their boat. They then went back to the business at hand, which was drifting lazily down the river and fishing.

The outcome proves that they really should have paid better attention back in school. Remember when a teacher said something like, "Someday you'll need to know this, and then you'll thank me for making you learn it?" This statement was often made in connection with a topic that was either really boring, really complicated, or really obscure, but the teacher was often right. These fishermen probably heard something similar in biology class when they were studying about reptiles being cold-blooded, but did they pay attention? Noooooo. Boy, would they be sorry!

As was often the case when something had gone awry in the park, my first inkling of trouble came when a couple of visitors flagged me down as I was on boat patrol on the upper end of Lake Mohave. "Hey, Ranger! I'm not exactly sure what's happening upriver, but maybe you'd better go check on . . . ."

In the great rattlesnake caper, the "reporting party," as he or she is often referred to in the subsequent report, said he had found a boat drifting down the river more or less unoccupied. It contained the normal assortment of fishing gear and a couple of partially consumed cans of beverages, but strangely enough, no people. It did, however, contain one unusual passenger: a rather feisty rattlesnake.

Since these boaters were quite a distance upstream from the ranger station and recognized that this situation just might suggest that someone was in difficulty, they decided to go have a look for themselves. This group *had* paid attention in class and quickly deduced that if there was a strong current in the river and the boat was drifting downstream, the trouble was probably *up*stream from the place they found the unmanned boat.

Keeping a close eye on the snake, they towed the (almost) empty boat to the bank and shoved it up on a sandbar, while they sent their buddies in a second boat downriver to look for a ranger. The first boatload then headed upriver. It didn't take them long to spot two guys on a gravel bar on the edge of the water. They were very wet and jumping up and down to get the attention of their potential rescuers. By the time I got the word and met up with the group, everybody had been reunited with their respective boats, and it didn't take long to get to the bottom of the story.

The water in the river was cold enough to put the snake into suspended animation, but once it was fished out and tossed into the full sun on the inside surface of that boat, it didn't take long for a revival of sorts to take place. A few minutes after the boaters pulled the snake out of the water and went back to fishing, they heard an ominous sound. If you've ever heard the warning "buzz" of a rattlesnake, you probably won't ever forget it. I've heard that sound myself quite a few times, but thankfully none of them were while I was sitting in a small boat in the middle of a river, with that chilling rattle coming from the immediate vicinity of my feet.

It apparently didn't take these two fishermen very long to come to a consensus—that their boat wasn't big enough for them and the snake, and he wasn't showing any interest in leaving. Fortunately, they were among the minority of boaters who take safety instructions seriously, and they were actually wearing their life jackets. If they hadn't been, this whole scenario might have had a tragic rather than a comic ending. As it was, they both jumped overboard and started swimming to the nearest bank of the river, which was thankfully only about thirty feet away. Their boat, which had been drifting along with the motor off, continued on its way downstream until their Good Samaritans intercepted it.

By the time I arrived on the scene, the snake was nowhere to be seen. The official version related to me was that it must have vacated the boat on its own before the fishermen returned to reclaim their craft. Whether the snake's exit, either from the boat or from the present world, was helped along by some of these guys, I'll never know. This is probably a good example of an appropriate use of the "don't ask, don't tell" rule, since I wasn't highly motivated to start beating the brush on the gravel bar looking for a reptilian *corpus delicti*. The fishermen were satisfied that their unwanted passenger was no longer onboard their boat, and, under the circumstances, that was good enough for me.

There is a story in *Aesop's Fables* about a peasant who found a snake half dead with cold and decided to help it out by holding it close to his body to warm it up. When the snake revived, the man was fatally bitten for his efforts, providing a classic example of ingratitude. You could probably draw a modern parallel to this fable in the experience of these two fishermen. See, and you didn't believe your English teacher years ago when you were told that there really was a practical application for all of those classic tales you had to study!

Similar snake encounters have occurred at other parks. Rangers at Bighorn Canyon National Recreation Area in Montana reported that on a summer day two men named Randy and Ryan were boating in Afterbay Reservoir. Randy spotted a rattlesnake in the water and apparently acting on the time-honored principle that the best defense is a good offense, whacked the snake with an oar.

His explanation later was that the snake might decide to climb into his boat. Ryan, apparently confident of his friend's prowess with an oar, made another of those infamous assumptions, and concluded that the snake was dead and grabbed it. Unfortunately for Ryan, the snake had only been temporarily stunned and it reacted as snakes are inclined to do after they have been whacked in a non-lethal fashion with a boat oar or any other object and then picked up by their assailant: It bit Ryan, in this particular case on his right index finger.

In retrospect, Ryan may have wished that he had paid more attention in English class in school, in which case he might have recalled a line from *Macbeth*: "We have scotch'd the snake, not kill'd it." The noble Macbeth had a slightly different context in mind, but the underlying point holds true: When it comes to snakes, things are not always as they appear.

Ranger Scott Taylor provided initial emergency care and removed a ring from Ryan's finger before the hand could swell and create further problems with the tight-fitting jewelry. Ryan was then taken to a hospital for further treatment. Both men admitted that they'd planned on killing the snake and taking its rattles.

The snake had his full measure of revenge for Randy's ungentlemanly use of that oar, since further investigation by Ranger Lance Twombly revealed that Randy was wanted on an outstanding warrant. As a result, he was placed under arrest and for good measure was also issued a citation for disturbing wildlife. The two men had also been cited for a traffic violation the previous night, and evidence in their camp site indicated that they'd consumed large quantities of alcohol, perhaps explaining in part how they got into this fix with the snake. They'd obviously have been better off if they'd avoided scotching the snake *and* themselves.

Another good example of the wisdom of "letting sleeping snakes lie" occurred at Lake Meredith National Recreation Area in Texas. A group was hiking on a trail above Harbor Bay on an early June morning and came across a rattlesnake. The snake did not move, even when prodded. One man in the group assumed that the snake was dead and apparently with the good intention of moving the snake so it wouldn't frighten anyone else who happened by, picked it up by the tail.

This provides a good opportunity to mention four highly recommended rules concerning snakes: 1) just leave them alone; 2) never make assumptions about whether a snake is dead or alive based on its level of activity, because looks can be very deceiving; 3) if it's just not in your genetic makeup to obey rules 1 and 2 or if the situation absolutely, positively, beyond a shadow of a doubt demands that you take some action concerning the snake, at least never pick it up; and 4) if for some reason beyond my comprehension you decide to break rules 1, 2 and 3, never pick up a snake by the tail, because that leaves the "business end" of the snake free to put you in a Melancholy Situation.

During my three decades of rangering, I occasionally encountered people who seemed determined to break all of the above rules, along with a number of other common-sense principles. The term "daredevil" applies to some of these people and comes from the root word "dares," which stands for **D**isregard **A**ll **R**easonable **E**xpert **S**uggestions.

In the situation at Lake Meredith, the "dead" snake suddenly became very much alive and did what most snakes do if picked up by the tail: It bit the man—not once, but twice. The man finally made a good decision and dropped the snake, which became aggressive and followed the group for a short distance up the slope. The victim was taken to a hospital, where he required five vials of anti-venom and surgery the following day due to extreme swelling in his hand, wrist, and elbow.

One last snake story took place back at Lake Mead, right in the middle of civilization. (Well, there were a few man-made structures in the vicinity, which certainly passes for "civilization" in the more remote sections of northwest Arizona.) The Willow Beach Ranger Station had a small exhibit and information area at one end and rest rooms at the other. Our limited office space was located in the middle, so the work area shared a common wall with the men's rest room. The rest rooms were left open 24 hours a day.

Early one summer morning, I had just walked into the office to take care of some of the inevitable paperwork. I had noticed a car parked out front, which was normal when a visitor stopped to use the comfort station. Through the wall I heard the familiar sound of the stall door in the men's rest room bang shut, but a couple of seconds later I heard a blood-curdling scream coming from that area. I dashed through the adjoining lobby and out onto the front porch of the building just in time to see a very large middle-aged man struggling mightily to make haste in leaving the comfort station. His struggle was mainly due to the fact that he was still trying to get his trousers pulled back up into their normal position, so his freedom of motion was severely restricted. Other than his awkward situation, I couldn't see any obvious reason for his panic.

The poor guy made it about half way to his car before he got his act together, so to speak, at which point he stopped and stood there, gasping for breath. I wasn't sure if he was having a heart attack or some other problem, but since I could now approach him without embarrassment on the part of either of us, I circled around to approach him from the front and asked the least compromising question I could think of under the circumstances.

"Is everything OK, sir?"

The man noticed me for the first time and raised a trembling hand back toward the rest room. This would normally be a prime moment for a "Hey, ranger!" greeting, but the man was still having trouble getting enough breath to speak. Finally, he was able to utter a single word in a quavering voice: "Rattlesnake!"

I glanced back toward the men's room door and saw that someone had propped it open during the night, using a large rock as a doorstop. Since the rest rooms were not air conditioned, this happened with some regularity during the hotter months of the year, although when even nighttime temperatures often remained above the century mark, any "cooling" effect provided by the open door was questionable.

A theory was already forming in my mind, but I continued over to the man to make sure he was really okay. As he calmed down, he was able to relate the following story. He had gone into the stall, closed the door, and was about to take his position on the appropriate plumbing fixture when he heard the rattle of a snake. As he turned his head, he spotted the rattler coiled up next to the wall, in the corner of the stall. The snake had obviously crawled in through the open door and found a cooler spot on the concrete floor to escape the heat. Having gotten comfortable, the reptile apparently objected to sharing its spot with anything, or anybody, else.

Now that the man had escaped unscathed, he was able to see some humor in his situation. Shaking his head, he commented, "I'm glad that I didn't get bitten, but I'm really glad I don't have to explain to anybody how I got bitten in the part of my anatomy that was closest to that snake!"

Just for the record, I was also very glad that I didn't have to administer first aid in such a situation.

Now, some of you may be wondering about the outcome for the snake. Removing rattlesnakes and similar critters from such situations are listed in a ranger's job description under that infamous catch-all category "Other Duties as Assigned." After it was captured, the snake was relocated to a spot far from the campground and other visitor facilities—and I definitely did not pick it up by its tail!

I trust the adventures of these visitors have been both entertaining and instructive, because there are some things in life that you just don't want to learn from first-hand experience! That's certainly true when it comes to snakes, an observation confirmed by Josh Billings, a nineteenth century American humorist and essayist. He noted, "It's a wise man who profits by his own experience, but it's a good deal wiser one who lets the rattlesnake bite the other fellow." Hopefully, you and any "other fellows" who happen to be around if a snake enters the picture will be the wisest of them all, so that nobody gets bitten. Just remember—when it comes to snakes, don't make any assumptions!

3

Leave It to the Beaver

Willow Beach, where I spent most of my assignment at Lake Mead National Recreation Area, is located on the Colorado River, about thirteen miles downstream from Hoover Dam. Technically the upper end of Lake Mohave, the river at this point flows through a steep, rocky canyon. The marina, campground, and other visitor facilities at Willow Beach were located at a point where several wide side canyons intersected the Colorado, creating enough level ground for those facilities. Over time, a long, sandy beach developed at the mouth of these side canyons, creating a place where a few hardy willow trees could actually grow. In addition to providing some welcome shade, this also saved the early settlers a lot of thought when it came time to naming the place.

Because the river is contained within the walls of Black Canyon in this area, water levels from Willow Beach upstream to the dam are determined by the discharge of water through Hoover Dam. When demand for electricity is higher, more water is released to drive the generators at the dam, and when demand drops, water releases also drop. As a general rule, weekends, when there was usually reduced need for electricity in places like Phoenix and Southern California, brought lower water.

This situation can cause fluctuations of several feet in the water level in Black Canyon in a matter of only a few hours, creating interesting challenges for boaters who fail to get—or listen to—some basic information before starting their trip. More than one group has ventured upstream, beached their boat on a nice sandbar on Friday evening, and set up camp for the weekend. When they woke up the next morning, they found that the river level had dropped and their boat was high and dry. Depending upon the size of the boat and how far it was from the water, they sometimes had to wait until Sunday night or even Monday morning for the river level to rise enough to float their boat.

Even at moderate water levels, the river can get pretty shallow in the last several miles below the big dam, and the rocky bottom can be pretty unforgiving to propellers on boat motors. A couple of visitors learned this the hard way one day, and I got caught in the aftermath.

I had just finished checking the campground and resort area and was about ready to head out for a patrol of the river when I saw a boat with a couple of guys approaching the dock next to the launch ramp. They had a rig favored by a lot of older fishermen on that part of the river—about a fourteen-foot aluminum boat with a small outboard. The motor seemed to be running pretty rough, so I waited to make sure they made it to the dock okay. As soon as they tied up, one of them spotted me, and I knew right off something was up.

When you work with the public for a while, you learn to spot an unhappy camper from quite a distance, and this guy had a good head of steam up as he headed my way. I decided to try the "disarming" approach. I put on my best ranger smile and headed his way.

"Hi, how's it going?"

No sale—this guy was loaded for bear! In no uncertain terms, I was told that it was a disgrace that the government didn't do something to control those awful beavers in the river, and I should get right to work and take care of that problem!

One of the interesting things about a ranger's job is that just when you think you've run into most of the weird situations, you find one that's totally off the map. Although there were in fact a few beavers that lived along the river, they had never caused a problem that I was aware of. (These beavers had dens in the banks of the river, and didn't try to dam up the Colorado!) As a result, I was totally mystified by this guy's comment.

Fortunately, I was saved from having to ask any additional questions when the second man chimed in from the boat.

"Yeah, just come have a look at this!" As he talked, the man tilted the outboard motor on the stern of the boat so the propeller was out of the water. I walked over to the dock, the first man right alongside, and saw a familiar sight—a metal prop with its blades badly chipped and bent from hitting the rocks on the bottom of the shallow river. This particular prop was in especially bad shape, but I was still having a hard time making any connection to beavers.

"We couldn't figure out what was going on until we talked to that other ranger up the river," the man said. "That's when he explained to us about the beavers."

Now I was stumped for sure, because I was the only ranger on duty within at least forty miles, and the mystery of the beavers was nowhere closer to being solved. There's an old saying that God gave people two ears and one mouth for a reason—that we should listen twice as much as we talk. In situations like this, I usually adopted this approach until I saw where the conversation was headed.

Boater number two quickly jumped back in. "Yes, you guys need to put up signs warning boaters to take this seriously, until you can trap those little *#@* and get them off the river! Who'd ever imagine that they could do this kind of damage to a prop?"

All eyes turned back to solemnly study the pitiful prop, and the conversation faltered. I realized this was a good chance for a noncommittal comment to try to keep things moving.

"Yes, it is hard to imagine, isn't it?" I agreed. This was easy to say, since I still had absolutely no clue what they were talking about.

Number two was now the expert commentator, and he rose to the occasion.

"Yeah, when the ranger explained it to us, it started to make sense. I've heard somewhere that beavers have to keep gnawing on something almost all the time, or their teeth will grow so fast that they can't shut their mouths, and then they'll die. Since there aren't enough trees along this river for them to gnaw on, they've had to start chomping anything they can find. That's why they'll even chew on props on boat motors out of desperation."

This last "fact" was delivered with a suitable glare in my direction, since it was obviously my fault as the local representative of the might and majesty of the United States Government that suitable trees were in such short supply here in the desert.

It was number one's turn now to hammer the point home. "It makes sense when you think about it. Those props are kinda shiny, and that's sure to attract the attention of those poor beavers. If you're just drifting along and fishing, that prop hanging down there in the water is bound to be too much for them beavers to resist. Besides, these new props are made out of that soft aluminum or somethin'—not like the good un's we used to get."

I read once that you should never consider a day to be a success unless you've learned something new. On that basis, today was certainly a winner for me—but I'll refrain from commenting about what I had just learned from this conversation.

Fortunately, I was saved from further discussion by the arrival of a couple of other boats who were waiting rather impatiently for their turn to tie up at the "courtesy dock" and unload their gear. I think their comment was along the lines of, "You guys gonna spend the night there, or what?" Number one took the hint and headed for the parking lot to bring down their truck and boat trailer, while number two lowered the motor back into the water and got ready to crank it up and back away from the dock. I was free to go, with the parting admonition to check into this situation "right away." I assured them that I would do just that, and I intended to start by heading upriver and seeing if I could locate this mystery ranger.

As it turned out, I didn't have far to go. Less than two miles upstream, I spotted a familiar boat headed back downriver. It was the local state game warden, who sometimes came out to help us check fishing licenses and do boating safety checks. He had put onto the river at the next launch ramp about twenty miles downstream, so I hadn't realized he was in the area. It didn't take long to put the pieces of the puzzle together.

I eased my outboard down to idle and waited for him to come alongside. We had a great working relationship, and I could tell that he was having to work pretty hard to suppress a grin. We exchanged greetings and there was a brief silence.

"So," I asked, "seen any beaver up toward the dam today?"

The warden burst out laughing, and I couldn't help but join in. "I can't believe you pulled such a wild tale on those guys. What in the world were you thinking?"

My friend at least had the grace to look a little sheepish. "Well, those guys wouldn't listen to any advice when I tried to warn them about the shallow water. Said they'd been boating before I was even born, but they couldn't figure out why their motor was vibrating so much. When I took a look at the prop, I knew right away what had happened. I can't believe they didn't feel the prop hitting all those rocks. I offered to make sure they got back OK, but they said they didn't need any help. I figured I'd catch up with them again before long if they had any trouble."

After a brief pause, he continued. "Sorry, but they were such a pain that I just couldn't resist. I take it you talked to them."

"Well, actually, they did most of the talking. And if I were you, I'd give them a few more minutes to make sure they're long gone before you show your face down there. Oh, and one last thing. If I run into those guys again, I'll be sure to give them your phone number if they need any follow-up on our 'beaver problem!'"

"Knock, Knock, Who's There?"

For several of my Park Service assignments, we had the somewhat dubious "benefit" of living in government housing right in the park. While most people assumed that our house was provided at no cost by the NPS, in fact we were just tenants, paying rent to Uncle Sam for places of widely varying quality. In recent years, park housing has come under considerable political scrutiny, and the NPS is under a lot of pressure to eliminate as much housing as possible.

The reality is that most rangers would prefer to have the chance to buy their own homes, which makes a lot more sense economically than being renters for most or all of their careers. Sometimes, however, this is virtually impossible, since at some parks there is no privately owned housing available for purchase within many, many miles of the ranger's duty station.

In other parks, the housing in reasonable proximity to the park is so expensive that even the most highly paid employee in the government could have trouble affording a place. Without park housing rangers would end up living an hour or two's drive, or more, away from the park. The politicians don't seem to feel that's a problem, but when an emergency arises late at night and a visitor has to wait two hours for someone to show up and help, I predict that there will be some mighty unhappy customers.

That ability to respond to emergencies 24/7 (that is, any time, any day) is the main reason some rangers end up living in park housing. How they get the call for help varies from place to place. Sometimes the houses are at least tucked away on a little side road, and some degree of privacy is possible. In those cases, visitors with a problem report it via a payphone in the campground or outside the ranger station—or these days often by cell phone. In other cases, the rangers have the chance to get notified by a knock on their front door.

At Lake Mead National Recreation Area, the isolated location for most of the developed areas makes park housing the only practical solution. At Willow Beach, there were four houses used by park employees. These were separate units connected by a common roofline—a kind of cozy quadraplex design—with rangers living in the two end units, and maintenance personnel living in the two center units. Each house had a large sign hanging over the front door, with our name and the words "Park Ranger" or similar title. We were directly behind the ranger station itself and right across from the entrance to the campground. In short, we were pretty "accessible," and virtually all of the regular visitors to the area knew where we lived, in case we were needed.

Sometimes there really were valid, life-threatening emergencies, and we were glad to be close by. Other times we recognized that the level of "emergency" was in the eye of the beholder, but some of these could provide a little comic relief, even at 2 a.m. In short, when there was a knock on the door, we never knew what to expect. There was one consolation—we could be pretty sure it wasn't someone wanting to sell us vinyl siding or magazine subscriptions.

One lesson we learned early on was to always keep the door locked, even if that meant securing the screen door when the front door was standing open. That was confirmed after I had been out early one morning to deal with a problem and had come back home long enough to clean up and have breakfast before heading back to work at the "official" starting time. I had obviously forgotten to lock the door when I came back in, because as I was standing in the bathroom shaving, a total stranger walked right in and asked if I was about finished, because he needed to use the john! I was glad I was almost completely dressed, but it was still a shock!

When I politely explained that he was in a private house, he countered with the fact that it was "owned by the taxpayers, one of which he happened to be," and he needed to use it, pronto. I think I still managed to be polite as I ushered him to the door and pointed the way across the street to his correct destination.

We should have kept a list of all of the reasons for late-night knocks. They included the expected missing children, missing pets, missing wallets, and missing spouses (usually overdue from a trip on the river). When the campground was filled to capacity, we'd get a fair number of disputes over who had the "rights" to a campsite. This often happened when one group would register for a site, go off for the day without leaving anything to show that it was taken, and return late at night to find somebody else set up and asleep in "their" site. Possession may be nine-tenths of the law according to some people, but that other tenth can be a sticky wicket in such situations.

In retrospect, many of the people we met at our front door could be grouped into two categories: the "haves" and the "have-nots." The "haves" included the problems that were often a little less pleasant for the visitors. They included people who had fishhooks in their fingers (and many other parts of their anatomy), cactus spines in their feet, sand in their eyes, bugs in their ears (more about that shortly), and keys in their car.

Now, what's so bad about having keys in their car—isn't that where they're supposed to be? Well, not if the car is locked, the keys are inside, and the people involved are "on the outside looking in." Back in the days before so many vehicles had electric locks, this problem could often be corrected by a helpful ranger with the right tools and a little time. But the newer models pose more of a problem. Here's some free financial advice: If you're looking for a potential business opportunity, you might see if there is already a locksmith in the vicinity of a large recreation area!

The "have-nots" were usually a little easier to solve and included people who had no air in a tire, no gas in their tank, no ice for their cooler, and no charge in their battery. A thankfully rarer problem was the person who had no money in his wallet, a situation which occurred occasionally and seemed to have some correlation with the fact that Willow Beach was in the general vicinity of Las Vegas.

That connection is illustrated by a group that was taking a conducted bus tour of several attractions in the Southwest, and spent one night in Las Vegas. As they pulled out of the hotel parking lot, the tour guide got on the vehicle's P.A. system and asked if they had learned anything during their night in Vegas. After a moment's silence, a rather mournful reply came from the back of the bus: "Never play a game you don't understand!"

The "no gas in the tank" scenario took an unusual twist around one holiday, because Thanksgiving weekend was always a busy one at Willow Beach. Since the place was so hot in the middle of the summer, but weather was more pleasant during the winter, our "busy season" ran from late October through March. It's amazing how many people manage to fix a full Thanksgiving dinner in a camper or motor home, and even more amazing what time they decide to start cooking.

We had more than one very early morning knock from people who said they had run out of propane before the turkey was done, and wanted to know where they could get some more. (At 5 a.m. in that remote corner of Arizona, their options were really limited!) They did sell propane at the nearby resort, but not at that time of the day. I drove past the propane filling spot around noon one Thanksgiving and saw about a dozen campers lined up, waiting to fill their tanks. I'm not sure just how big a turkey you can get in the oven in one of those RV's, but they either used a lot of fuel or more than a few folks forgot to plan ahead and top off their tank before leaving home.

When you live a long way from town and associated conveniences like doctors and hospitals, it's useful to build up your list of remedies for simple emergencies. One of my favorite knock-on-the-door stories used one of those common-sense solutions.

It was sometime after midnight in the early summer, and I opened the front door to find two guys in their early twenties standing there. One was in obvious distress of some kind, since he couldn't stand still and kept slapping the sides of his head with both hands. Since this was in the early 1970s and we got a lot of visitors from Southern California, my first reaction was to run through a quick mental checklist of the symptoms of a bad drug trip. There were several possibilities, but since the "victim" didn't seem to be violent, I decided to wait for a little more information. The second man was obviously elected as spokesman.

"Hey, ranger, we need you to take us to the hospital."

"What's the problem?"

"Well, my buddy here has a big bug in his ear, and it won't come out. It's driving him crazy!"

We had several similar "bugs in ears" situations during our stay at Lake Mead, and my first question was always, "What have you done to try to take care of it?" If the answer was something like, "We tried to wash it out by pouring a lot of water in the ear," I almost always knew the answer to question number two, which was, "Can you still hear it or feel it moving around?"

The answer was probably "no," because they had managed to drown the little pest, which was now definitely not going to come under its own power. At that point, I always declined a request to go on a fishing expedition with a pair of tweezers and gave them the lecture on the risks of trying that themselves. I had to talk one guy out of trying to remove a "foreign object" from his ear with a pair of needle-nose pliers! It's amazing what some people will try to do in order to save a trip to the doctor.

I glanced back at the victim and agreed that he was definitely agitated. The good news was that they hadn't yet tried any direct action. "You sure you can feel or hear it actually moving around?"

"Yeah, man, it's beating a BIG drum inside my head. You've gotta get me to the doctor fast!"

"Wait right there, and try to leave it alone for a few seconds," I replied. "I'll be right back."

I grabbed my keys and pulled a big, five-cell flashlight from the front seat of my truck. Hurrying back to the front porch, I looked at the fidgeting man.

"Okay, you've got to manage to stand real still for just a little bit."

He looked at me with some alarm. "What are you gonna do?"

"I'm going to try to solve your problem, and I promise this won't hurt a bit." (How many times have you heard that one from someone about to render "medical care" of some variety or another?) "Now, you've just got to stand still while I hold this flashlight up to your ear. Which one is it?"

He looked at me with considerable suspicion, but replied, "The right one."

I turned on the powerful light and held it a few inches away from the man's ear.

"You feel anything?" I asked.

"Yeah, it's really moving around in there!"

In only a couple of seconds, the bug struggled its way to the "surface" and flew off. The man looked at me in total amazement. "Hey, I think it's gone!"

"I think you're right. How's it feel now?" I asked.

"Great! I can't hear a thing. Uh, I mean I can't hear that bug anymore. How'd you do that?"

"Pretty simple, actually," I said, "A lot of insects are attracted to light. I figured we'd just make it easy for him to find his way back out."

At this point, his buddy spoke up and added the final comic relief to the scene. "Hey, ranger, hold that light up to his ear again."

"Why's that?" I asked.

"Because when you did it the first time, I think I saw the light coming out through his other ear!"

I'm not sure the victim ever figured out the joke at his expense, which tended to confirm that there might be something to his friend's observation after all!

"Head for the Hills"

It was a nice weekend evening, not long after dark, and the Willow Beach campground at Lake Mead National Recreation Area in Arizona was just about full. With 187 campsites, that meant somewhere between 750 and 1,000 people were tucked away in a side canyon just above the edge of the lake. As far as desert campgrounds go, this one was one of the prettiest. The maintenance foreman assigned there for many years had diligently cultivated a virtual oasis of shrubs and trees that provided welcome shade and a nice, natural screen between every campsite. This was possible due to a combination of truly dedicated effort and plentiful water from the lake for irrigation.

The air was full of that post-sunset fragrance unique to a campground, a mix of wood smoke, charcoal starter, and meat on the grill, mingled with the aroma of dozens of different supper menus. The hum of conversations and the excited laughter of kids were occasionally punctuated by the sound of metal striking a very unforgiving rock, as a few late arrivals tried to hammer tent stakes into that stony desert ground. The cheerful glow of Coleman lanterns pushed back the night around each campsite, the crowd was well behaved, and life was good at Willow Beach. Unfortunately, that was about to change.

The call over the two-way radio came from the assistant chief ranger at park headquarters up in Boulder City. That was unusual in itself, since the chiefs usually managed to take the weekend off. What was even more unusual was the message: "Give me a 10-21 (phone call) at headquarters as soon as possible." This was way before the days of cell phones, and the boss knew that having to drive back to the office to take a phone call was an interruption in our busy schedule. The fact that the message couldn't simply be transmitted over the radio was ominous, since it meant the contents were something not intended for the ears of the general public or the news media, both of which often monitor such radio messages via scanners.

After you work in the ranger business for a while, you're occasionally tempted to think that surely you've already encountered most of the weird situations that could occur in a park. You know, of course, that isn't true, but you can always hope. That phone call from headquarters proved once again that the human mind seems to hold boundless possibilities for mischief.

If you're old enough to recall some newsworthy items from back in the early 1970s, or if you paid attention in American history class, you may recall that during that era the United States went though some challenging times with several radical groups. Those events pale in comparison to September 11th, of course, but at the time, some occasionally violent demonstrations and threats to disrupt various government activities were a cause for concern. One of the more bizarre examples of such threats was the reason for that after-hours phone call from headquarters.

The essence of the conversation was as follows: A bomb threat had been received at Hoover Dam. The caller said that their group had managed to get their hands on the means (implying a small nuclear device) to blow up the dam the next morning. Presumably because they were such nice people, the bombers had called in their warning to give authorities time to evacuate areas downstream that would be wiped out if the dam released all of that water currently resting placidly behind it.

The expert opinion was that the call was a hoax and that it was very unlikely any group had the capability to actually blow up the dam or even do serious damage to it. However, the official position was that we were to notify all of the visitors in our area, tell them about the threat and the likelihood that it was a hoax, and let them make their own decision about whether to stay or leave. The emphasis, of course, was on maintaining calm.

A quick geography review will help you understand why there was at least some concern about this threat. The site for Hoover Dam was selected because the Colorado River was confined at that point by a deep, narrow canyon that continues downstream for about twenty miles. Willow Beach was located a little past the half-way point, thirteen miles downriver from the dam. About the height of a seventy-story building, the dam impounds Lake Mead, one of the largest artificially created bodies of water in the world. When more or less full, Lake Mead holds about 28,537,000 acre feet of water, give or take a gallon or two.

So how much water is that, you might ask? Most of us can't really visualize twenty-eight million of anything, much less "acre feet," so I checked with the experts for a little clarification. According to the

Hoover Dam impounds Lake Mead, one of the largest man-made reservoirs in the world. Below the dam, the Colorado River and the upper twenty miles of Lake Mohave are confined by the sheer cliffs of Black Canyon. Willow Beach, the setting for this story, is thirteen miles downstream from the dam. (Bureau of Reclamation)

Bureau of Reclamation, that's enough liquid to cover the state of Pennsylvania to a depth of one foot, which would be a considerable inconvenience for those folks, but not a total disaster. However, since you couldn't fit even a small fraction of Pennsylvania into the portion of Black Canyon between Willow Beach and Hoover Dam, "removing" the dam would result in a wall of water considerably deeper than one foot. As unlikely as it seemed that this would actually happen, we still had the responsibility to inform people who would be affected, and let them make their own decisions.

In this case our job was mainly one of racing the clock. In addition to the people in the campground, I was also responsible for delivering this cheering news to the staff and guests at the Willow Beach Resort, the people at a nearby federal fish hatchery, and any backcountry campers who might be spending the evening on any number of gravel bars scattered up and down twenty miles of the river below the dam. Rangers assigned to the next subdistrict downstream would take it from there.

As is usually the case, our situation included both good news and bad news. On the plus side it was a weekend, which meant that the entire ranger staff assigned to my area of responsibility was available to help. The downside was that this staff consisted of me and one other ranger, who had already finished his "day shift" and was by then at home hoping to get a little time off.

Stan was a good ranger and didn't waste any time meeting me at the campground when I gave him the news. He understood the time challenge, but I'll do the math to save you a little work. With 187 campsites, we each had groups in about 93 sites to contact. We discussed our message before we started to try to keep it quick, concise, and uniform—and, of course, low-key. If we could manage to finish up at each campsite within two minutes, we'd cover the whole campground in just about three hours. After we finished that, we'd deal with looking for campers in those twenty plus miles of very dark canyon.

Two minutes per campsite was, of course, a bit optimistic. If you've ever spent any time around campers, you know that most of them are friendly, talkative folks. While that's usually a plus in dealing with these visitors, in the current scenario, extended conversations were not high on our list of the night's activities. As you might expect, about 99.999% of the people we contacted also had at least one question, even if they otherwise scored a "0" on the sociability scale. In short, it was going to be a challenge to keep things moving along.

All in all, things went really well, and everybody seemed to take the news in stride. We got a lot of "what do you really think?" questions, and we heard similar conversations going on between campers as we made our way through the area, but by the time we were finished, nobody had made a move. In retrospect, I realize that this episode provided a great study in human behavior. Some academic type has probably already written a doctoral dissertation on this, which would be entitled something like, "The Influence of the North American Entertainment Industry and the Settlement of the American West on Group Dynamics When External Stressful Stimuli of Unknown Validity Are Introduced Into the Sociological Milieu of Late 20th Century Middle and Upper Class Recreational Users."

Loosely translated, that means when they pull into the campground and circle their travel trailers and motor homes, most Americans take on at least a little of the persona of John Wayne, Clint Eastwood, or whatever Hollywood hero from the Western genre you might choose. When a cowboy bursts into the back room of the Rusty Nickel Saloon, interrupts the card game and says, "Boys, I hear that Black Bart and his gang are headed our way," Big John Wayne takes it all in stride. After all, maybe it's just a rumor, and nobody else wants to be the first one to pull out of the big game.

Between Hollywood and something very real in the subconscious makeup of most Americans, nobody really wants to be the "first to blink" in the face of adversity, especially if you're in a group with a bunch of similar people in a campground Out West.

In short, there was a general undercurrent of uncertainty among our crowd of campers, but nobody wanted to make the first move.

This lasted for about five minutes after we finished our rounds of the campground. Ironically, it was the people in a campsite very close to the entrance to the area who cracked first, so I got to see it happen. My partner Stan and I had pulled our vehicles up at the campground entrance and were planning our strategy for trying to locate any campers scattered up and down the river. Perhaps the guy in campsite number three saw us there, deep in what was obviously an important discussion, and decided that maybe we knew more than we were telling.

We'll never know what tipped his decision in favor of leaving, but all at once he jumped up from his lawn chair, hollered to his wife to "pack it up," and cranked up his truck to hook up their trailer. In what was probably record time for breaking camp, they were headed through the gate and up the canyon for high ground. At that point, the dam broke, at least figuratively!

If we had been able to view the scene from the Goodyear Blimp, I'm sure we would have seen a definite ripple effect, something like one of those group "waves" that moves through the crowd at a big sporting event. Now that somebody else had blinked when faced with the evil gaze of Black Bart, it was okay for everybody else in Dodge City to pack it up, too. Starting at campsite #1 and moving steadily up the canyon all the way to site #187, the sounds of preparations to hit the road were clearly heard. I'm happy to report that it was still calm and orderly, and nobody got run over or cut off at the intersection.

When all was said and done, only a handful of hardy souls were left. They're probably related to the people you see on the Weather Channel when a Category 4 hurricane is bearing down on some stretch of coastline. "Yes sir, I've rode out every hurricane right here in this 'ol beach house, and this storm will probably turn and go up the coast, just like most of 'em do. If it don't, I'll just ride it out, and I'm staying right here!"

As we all know now, the call turned out to be a hoax, just as everybody expected. By late morning, many of our campers returned, life got back to normal, and we could all shake our heads and laugh about the crazy people who would dream up such a stunt. At least most of our visitors kept their sense of humor, and more than one of our regulars from California came up with the same line. When asked what they would have said if the dam had actually been taken out, the answer was: "Surf's up!"

"Can You Hear Me Now?"

It's hard to imagine in today's world of cell phones, e-mail, and similar technology, but back in the early 1970s even basic telephone service was a challenge in some remote areas of the West. That was often the case for us at Willow Beach, one of the ranger stations at Lake Mead National Recreation Area. We were served (or at least they tried) by a small, local phone company.

Our phone lines originated in the town of Kingman, Arizona, about sixty miles to the south, and there wasn't very much in the way of civilization between us and Kingman. With so few customers, there was obviously little financial incentive for the phone company to upgrade equipment or install additional lines. As a result, the few existing lines had to be shared, so we had the opportunity to experience life on the "party line."

Now I realize that at least some of you won't recognize that term, which incidentally has no connection to "party time." A party line is a telephone line that is shared by two or more different customers. In our case, we shared both the phone number and the line with the ranger station and the second ranger family who lived at Willow Beach. We also shared that same line with a family who lived about a mile away, at a federal fish hatchery. They had a different phone number, but not a separate line. Here's how it worked.

Each phone number on the shared line had its own distinctive "ring" pattern. For example, if the call was for the ranger station, the phone might ring only once, followed by a pause, then by a single ring, another pause, and so on. If the call was for the family down the road, the phone would give two quick rings, followed by a pause, then two quick rings. You simply had to let incoming calls ring a couple of times to be sure you heard the correct pattern. The more customers on the line, the more complicated the ring pattern became (one long and one short, or long, short, long, etc.), so that every number had its own pattern.

The real fun comes when you understand that if one "party" is talking on the phone and you pick up your phone, you have now joined the conversation, albeit uninvited. If you pick up the phone carefully and keep the mouthpiece on your phone covered, it's usually possible to listen in on the conversation without the other parties being aware of this fact. When party lines were the norm all over the country, this situation provided lots of material for comedy writers, and was a huge boon to anyone who enjoyed keeping up with the latest gossip. (I suspect it was also at the root of many a neighborhood dispute!)

If the line is already in use, you have to wait, of course, for that conversation to end before you can make a call yourself or before you could receive any incoming calls. How well this whole situation worked (or didn't) depended largely on the cooperation of everybody on the party line. Fortunately, in our case at Willow Beach, it worked fine. It's hard to imagine how someone wanting to use a computer modem would cope with that situation today!

The phones in the two ranger houses were simply extensions of the number for the nearby ranger station. If we wanted to make a personal, long-distance call (and that included calls to all but a handful of people at Willow Beach) we charged those to a credit card. Since neither of the rangers living at Willow Beach spent much time in the office (we were out "ranging," of course), this gave the two wives something really fun to do, which was to take most of the phone calls on behalf of the U.S. Government.

Since this was before the days of a 24-hour dispatch center for the park, both houses also had a speaker installed that allowed the occupants to monitor all the "traffic" on the park's radio system around the clock. In effect, spouses and off-duty rangers around the park had to function as "dispatch" sixteen hours a day and listen for any urgent calls for help from rangers out in the field.

We got only one very fuzzy picture on TV and had minimal radio reception, so the NPS generously provided this chance to answer official phone calls and keep an ear on the radio as a form of entertainment for the spouses—and for the rangers when we were home. By mutual agreement, if the phone rang on a day we were supposedly off-duty, the other family tried to catch the calls. As we'd tell people inquiring about how to get one of those great jobs as a ranger, "The pay wasn't much, but you wouldn't believe some of the fringe benefits."

This is only one of many examples of the way spouses of rangers are among the unsung heroes of parks. My wife got plenty of practice answering those phone calls while taking care of our first-born when we lived at Lake Mead. She got so good at it that we still tease her sometimes about an experience during a visit back home to see family members in Texas.

The phone rang in her parents' house, and Velma happened to be the one closest to it. She picked up the phone and automatically said, "Willow Beach Ranger Station." There was a puzzled silence on the other end of the line until Velma realized what she had said and corrected herself in time to keep the caller from figuring they had a wrong number and hanging up!

In addition to the potential perils of the party line, we also had to contend with some amazing technology—or the lack thereof. In the process of sorting out various phone problems, we learned from the repairman that our phone line was actually two strands of wire, separated by insulators and strung from pole to pole across sixty miles of rough desert mountains. This system was apparently not uncommon "way back then," at least in remote sections of the West, because we encountered a similar situation with another phone company elsewhere at Lake Mead. Depending on how much slack had developed in the wires and how hard the wind was blowing at any given time, the distance between these two wires could vary quite a bit. That spacing made quite a difference in the quality of the phone connection, because if the lines came really close together (or sometimes even touched), the result was some really amazing patterns of static on the line.

The poor repairman assigned to try to maintain this section of phone line didn't have an easy life, and I got pretty well acquainted with him and with the operators who took "trouble reports" about the phones. "Trouble" usually meant you couldn't hear the conversation due to the static on the line or you or the person calling (or both) couldn't hear much of anything at all. While that was an inconvenience for any customer, this was a more serious problem when the phone number in question was used to receive emergency calls. As a result, we felt obligated to at least report it when the line became more or less unusable. It was during one of these times that I had the following conversation with the telephone operator.

"Operator."

Me, speaking loudly: "I need to report a problem with our phone."

Telephone operator: "Hello?"

Much louder on my end: "I need to report a problem with our phone."

Telephone operator: "Hello, hello?"

Considerably louder on my part: "I'm having a problem with our phone."

Operator: "You'll have to speak up, I can't hear you."

Seriously louder this time: "That's the problem!"

Operator: "Okay, you don't have to yell. Why didn't you just say so?"

Later during my stint at Lake Mead, we moved from Willow Beach about a hundred miles or so up the road to another ranger station at a place named Echo Bay. While Willow Beach was located downstream from Hoover Dam on the upper reaches of Lake Mohave, Echo Bay is located in Nevada on the north side of Lake Mead. About an hour's drive from Las Vegas, it wasn't exactly "downtown" either. The phone situation wasn't radically different from our previous duty station, although we had a different small, independent phone company.

One day everyone on our line began to experience a periodic "buzz" that lasted about a second, then went away for a few seconds, then returned. The buzz came at very regular intervals, and was loud enough to completely interrupt your conversation. When we first reported this, the phone company suggested helpfully (hopefully?) that since the buzz was so regularly timed, we could just build short interruptions into our conversation every few seconds, and go on about our business. I guess this would work if you really practiced, but it made for a pretty disjointed conversation. It also made for some interesting dialogue when the other person on the line didn't realize what was going on.

(Phone rings.) "Echo Bay Ranger Station (buzz)."

"Hey, ranger, this is (buzz), calling from down at (buzz)."

(Trying to see if I recognize the voice, so I'll know who's on the line). "Hi, what can I (buzz) you?"

"We need to know (buzz) campsites you have (buzz) now."

"Are you asking how (buzz) have open or taken?"

"Open."

"Sure. I checked (buzz) hour ago."

"How many hours (buzz) you check?"

"Half an (buzz) ago."

"What was that? I didn't quite (buzz) it."

"Half an hour (buzz). We had fif...(buzz) sites."

"Did you say fifty or five (buzz)?"

"Yeah, fifteen (buzz) open."

"Oh, fifteen. Thanks. Say, (buzz) you've really got a bad (buzz) on your phone line. Have you (buzz) that to the (buzz)?"

After we buzzed the phone company a few times, they finally sent the repairman out on his rounds. Considering how many miles of wire he had to check, he actually solved the problem pretty fast. By the end of the day, he discovered that a rancher about thirty miles away, outside the park, had set up a new charger on an electric fence at a corral on his ranch. One side of the fence ran right next to the phone line, which had sagged badly and was almost touching part of the fence. Every time the electric charger cycled on and off, it caused the buzz on the phone lines. So went life in the Old West of 1975.

The main reason we wanted the phone to work reasonably well at all of these ranger outposts was that these were emergency numbers as well as our own link to the rest of the world, and on occasion we actually did get some valid emergency calls. Many other calls were at least legitimate requests for information (such as, "Is the campground full yet?"). Some, however, tested our ability to maintain the friendly park ranger image.

We'd get a surprising number of calls that went something like this, often well past bedtime by almost anyone's standards: "Hey, ranger, I need to get a message to some relatives in your campground. It's really, really urgent."

Okay, we're here to help out for really, really urgent problems, so I fished for a little information: "What's their name, and do you know which campsite they're in?"

"Well, his name is Jim-Bob Jones, but he usually just goes by 'J.R.' That's because his name's really James Robert, except the family usually calls him Jim-Bob for short. They camped there on Labor Day weekend about four or five years ago, or maybe it was six, I'm not sure, so I figured you'd remember them."

I suppressed a sigh and went back to the second half of my original question. My odds at getting a good answer would have been better at one of those casinos up the road in Vegas, but I had to try anyway.

"Do you know which campsite they're in?" (Here's a free tip—if you've gone camping and think there's even a remote chance someone might need to get a message to you, at least call and let them know the name of the campground and your site number.)

"Well, of course not, I figured you did."

Unfortunately, I had no idea where J.R. was located. Like many NPS campgrounds with limited staffing, this one was on a "self-registration" basis. Campers would find an empty site, set up camp, fill out a registration envelope with their name, site number, and other basic information, enclose their fee, and drop the envelope into a slot in a device known in the trade as a "pipe safe." Just think of it as a low-tech night depository that was actually quite sturdy and pretty burglar-proof.

At regular intervals we'd empty the pipe safe and move the money to a real safe elsewhere. (Don't ask where it's located—that's classified information under the new Homeland Security guidelines, so if I told you, I'd have to shoot you.) We'd then check the campground each morning and compare occupied sites with the registration envelopes to make sure we didn't have any freeloaders.

A major drawback to this system was that the only way to find out the name of a person in a specific campsite was to look through all the envelopes, a pretty tedious task when you have 187 sites. It was made even more challenging because some people would pay for several days or even a week at a time on one envelope, so finding a specific person might require looking through as many as a thousand envelopes.

In an effort to simplify this process, campers were also invited to sign a sheet kept on a clipboard at the registration point, listing their name and site number. This was especially encouraged if they were expecting friends to meet them there later, or if they might be expecting a phone call at the ranger station from that third cousin. Probably a violation of privacy these days according to the American Civil Liberties Union, but a system that actually worked pretty well for those who chose to use it.

There was one other small hurdle in this game of locating people in the campground. I was always amazed at the number of doctors who apparently stayed in our campground. I based that observation on the hieroglyphic handwriting that frequently appeared on both the registration envelopes and the sign-up sheet for the campground. In accordance with my experience in trying to decipher the scrawl on a prescription form that I've received from various physicians in the past, no other group of people in the known world has handwriting that bad, so most of our campers must have been doctors!

We tried to keep a pen or at least a sharp pencil at the registration station, but some people insisted on filling out the information with what must have been a blunt crayon, which has a rather detrimental effect on the legibility of a name written in a small space on the envelope. As a result, even checking the registration envelopes and sign-up sheet to try to locate someone was often an exercise in futility.

With that information in hand, you can now join me back on the phone late at night, as I'm trying to get enough information to locate the caller's elusive relative J.R. We've already established that the camper's site number is not known.

I decide to try another approach. "Can you give me a description and license plate number on their vehicle, and do you know if they're in a tent or an RV?"

There's a brief pause while the caller yells to someone else on his end of the line. His response was pretty typical for such situations:

"Well, we've never actually camped with them before, so I don't really know. I think Jim-Bob said he was going to buy a pickup, but I'm not sure if they ever did, so they might be in their van. I think their van is a dark color, maybe blue or green, but it might be red. Well, not real dark... you know, that kinda medium shade. Wait, I just remembered. The reason he was thinking about buying a truck was because their van hasn't been running real good lately, so if didn't buy a truck yet, they might have come in their car. I think it's white, or silver, and I'm pretty sure it's a Ford."

Recalling that I'm a servant of the public, even though I'm actually off the payroll at the moment, I try again. By this point, I'm not overly optimistic.

"In that case, I don't suppose you know their license plate number, or at least the state for their plate?" Maybe I'd get lucky and they'd be the only people in the campground that night from Rhode Island.

There's another brief pause. "Say, that's a really good question. They used to live in California before they moved to Nevada, but I remember J.R. saying he was going to try to get away with not buying Nevada tags until his California plates were about to expire. Those things have gotten awfully expensive, you know."

Given the fact that about eighty percent of the vehicles in the campground that night had either California or Nevada tags, this was not a whole lot of help. While I was pondering my next move, my caller jumped back into the conversation.

"So, can you go find them and ask J.R. to give me a call right back. It's really important!"

Recognizing by now that my only chances of locating J.R. at close to midnight in a jam-packed campground were going to be based on a search of those campground envelopes and sign-up sheets, I had to ask the next question. This was potentially delicate, because occasionally we would get a legitimate emergency, such as a serious illness or a death in the family.

"It may take quite a while to find them, and I can't promise that I can if they didn't sign up for their campsite, but I can try if it's really important. What's the problem, so I'll know what to tell them if I locate them?"

"Well, I need to know if he found out if they have any live minnows down there at the marina or if I need to wait until the bait shop opens up in town and get some before I drive down in the morning. You know how long it takes to drive all the way back up here to Vegas, and I sure don't want to have to make an extra trip tomorrow."

My former supervisor would have been proud of the way I managed to politely close out that conversation. I might also add that this conversation occurred very early in my career, and I quickly learned to find out the nature of the "emergency" before I bothered to go though all the other questions. Since honesty is the best policy, I'll have to admit that there were some occasions where I just had to explain that unfortunately we just couldn't go look for J.R. in the middle of the night.

We always tried to keep in mind that when someone looked in the phone book or called "information" to get our number, they didn't realize that the phone was ringing in our house as well as at the office and that this particular arm of the U. S. Government didn't have operators standing by to take your call, no matter what time of the day or night. Despite our best efforts, it was sometimes a challenge to keep that "smile" in our voice.

Ring...ring. (Trying not to sound too sleepy.) "Willow Beach Ranger Station."

"Say, we're thinking about coming out to fish today. How hard is the wind blowing down there right now?" (Alternative questions: "Have they been catching any big ones lately?" or "How's the water level?")

(Look at the clock: 4:15 a.m. I'd finished convincing the last noisy group in the campground to call it a night at about 11:30 p.m. and was in bed by midnight. Wonder if the caller can hear what the nice ranger is thinking over the phone line?)

One of my fellow rangers once admitted that after several such calls in the middle of the same night, he finally told one individual that he was sorry, but he didn't know if the wind was blowing or not. When the man asked why not, the ranger replied it was because it was still really dark outside at 4:30 a.m. and he just hadn't gotten out of bed yet to check!

Since we got quite a number of these calls, most of the rangers made sure there was a phone located right next to the bed. One of my co-workers had just moved into park housing where the only phone was in the living room. The floor plan had a fairly large closet located right beside the bedroom door. About the third night in his new house, he got one of those middle-of-the-night calls, jumped out of bed, and dashed for the phone in the dark, hoping to avoid waking up the rest of the household. He grabbed the wrong door in the dark, ended up in the closet instead of the hall, and got all tangled up in the clothes hanging there. He didn't escape until his wife heard all the commotion and turned on the light to see what was going on.

Like many others, this story would have never been told if the caller hadn't turned out to be his boss, at the next ranger station down the lake. When he wanted to know why it took so long to answer the phone, and what all the laughter was about in the background at that hour of the night, the poor guy 'fessed up.

So, if you're going to a park and want to know if the wind is blowing, if the campground is full, or if the fish are biting, give the poor folks there a break, and call at a decent hour. Oh, and just for good measure—bring some extra minnows if you're planning to do a little fishing.

"Back It Up Right Here"

On the list of facilities people use in the pursuit of outdoor recreation, few offer more opportunities for confusion, chaos, and calamity than a boat ramp. If you don't believe me, just spend a couple of hours on a sunny, summer Saturday morning at a busy boat ramp in your part of the country. While you're at it, take along a video camera, and you might have some award-winning footage for "America's Funniest Home Videos." An even better time would be the first warm weekend of the spring, when many of the boaters are either: 1) out of practice since last summer, or 2) novices who just bought their first boat and are ready for their maiden voyage.

Now, in fairness to all involved, let me say right now that no one—including rangers and others who do this for a living—is born with the ability to launch or operate a boat safely and with finesse. Like anything else, it's an acquired skill, and practice makes perfect. Unfortunately, too many people buy, borrow, or rent a boat and hit the waterways without bothering to get any instruction. That's when life can get interesting.

In case you aren't a boater, let me describe a boat ramp and what is supposed to happen there. Bear with me for about a page or so, and we'll get into the really fun stuff. Although they come in a variety of shapes and sizes, a boat ramp is basically a road that runs down a slope and ends up in the water, whether it be a river, lake, or even the ocean. A well-designed ramp has a nice even grade, but isn't too steep; has a firm paved surface instead of gravel or dirt, with the pavement extending out for some distance into the water; and has plenty of width to accommodate several boaters at once. The purpose of the ramp is to make it safe and easy to launch a boat off of a trailer into the water, or to retrieve a boat from the water and load it back onto a trailer, so it can be towed back home or wherever it's kept when it's not in use.

The principle is really very logical. When it isn't in the water, the boat sits on a trailer, which the boater tows behind his truck, car, or SUV to the ramp. Upon arriving at the ramp, the boater makes sure the boat is ready to launch, then backs the trailer down the ramp until most or all of the trailer is under water. If the ramp is well designed (and water levels are cooperative), that allows the boat to float off the trailer, but the back wheels of the towing vehicle won't be very far into the water. The driver then pulls back up the ramp, sliding the trailer out from under the now floating boat. He then parks the tow vehicle and trailer nearby and strolls back down to the water to join the rest of his group for a happy day afloat.

If you were paying attention to the previous paragraph, you may have picked up a couple of points that can make this process a little more complicated than it seems. First, backing a trailer behind a tow vehicle is a learned skill and takes some practice, especially if you're doing so on a steep slope that ends up in the water. More about that in a minute.

Second, it's important to be sure the boat is ready to go in the water before you launch it. Yes, I realize that seems obvious, and I'm really not trying to insult your intelligence. We'll talk about that in a little more detail soon, and when you read that section you'll realize that there's more to this process than you might expect.

Finally, this whole process is a lot easier if you have two or maybe three people who have done it before—but no more. Friendships, marriages, family harmony, and perhaps world peace are all in jeopardy if too many people try to get into the act when launching a boat.

Let's talk about those points in reverse order. If you have two people to launch the boat, one can drive the tow vehicle and the other can maintain control of the boat once it's in the water. That leaves the driver of the vehicle free to concentrate on driving, which is a good idea for someone backing down a steep and often wet and slippery slope with several hundred (or thousand) pounds of extra weight attached to the back of the vehicle.

Meanwhile, the person in charge of the boat can simply sit in the boat as it's backed down to the water, then start the boat's motor, put it in reverse, and ease the boat off the trailer when there's enough water under the craft to lift it free of the trailer. The "captain" of the boat then moves it to a nearby dock or eases it over to the bank, out of the way of the boat ramp, until the vehicle driver returns to get on board. Sounds easy, doesn't it? With practice, it is.

An alternative approach is for the person in charge of the boat to walk alongside the boat as the trailer is being backed down the ramp. (Note: This person should never walk behind the tow vehicle. This important safety disclaimer is brought to you at the advice of the lawyer that I don't currently have and hope never to need.) This person is holding a long rope, one end of which is tied securely to the bow (that's nautical talk for front) of the boat. When this person gets to the edge of the water, he or she stands there and waits until the boat floats free of the trailer and the trailer has been pulled back up the ramp. He then uses the rope to pull the boat over to the bank or nearby dock for boarding.

This one can be a little trickier, because sometimes (oftentimes) the boat needs a little nudge to come free of the trailer. This means the person has to wade into the water and shove the boat free of the trailer. Depending on the size of the boat, this might be pretty easy or really hard, but the main problem is that for some reason many people who are about to spend the rest of the day on the water seem to have a strong aversion to getting their feet wet.

As proof positive that American ingenuity is still alive and well, some boaters have developed an "easy" way to get the boat off the trailer without getting anybody wet in the process. Since many of our visitors to Lake Mead came from Southern California, we sometimes called this method the "L.A. Launch." It worked like the alternative approach I described above, with one little refinement.

With this technique, a rope is secured to the bow of the boat, and the launch assistant holds the other end of the rope. The assistant walks alongside the trailer and boat as they are being backed down the ramp. (The same safety disclaimer given a little earlier still applies, but it becomes more important here!) The driver backs down at a somewhat higher rate of speed, then slams on the brakes of the tow vehicle just before the trailer gets far enough into the water for the boat to start to float free of the trailer.

If done correctly, this brings the tow vehicle to an abrupt stop right at the edge of the water and causes the boat to be propelled off the trailer with just enough force to slide smoothly into the water. The assistant, who is standing on the ramp with nice dry feet, uses the rope to maintain control of the boat and pull it back to shore once the trailer is out of the way. Advocates of this approach think it's really clever, and it can be pretty impressive—when it's performed as intended.

The L.A. Launch uses some basic principles of physics, including momentum, which suggests that a graduate of one of California's fine institutions of higher education probably came up with it in the first place. For those of you who slept through that physics lecture, "momentum" means that if the boat and trailer are moving backwards (toward the water) at five miles per hour, and the trailer suddenly stops when the driver of the tow vehicle hits the brakes, the boat will continue to move backwards for a little while longer at five miles per hour, minus the effect of factors such as friction on the bottom of the boat and the resistance of the water on the stern. (I warned you that a scientific type came up with this.)

The L.A. Launch does have a couple of potential perils. Depending upon conditions at the launch ramp and how many vehicles have already used that area recently, the part of the ramp closest to the water can be wet and therefore a little slick. Sometimes it can be really slick. So what, you may ask? An occasional boater will fail to ask that same question. Here's the answer: If you are backing your tow vehicle and boat trailer downhill toward the water at a fairly vigorous speed, and you slam on the brakes right at a point where the back wheels of your tow vehicle just happen to be rolling over a slick spot, two of those old physics principles will come into play.

Since there isn't enough friction between the tires and the ramp on that slick spot, jamming on the brakes just won't stop the tow vehicle. In this situation our old buddy momentum will not only cause the boat to continue backwards into the water, it can also cause the tow vehicle to do the same thing. The identical result occurs if the driver of the tow vehicle backs up with too much speed or fails to put on the brakes soon enough.

If any of those situations prevail, you have a variation on the L.A. Launch known as the "car launch." This is not a desirable outcome and definitely qualifies as a Melancholy Situation. Not only is it hard on the car (or truck, or SUV), it can tie up the boat ramp for some time, until a wrecker shows up to retrieve the tow vehicle.

A boat ramp is intended for launching watercraft, not vehicles, and a "car launch" always qualifies as a Melancholy Situation! This one occurred at the Hemenway ramp in Lake Mead National Recreation Area. (Bob McKeever)

Car launches can also occur when the driver of the tow vehicle gets out of the vehicle while it is parked on the incline of the boat ramp and forgets to set the parking brake. This slow-motion car launch is much less spectacular than the previous format but still has the same result.

The third most common variation, the "oops gear" car launch, usually involves a tow vehicle with a standard transmission, although an automatic model isn't excluded from playing this game. This version can occur when the vehicle driver backs down to the edge of the water, pushes in the clutch, and then holds the vehicle in place with constant pressure on the brake while the boat is being taken off the trailer.

Unfortunately, one important step is sometimes overlooked before driving back up the ramp—you have to shift from reverse into first gear. Most people tend to give it the gas pretty vigorously when they're ready to start back up the steep ramp. If the transmission is still in reverse when you hit the gas and engage the clutch, you can conduct a very impressive car launch indeed.

There is a certain amount of irony to all of the above undesirable outcomes—you may recall that the whole purpose of the L.A. Launch and related techniques is to get the boat into the water without anyone having to get their feet wet. If the end result is a car launch instead of damp shoes, there is a definite opportunity to evaluate priorities.

A related potential pitfall to the L.A. Launch is aptly illustrated by the experience of one couple who arrived at the Willow Beach ramp one nice spring day. At the risk of sounding tacky, I will simply describe him as the stereotypical tourist from a sitcom or comic strip. About fifty-five years old, he was wearing a bright, floral Hawaiian-type shirt, size XXL, which barely covered his generous waistline. His Bermuda shorts, size XL, didn't hide a pair of knobby knees, and it was safe to guess from his dress socks and expensive shoes that he had absolutely no intention of getting his feet wet while launching his boat.

As he got out of their luxury sedan, our hero slapped a hat on top of his balding head, clamped a very large cigar between his teeth, and began to give instructions to the woman driving the car, who I assume (yes, I'm guilty as charged) was his wife. She was apparently assigned to drive the tow vehicle while he tended to the rope tied to the bow of their boat. He had obviously gotten advice from somebody about how to conduct an L.A. Launch.

If you've ever seen the character Archie Bunker on some old TV reruns, you'll have a mental picture of the character in this story, except that Archie was a lot more polite than this guy. It didn't take long for everybody in the vicinity to realize that the lady behind the wheel had absolutely zero experience in backing a trailer. If you've never tried it yourself, you can take my word for it—backing a trailer is not easy until you get some practice. It also didn't take long for her husband, whom we'll just call Archie for the sake of this account, to start to offer advice to Edith. Either the lady was hard of hearing or Archie assumed she was, because the advice started at a fairly high volume and just kept getting louder.

"Cut your wheels the other way . . . no, the other way, you idiot!" Each attempt at backing quickly resulted in the car and trailer being jack-knifed on the ramp, many feet away from the water. With each try, Archie's advice became more and more vocal, and less and less complimentary about the lady's driving skills. It was amazing how Archie could shout such a variety of instructions without losing control of that cigar, which remained firmly clamped between his teeth. Through it all, the lady behind the wheel seemed to maintain a remarkably calm demeanor. She apparently had considerable previous experience in dealing with Archie.

Fortunately, there was only one other boater waiting to launch, and that group wisely just shut off their truck's engine and sat back out of the way. Now, you're probably wondering, where was the trusty ranger during all of this activity? Well, he was standing by, well out of the line of fire and discreetly mostly out of sight, waiting to be sure the situation didn't get seriously out of hand.

One thing I had quickly learned was that it did not pay to jump into the middle of one of these little family situations and offer unsolicited advice, which usually had one of two outcomes. In some cases, the people don't want any advice simply because they are skeptics (**S**omeone **K**eeping **E**ven **P**ositively **T**ruthful **I**nformation under **C**onstant **S**uspicion.) In other cases, well-intentioned advice falls under the category of adding fuel to the fire, and I was not in a position to take the visitor up on the heated offer that usually resulted: "If you think you know so much about it, let's see *you* back up this rig!" I suspect strongly that Archie would fall into the second category.

Keep in mind that Archie and his bride were attempting the infamous L.A. Launch, so he was holding one end of that rope that was tied to their boat. After a number of tries, the lady behind the wheel finally got that trailer and car lined up straight. Recognizing that opportunity would probably only knock once, she seized the moment and backed up with vigor.

I will have to say that she got the timing exactly right. At the last possible second, she slammed on the brakes, and the trailer and car came to an almost instant stop. This was a sizeable boat, and it shot off that trailer like it had been fired from a slingshot. It was a textbook L.A. Launch. Archie was standing with his back to the water so he could give advice to the driver if needed, and for about one second he was all smiles.

Then he ran out of rope.

In retrospect, it was fortunate that he wasn't seriously hurt, because our old friend momentum came into play once again. Archie must have tied his end of the rope around his wrist, or he had an incredible death-grip on it, because when the slack was all gone out of that rope, Archie was literally yanked off his feet and right out into the water!

He came up almost immediately, about knee-deep in the lake, and very, very wet. His hat was slowly drifting away, apparently in pursuit of the boat. He still had the soggy cigar clenched between those teeth, but it was already looking pretty bedraggled, with a definite droop. For a few moments, he was at a loss for words, but his wife filled the silence nicely.

Leaning out the car window and looking back at her husband, she asked sweetly, "Did I do it right, dear?"

Somewhat to my surprise (and relief), they finished their preparations and headed out on the river, both of them seemingly in good spirits. I really wanted to be on hand later to watch them take the boat back out of the water and load it on the trailer, but duty called elsewhere and I missed that potential show. Since I didn't get any calls about altercations on the boat ramp for the rest of the day, it apparently went okay.

Near the beginning of this chapter, I mentioned three common pitfalls associated with launching a boat. The second involved making sure the boat was ready to launch before the trailer was backed down into the water. While this seems pretty obvious, a different kind of misadventure occurs fairly often at this stage.

Almost every boat has a "drain plug" located in the stern (that's nautical for back of the boat) down near the point where the stern meets the deck (floor) of the boat. This plug serves a couple of purposes. First, boats tend to get dirty when they are used. Sand and mud get tracked on board, salt spray blows on board if you're in salt water, and other unsightly stuff ends up all over the inside of your nice, shiny boat. A prudent boater washes his craft inside and out after each trip. This little chore is easiest if the boat is sitting on its trailer on dry ground. However, once you finish that nice wash job, you have several inches of water captured inside the bottom of the boat.

The solution: Just pull out that handy drain plug, crank up the front of the trailer so the bow is higher than the stern, and let all that water run out. The same situation prevails if you store the boat uncovered, out-of-doors. Rainwater collects inside the boat and must be drained out, unless one of your hobbies is raising mosquitoes. As a result, most boaters leave the plug out when the boat is stored on its trailer and out in the weather.

We had all of that discourse about drain plugs to prepare you for one key point: Before you launch the boat, be sure the drain plug is back in place! You'd probably be amazed at the number of boaters who forget this little detail, which occurs most often the first time people put their boats back in the water in the spring. They probably left the plug out all winter, so rainwater would just drain out as needed, and then forgot about it on their first trip of the year.

This really gets interesting if the person who first notices the fact that the boat is filling up with water at an amazing rate can't find the plug. In an apparent violation of another law of physics, it always seems to take forever to drain water out of a boat after you've washed it on dry land, but it's absolutely amazing how quickly water can flood back into a boat through that very same drain hole if the plug isn't in place when the boat is launched.

Whatever the reason, launching a boat without a drain plug in place almost always puts those boaters in the same frame of mind as Vice-Admiral Sir David Beatty, who is reported to have said during the Battle of Jutland in 1916, "There's something wrong with our bloody ships today." If a day on the water is part of your future plans, I trust you can use the information in this chapter to help make your trip much more enjoyable!

"There's a Burglary at the Marina"

The Willow Beach Resort was a pretty well-run operation back when we were assigned there in the early 1970s, with a motel, restaurant, a small trailer park for semi-permanent residents, a gas station, a small store with basic groceries, camping, and fishing items, and of course, a marina with rental boats and slips where regular customers could tie up their boats.

Today the operation has been scaled back and the current owners and staff have no connection to the folks who ran it during my stay, so I can tell this story without causing any embarrassment to the present management.

Because this particular site primarily attracted fishermen, family groups, and older campers, it was a little more laid back than most of the other spots in the park, which got more of a younger, fast boat and party crowd. Unfortunately, it also proved than any of us can let our guard down when we feel really secure in our "neighborhood."

One Monday morning I got a frantic call from the cook at the resort, who upon opening for the day had discovered that they had been the victims of a burglary. I hustled down in the dawn's early light and was met at the door by the manager, who had also arrived by then. He took me back to the office and pointed to a safe, which was standing wide open and did in fact look very, very empty. The reason for the manager's long face was even more apparent when he explained that they had just finished a really good weekend of business, and the safe had held all of the money they had taken in since the last trip to the bank Friday afternoon.

I asked him to be sure no one touched anything in the building until we had time to collect any evidence and took a quick look around. The point of entry was easy to spot—broken glass from a window was scattered over the floor of an adjoining storeroom, and there was a muddy footprint on a counter directly under the window. That gave us hope that this was a pretty amateur job and that more evidence, such as fingerprints, might also have been left behind by the careless burglar. If that was the case, I was a little surprised that he (or she, or they) hadn't seemed to have any problem getting into the safe, since it didn't appeared to be damaged.

I went back to take a closer look at the safe and confirmed that there was absolutely no sign of forced entry. An expert safe cracker smashing windows and leaving muddy footprints out here in the middle of the Arizona desert? I looked at the unscathed dial of the combination lock and the open door from several angles, and then my attention was drawn to a detail on the front of the safe, right above the door. I glanced over my shoulder at the manager, who was looking very sheepish as well as unhappy.

After asking the manager to help me look around the rest of the building, we moved to a spot out of earshot of the cook. A couple of questions confirmed my theory about the safe and determined that so far the only other item missing was a pickup truck from the resort parking lot. It was time to make a phone call to the county sheriff's office, sixty miles away in Kingman, to get some help with processing the scene and put out a lookout for the stolen truck.

I left a message with the dispatcher and before long got a call back from the lucky investigator who was probably dragged out of bed as a result of my call. After I had given him the basic facts, my conversation with the detective went something like this:

"A safe job, huh? We don't get a whole lot of those in the county. I gather they didn't blow the door [with explosives] or somebody would have heard that. Did they peel the door, or are we looking for somebody with the skills to actually crack the combination?"

"Well, actually, it didn't require much skill," I replied.

"How so?" asked the detective. "Was the safe that cheap?"

"You probably won't believe this one, but the burglar just dialed up the combination and opened the door."

"Oh, yeah, what do we have, an inside job, then?"

"Hard to say. It could have been anybody," I replied, "since they had the combination written on the front of the safe with a magic marker."

There was a brief silence on the line. "You've got to be kidding!"

" 'fraid not. They have a fair amount of turnover on their staff, and it seems that some of the new help were having a hard time remembering the combination, so they just wrote it down in a place where they wouldn't have any trouble finding it."

I wasn't sure if the sound on the line was a sigh or a suppressed laugh. "Anything else missing?"

"Just a pickup truck." I gave him the description so they could put out a "BOLO" (Be on the lookout for).

"They hot-wired it, I suppose."

"Not exactly. They just took the keys off of a row of hooks on the office wall. Every vehicle they have is neatly labeled with the vehicle description and tag number right over the set of keys, so they didn't have to waste any time finding the keys for the newest one."

I believe the detective made some comment related to candy and babies, told me he'd be up in a bit and hung up.

Well, to make a long story short, there were plenty of fingerprints to go along with the footprint, the pickup was recovered before long in pretty good shape, and as I recall, an arrest was finally made. Suffice it to say that procedures were tightened up considerably at this place of business! In the aftermath of this little episode, the resort owner also decided to install an alarm system.

As the saying goes, it seemed like a good idea at the time, but the results of that effort confirmed the truth of another platitude: You get what you pay for. Their security system wasn't totally bad, it just had a few major bugs that resulted in a lot of false alarms. That was bad, because guess who got to answer all of those alarms? When the system was activated, an automatic phone dialer would go into action, and, just as the alarm system salesman promised, promptly send a recorded message to the local police department. At Willow Beach, that happened to be the two rangers who lived there.

As a result, we had a new attraction added to our list of possible reasons the phone was ringing in the dark of night. At least it was pretty basic: We answered the phone and heard a familiar voice repeating over and over, "There's a burglary at the marina." This message kept going until we hung up the phone. I guess the only small consolation was that they didn't begin the taped message with, "Hey, ranger, there's a burglary. . . ." After several nights in a row of multiple calls, we insisted that the manager of the marina also get all of those calls. This is otherwise known as the "incentive plan" to make the system perform more efficiently. As it turned out, the system itself soon had a nervous breakdown of sorts, which prompted a much-needed overhaul.

In the wee hours of the morning several days into this process, I answered the phone to hear something that sounded like a "Chipmunks" record gone berserk. You may remember a song or two by this group, which had a couple of high-pitched voices that were supposed to be a cute pair of the little animals, or maybe you recall the Chip and Dale cartoons, which had a similar pair of characters. If you're old enough to remember phonograph records (yeah, I know we're talking ancient history here), you will be able to visualize how it sounded if you took a 33 rpm record and played it at 78 rpm speed. For you younger readers, try to imagine listening to the soundtrack on a cassette tape if you could hear the audio while the tape is being run at fast forward or rewind speed.

It took me a few seconds to realize that the strange sound coming from my phone was the now familiar "there's a burglary at the marina," but being played at about six times the normal speed. This happened twice in the space of about an hour, just long enough for everybody to get back home and into bed in between times. When I got down to the store on the second trip, I think I asked the haggard manager something like, "Do you want me to shoot the dialer and put it out of its misery, or do you just want to turn it off until it gets fixed?" Fortunately, he opted to turn it off, and thankfully it did get fixed without any more break-ins during the interim. In the process, the repairman also figured out what was causing so many false alarms, and the system worked pretty well after that time.

There are at least two morals to this story: Don't cut corners if you want to install an alarm system, and more importantly, if you can't remember your safe combination, at least use a little imagination when you pick a spot to write it down!

9

Too Hot to Handle

If you spend much time watching the weather on TV, you already know that the desert Southwest can be a pretty hot place in the summer. Now, just in case you make it to the hot seat for one of those quiz shows, here's your question: What place holds the record for the highest temperature ever recorded in the United States?

A. Death Valley, California
B. Lake Havasu City, Arizona
C. Parker, Arizona
D. Greenland Ranch, California

According to the National Climatic Data Center, the highest temperature officially recorded in the continental United States was 134° on July 10, 1913, at a place ironically named Greenland Ranch. That's in the neighborhood of Death Valley National Park in California. For you trivia buffs, that's a mere two degrees below the all-time world record of 136° in Libya. All those other places listed above hold the dubious distinction of having the highest temperature in their respective states at least one month out of the year. Take my word for it, once it gets much over 120 degrees, it really doesn't matter a whole lot anyway—it's hot, no matter how you slice it!

One spot that's not on the above official list is the subject of this little story. The National Weather Service has a network of hundreds (maybe thousands?) of cooperators scattered across the United States. Each of them faithfully records weather information, such as the highest and lowest temperature and the amount of any rain or snow on a daily basis. That information is noted on a form and then mailed after the end of each month to the weather service.

In order to help standardize the data, every cooperator has the same type of rain gauge and an identical instrument shelter (a louvered box on legs) to house items such as maximum and minimum thermometers. The thermometers are housed in these shelters not only to protect them, but to provide a standard way to measure temperature in the shade. A lot of national park ranger stations serve as cooperators in this network. This information is not normally included in the weather report you see on TV or in the newspaper, because it isn't reported by the cooperators to the weather bureau on a daily basis.

Willow Beach was one of these cooperator sites, as were the other ranger stations at Lake Mead. Every afternoon, each ranger station would contact the dispatcher at park headquarters by radio and report the current temperature, number of campsites available, and any other pertinent information. During the summertime, it became something of a perverse badge of honor to have the hottest temperature for the day.

For a brief period of time during my assignment at Willow Beach during the early 1970s, we had a little fling at national stardom of sorts in the world of weather.

Back in those days, we sent our monthly reports to the weather bureau office in Phoenix, where we assumed they were filed and never really analyzed in much detail. As a result, I was surprised one summer day to get a phone call from a man at that office in Phoenix.

He was inquiring, albeit politely, about the maximum temperature readings we had been reporting from Willow Beach. He quizzed me about our methods and our instrument shelter set-up, to try to see if we were doing everything correctly. I soon realized that he thought our readings for recent months were too high. The previous year my predecessor had recorded a daily maximum of 125° and readings in the vicinity of 120° were not uncommon. After further conversation, the guy from the weather bureau said he had some business in our part of the state anyway, so he'd bring up a new set of thermometers which he knew were absolutely accurate. I assured him we'd have the iced tea ready.

Sure enough, in a couple of days our man from Phoenix showed up, just in time to cast a dubious eye upon the afternoon's reading on our instruments. Now thoroughly convinced that our equipment was faulty, he installed a new set of thermometers and checked my technique for taking a reading. We adjourned inside to the air conditioning to test the iced tea and give the new equipment time to register the current data. I wish I had a photo of his face when we went back to check—the new, "guaranteed accurate" thermometer read 123°, which was a little higher than our old one.

Convinced now that he had stumbled onto a little weather lore gold mine, the weatherman asked if I could call his office every day as close to 4 p.m. as possible, which should allow ample time for the highest reading of the day to occur. His theory was that Willow Beach actually had the high in the nation at least some days, and he wanted to put that "out on the weather wire." I told him I'd be glad to do so, barring some emergency at that time of day.

Well, the man from Phoenix was right, and several times for a week or two we had the dubious honor of beating out those other heavy hitters like Bullhead City and Lake Havasu City for the nation's hot spot. (Even hotter spots like Death Valley don't normally report on a daily basis either.) One day I got another phone call from Phoenix and was told with some sadness that we'd have to discontinue our daily reports. When I asked why, he was a little guarded in his explanation, but I finally realized that the folks who ran the resort down the road had complained about the publicity. Seems that customers were starting to call up and cancel their reservations for the resort after they heard how hot it was in our little piece of desert paradise!

The funny thing about that situation was that some of these visitors had been coming back year after year—they just never realized how hot it was, but once they knew, it seemed a lot worse! By the way, for you skeptics or weather buffs, you can check out the official temperature readings for Willow Beach, and just about anyplace else in the West, on the website for the Western Regional Climate Center at www.wrcc.dri.edu.

We've all heard the phrase, "It's not the heat, it's the humidity," or its first cousin, "It's not so bad here, because it's a dry heat." There is some truth to that, up to a point. It was not unusual to have a relative humidity of less than ten percent during the summertime at Willow Beach (as long as you didn't measure it right next to the river). That is dry! My wife Velma used to comment that we definitely didn't need a clothes dryer, because by the time she finished hanging a load of clothes outside, the first pieces she had hung up were already dry. What did we do on rainy days? Well, with under five and a half inches of rain a year, that wasn't a real problem!

A dry heat can in fact be more bearable than the same temperature reading in a humid climate, in part because perspiration evaporates so quickly off your skin, resulting in more efficient natural cooling. This is especially true if you can find a shady place with a little breeze, in which case temperatures well over a hundred were not all that unpleasant.

The other part of that equation is that you have to work really hard to be sure you drink enough fluids to keep up with all that evaporation, and we always had to warn visitors of that fact, especially if they came from more moderate climes. We'd often hear something like, "I don't need to drink so much, because I'm not sweating." The answer was, "Yes, you are, it's just evaporating so fast you don't realize it!" We became serious iced tea drinkers while living and working in the desert, and I never left the house during hot weather without my two-gallon jug filled to the brim with ice water. I developed my "two rules for summer living" while working there, which we shared with a lot of friends and visitors:

1. Never stand in the sun when you can stand in the shade.
2. Never pass up a cold drink, because you don't know how long it might be until you get another one!

That's good advice if you happen to be visiting anyplace that's really hot.

Before you decide to cancel your summer trip to the desert, you can take some comfort in the fact that it's a little cooler up on the "big lake" at Lake Mead, and even further south on Lake Mohave. That's because Willow Beach is located at the bottom of a place called Black Canyon, which is located in the vicinity of the Black Mountains. Maybe that gives you a hint about the general tint of the landscape!

Actually, we did have a mix of colors in the surrounding rocks, ranging from brown, to dark brown, to occasionally dark red, to gray, to just plain ole black. There's no way to fancy it up—that area is a world of dark colored, mostly bare, rock. During the day, all that exposed rock did a great job of soaking up the solar radiation, which then continued to radiate back long after the sun had set. That accounts in large measure for the lack of campers at Willow Beach during the summer months. (For anyone who just has to experience camping out in those temperatures, you need to know that the campground at Willow Beach was closed several years after I moved on due to flash flood danger, but Death Valley is just up the road a piece in California.)

I will have to admit to having a little fun, in a perverse sort of way, with the hot weather. Occasionally during the summer, a car would wind its way down our four miles of steep, winding road from US 93 to Willow Beach. With the air conditioning going full blast, it really was an interesting drive of sorts, and it was nice and comfortable inside the car. Probably their last stop had been about sixty miles down the road at Kingman, where things were a little more moderate, or up north in Las Vegas.

These folks would pull up in front of the ranger station, or perhaps spot me on the road, making my rounds of the area. They'd stop, roll down a window, or maybe even get out of the car. When they did, you could see a little expression of surprise as all of the cool air was instantly sucked out of their vehicle and replaced with a hot shock wave, apparently straight out of an unseen blast furnace. Even so, they expected it to be hot—this was the Great American Desert, after all.

"Hey, ranger, it's pretty warm, isn't it?"

I'd, of course, agree with that size-up. The fun came with the psychological impact when they'd ask the inevitable second question.

"Say, how hot is it, anyway?"

I'd check my watch to be sure I'd give them a good estimate, then say something like, "Well, I haven't checked the official thermometer this morning, but our high yesterday was 121°, so this time of day, it's probably about 120°." I'd have a short pause for effect, and then add, "Of course, that's measured in the shade."

It was not unusual for people to actually stagger back about half a step at this little bit of news, but it didn't usually take them long to recover, get back in the car, roll those windows up fast, and hit the "maximum AC" button! The truth was, it didn't feel quite that hot, but there was just something about hearing the temperature reading that made it seem a lot worse. Lest I'd seem to be a poor host, I would always manage to let them know that it was nice and cool down at the restaurant if they wanted to enjoy the view of the river before they headed back up the mountain, and that our weather was great the other half of the year.

Most of us occasionally say something about the good ol' days, but I'm casting my vote on the side of modern air conditioning! We had one other funny experience due to the heat at Willow Beach. The park housing there was well designed to blend into the surroundings, but it was not great from an energy efficiency standpoint. The houses had cinderblock exterior walls and a flat roof. For aesthetics, the exterior was painted a medium reddish brown, very similar to the color of the surrounding rocks. The roof originally had a layer of light-colored gravel, which had been applied over a tar base, to help reflect some of the direct sunlight. Most of the gravel was long gone, so we had a great opportunity to prove some of those lessons from that long-ago physics class: A dark-colored concrete house with a dark-colored roof would definitely capture some serious solar radiation!

The first summer we lived there, the air conditioning unit died. Thankfully, the maintenance staff responded quickly with a new compressor. Later that summer, however, the new compressor also gave up the ghost. At that point, they concluded that the compressor, which was installed on the west side of the house (in the "back yard") was getting too much sun. The solution was to build a little wooden lattice shelter over the exterior AC unit to provide some shade and install a small cooling fan to blow on the compressor. I figured it was hot when even the air conditioning needed some air conditioning!

Hey, this is a great spot if you don't like cold weather. For the past thirty-five years, the maximum amount of snow recorded at Willow Beach was 0.8 inches and that was a rare event indeed! The fact that the state of Arizona (except for the Navajo Indian Reservation) does not observe Daylight Savings Time causes occasional confusion for people arriving in the state from other locations. Although I've not read an official explanation for this decision, I have a pretty good theory—when you have this kind of serious summer weather, an extra hour's sunlight at the end of the day is not necessarily an advantage!

10

Setting the Stage: Buffalo National River

The Buffalo River begins in the Boston Mountains of northwest Arkansas and winds eastward through pastoral valleys and past rugged limestone bluffs for 150 miles before it merges with the White River. About 135 miles of the river and 94,000 acres of adjoining land are now protected within the boundaries of the Buffalo National River, which was established on March 1, 1972—exactly one hundred years after the designation of Yellowstone National Park. A congressional report noted that the Buffalo "is a pure, free-flowing stream which has not been significantly altered by industry or man; it is considered to be one of the country's last significant natural rivers."

It's probably safe to classify the Buffalo as one of the undiscovered gems of our national park system. Even though warm weekends can be crowded at popular sites, it's not yet as overrun as its more famous brethren like Yosemite and Shenandoah. The primary attraction here is canoeing, although plenty of visitors also come to camp, fish, picnic, hike, swim, or just enjoy the scenery. A number of commercial outfitters in the area rent canoes and shuttle their customers to and from the river.

Local folks and regular visitors alike often refer to various sections of the river as the Upper, Middle, or Lower Buffalo, running from west to east. Depending on the time of year and amount of rainfall received, the Buffalo offers a range of canoeing, from Class II rapids that attract serious paddlers to many quiet stretches suitable for families and more casual floating. As a general rule, canoeing is best from late spring into mid-summer, with the easier sections located on the eastern, or lower end of the river. Almost every curve in the river has a nice gravel bar

The clear water, soaring bluffs, and beautiful forests of the Buffalo National River in north central Arkansas provide a prime location for canoeing and a variety of other recreational activities. (Arkansas Dept. of Parks & Tourism)

or sandbar for camping or a picnic, and there are plenty of big trees along the shoreline to provide welcome shade on a summer day.

Due to the steep terrain in and around the park, river conditions can change quickly following a rain, and the river can be challenging or even downright dangerous when it's running high. In late April 2004, about ten inches of rain fell in the area over a three day period, causing the river to rise from a depth of five feet to over fifty feet, its highest level since record floods in 1982. If you're planning a river trip to this or any park, it's always prudent to call ahead and check on river conditions.

The park has thirteen official camping areas, ranging from primitive sites offering little more than fire grates and vault toilets to one of the most attractive and best-equipped campgrounds in the NPS at Buffalo Point on the lower end of the river. That area also includes cabins, a restaurant, and a small visitor center. For additional information, see the park's website at www.nps.gov/buff or write for information to Buffalo National River, 402 N. Walnut, Suite 136, Harrison, AR 72601.

Don't Feed the Skunks

One of the "fringe benefits" of the ranger's job at several of my assignments was the opportunity to let Uncle Sam have a phone installed in our house for the purpose of making and receiving official U. S. Government calls. Now, before you get your ire up at yet another extravagant use of your hard-earned tax dollars, I need to point out that Will Rogers was right. There is no free lunch, especially if you're dealing with the government, and that of course applied to our "free" telephone. Unless we were in a situation like those I described in an earlier chapter where private phone lines just weren't available, we still provided our own phone line for personal use at our own expense.

The reason that you the taxpayers were willing to graciously provide this phone was to give both my wife and me the chance to answer business and emergency calls for the ranger station around the clock, seven days a week, right in the comfort of our own home. Now, I ask you, is this a great country, or what?

As an added bonus, this phone number was usually listed in several really prime spots in the phone book, under headings such as "In Case of Emergency Call" and "National Park Service, After-Hours Emergencies." In some parks, we were even listed in the yellow pages, right there under "Government Offices-U.S." I'm willing to bet that most of you don't have a phone in your house listed in the yellow pages—and trust me, you can be glad you don't! Last but certainly not least, this "call in case of emergency" number was posted at key locations all over the surrounding area, such as campground bulletin boards and pay phones.

In some areas, ranger stations made the really big time and were listed right there on the inside front cover of the phone book, along with other notables such as the County Sheriff and the Fire Department. Now that will really open up almost limitless opportunities for interesting conversations with some very unusual people. When the phone company operator couldn't decide where to send weird questions on almost any subject, he or she apparently assumed that surely a park ranger would know the answer and would direct the call to us.

If you haven't figured this out in terms of today's world, not only are we talking about the days before anybody thought up the concept of 911, we're also talking about some pretty rural areas. (Okay, in some cases, we're talking about some areas that were seriously in the boondocks.) These parks didn't have the staff for a "dispatch" center or even anybody to answer the phone at the ranger station, unless one of us happened to be in the office doing some paperwork. So, Uncle Sam just "drafted" the ranger's spouse and family to help pick up the slack. Fair or not, it was just assumed to go along with the job.

This is just one more piece of irrefutable evidence that ranger's wives in general and mine in particular are worthy of sainthood, and Velma took more than her share of calls on those "government phones." I at least volunteered to have the phone on my side of the bed, and so it was that I had the following conversation when the phone rang very early one summer morning when I worked at the Buffalo National River in Arkansas.

"Hey, ranger, we've got two problems out here at the campground."

I glanced at the clock radio, which confirmed that it was still the wrong side of 6 a.m. "Okay, let's take them one at a time."

"Well, you know those signs you put up that say, 'Don't feed the skunks and other animals,' and 'Don't store any food in your tent'?"

"Sure," I replied. I helped replace those signs on a regular basis after tourists apparently couldn't resist taking them home as a souvenir of their visit—or maybe the raccoons, skunks, and other denizens of the wild objected to our advice and removed the signs in order to increase their dining opportunities. I occasionally suspected that this was a job assigned to local members of the RAIDERS organization (**R**avenous **A**nimals **I**ncessantly **D**evouring **E**very **R**emaining **S**nack).

The caller at least had the grace to sound a little sheepish. "Well, we should have listened to your advice."

"What happened?"

Let's take a brief time-out from this little story to give you some background. I realize this probably sounds pretty unbelievable to a few of you, but skunks had become quite a problem in our campground at Buffalo Point, as they had at some other parks in the country. Why, you might ask? Because a lot of people seemed to find skunks to be irresistibly "cute." Skunks are like most wildlife and are very adaptable in terms of locating things to eat. They find it much easier to panhandle from the tourists than to search for real food out there in the woods. The rangers spend a lot of time trying to convince people that marshmallows, cookies, and other staples of the campers' diet were not good for the animals, not to mention the risk of getting a nasty bite from one of these little beggars.

In addition, once the critters got used to these free handouts, they tended to become bolder and bolder about hanging around and looking for more goodies. If you left food outside, or even stored it in your tent, they were likely to decide to help themselves whenever hunger pangs struck. For most wild animals, dinnertime usually runs way past bedtime for us humans. When you're dealing with skunks, this opens up a whole realm of interesting, but undesirable, possibilities. My early morning caller confirmed that as he continued his story.

"Well, when we were getting ready to go to bed, we decided it would be easier to just store our food in our tent, and besides, we had our dog to keep any animals away."

A premonition about what was coming began to form in my mind, but I figured I'd just keep quiet and find out soon enough.

"So," the caller continued, "We went to bed and tied the dog's leash to one of the tent poles. A little while ago, this skunk showed up and must have wanted to get in the other end of the tent to get to the food. To make a long story short, the dog and the skunk got into a fight, and the dog pulled the tent down on top of himself, the skunk and us. We all ended up in a great big pile, and now we all smell like skunk."

After learning that thankfully neither the people nor the dog, as well as could be determined, had been bitten, I agreed that this definitely sounded like a problem. Wanting to get the whole picture, I said, "Okay, what's the second problem?"

"We managed to get out of that mess pretty quickly, and figured we better get into the shower as fast as we could. However, when we got to the bathhouse, we found out that the skunk had gone into the men's side, and won't come out. We need you to come out and get him to leave, so we can get in there." Implied in his tone of voice was the idea that I should make all possible haste in doing so.

One of the interesting things about the public's perception of park rangers is that we are assumed to know the answer to just about everything, from "What tree (or bird, or flower, or rock) is that?" to "Will it rain on Memorial Day weekend next year?" Our body of knowledge is assumed to be especially deep when it comes to the secrets of animal behavior. As a result, there was absolutely no question in this gentleman's mind that I could drive out to the campground, walk right into the comfort station, and simply tell that pesky skunk to "hit the trail, Jack, these nice folks are waiting to take a shower." I, of course, could not be the one to burst his bubble concerning the ranger mystique.

I told the caller that I'd be there shortly, hung up the phone, and started getting dressed. The thought crossed my mind, ever so briefly, that maybe I shouldn't wear one of my newer uniforms for this little job, but I immediately dismissed that as lack of faith on my part.

Now even though the U.S. government requires its rangers to have a college degree, I'm here to tell you that most of what I need to know in this job I didn't learn in college—or in kindergarten. One of the benefits of trying to answer all of those weird questions over the years is that in the process of finding the answers, you can pick up some pretty obscure facts. Several of them actually have to do with skunks.

As your reward for hanging in there to this point you are going to learn, absolutely free of charge, a really obscure fact about skunks. Well, okay, it may not be a "guaranteed true fact," because I've never actually had a chance to test this one, but it does come from a reliable source, which will remain anonymous in case you try this and it doesn't work out.

I've been told that if you ever get a skunk in the crawlspace under your house or another building, you can toss a bunch of mothballs under there, and the skunk will soon leave. This approach is based on the belief that skunks can't stand the smell of mothballs. I presume it's preferable to get the mothballs as close to the skunk's location as possible, and I'll leave it up to your ingenuity to decide how to accomplish that.

The number of mothballs needed for the smell to reach critical mass will depend on the size of the area involved. In areas like Florida some structures are built on piers with an unenclosed crawlspace so the cooling breezes can waft around under there year-round. In those cases this technique won't work, since the mothball fumes won't reach the required concentration. Otherwise, this approach is at least worth a shot, unless you object to the possibility that you'll trade the smell of skunk for that of mothballs for an unknown period of time.

Even though I tend to be a night person rather than an early riser, the need to evict the skunk from that building before the crowd of witnesses grew much larger was sufficient incentive to get my mind in gear pretty quickly. The good news was that the mothball remedy that I had heard about in the distant past came almost immediately to mind. The bad news was that we didn't happen to have any mothballs at our house at that particular moment, and there were severely limited shopping opportunities in the rural area between home and the campground—especially at this hour of the morning.

The drive to the park gave me some time to consider possibilities, both good and bad. The quotation "necessity is the mother of invention" is sometimes attributed to Richard Franck in *Northern Memoirs,* which dates way back to 1658, but regardless of who said it, I was definitely in need of some "invention." I'm glad I didn't know at the time that the French essayist Montaigne phrased it slightly differently: "Necessity is a violent school-mistress and teacheth strange lessons." My task that morning had definite potential for a strange if not a violent end!

In retrospect, it was a rather heart-warming reception that greeted me upon my arrival at the campground. A score or more of campers were lined up outside the comfort station in the dawn's early light, towels draped over arms, shaving kits grasped in one hand, ready to descend upon the sinks and showers as soon as the coast was clear. I noticed that the crowd was keeping a respectful distance from one man, whom I assumed was the one who had already met the skunk.

As I climbed out of my truck, a small, relieved cheer went up from the crowd—"Hey, the ranger's here, he'll know what to do," and similar expressions of confidence. The one skeptic was a small boy near the back of the line. "Hey, Mister, whatcha' gonna do to get that ol' skunk outta there, anyway?"

One of the key techniques in dealing with a crowd in any crisis situation is projecting an air of confidence. "Don't worry," I assured him. "We'll take care of it." (I suppose that "we" was a subconscious reference to the collective body of rangers around the world, and somehow implied that I was not alone in facing this little challenge.)

I did, in fact, have a plan, which I can attribute only to divine inspiration. Sizing up the situation, I suggested that the bystanders "move back a bit, so when the skunk comes out he'll have a good escape route." You proponents of the power of positive thinking will recognize this technique as "visualizing the desired results before they occur." In this case, I was hoping it wasn't just wishful thinking. Thankfully, the assembled crowd took my advice and backed up at least a few steps without any further prompting. I wasn't sure if this was in response to my confident attitude or the realization that a skunk could appear in their midst on short notice.

Yes, I did have a plan. I sure hoped it worked, because I didn't yet have a backup strategy.

The building in question was divided into the usual men's and women's sides, with a narrow passageway between the two called a chase. The chase provided a route for the building's plumbing and was reached via a door on one end of the building. Just inside this door was a service sink and storage area for mops, buckets, and cleaning supplies. My hope for a quick and decisive victory was located just inside that door.

The federal government includes an agency called GSA that buys lots of stuff for official use, supposedly at a discount. Some of these items are reportedly specially formulated for government use, which probably explains why they sometimes seem to cost a lot more than their civilian counterparts. For example, GSA used to provide insect repellent that contained ninety-nine percent of the active ingredient DEET. (For comparison purposes, a can of "super duty" repellent I bought recently at America's favorite discount retailer touts the claim that it contains an amazing twenty-nine percent DEET.) I decided to quit using the GSA ninety-nine percent version after a fellow ranger accidentally spilled some on a plastic canteen, which dissolved almost immediately. That outcome gave us some pause about having the product in close proximity to our bodies.

I mention that information so you can understand that my hoped-for secret weapon in the upcoming skunk ejection was some of the concentrated GSA version of a well known, pine-scented, all-purpose cleaner. A container of this mega-disinfectant was supposed to be stored in the chase of that comfort station. I recalled hearing the maintenance guys talking about the fact that a couple of ounces in five gallons of water were all that was needed for disinfecting the floors.

If skunks didn't like the smell of mothballs, I reasoned, they probably wouldn't care much for concentrated pine scent either. Furthermore, I had no intention of using a capful in that mop bucket. This was war, the reputation of rangers around the world was at stake, and I planned to pull out all the stops. I dumped the whole bottle of concentrate into the bucket and topped it off with water. I had just created a W.M.D. (**W**eapon of **M**alodorous **D**isinfectant).

Entry to each half of the building was on the side, near one end of the structure. An L-shaped partition just outside the doorway provided privacy when the door was open. The door had an automatic closing device, but clever campers soon learned they could defeat this mechanism by propping the door open with a large rock, an item conveniently found in abundance in this part of the Ozarks.

Leaving the comfort station door open has at least two results. The intended effect is to try to improve ventilation and make it a little less muggy inside in warm weather. An unintended side effect is to provide easy access for skunks and other trespassers, which is how we got into this Melancholy Situation in the first place.

Like any good soldier embarking on a dangerous mission, I made sure I obtained as much advance intelligence as possible. After confirming that the bucket of my secret formula was close at hand, I turned back to the crowd, which was now standing a respectful distance away.

"Anybody actually seen this skunk in the building?" I asked.

A hand went up. As I suspected, it was the man standing somewhat apart from the rest of the group. This was my early morning phone caller, who had already "met" the skunk up close and personal. I followed the crowd's example and quizzed him from a safe distance, upwind. His situation gave me hope that if this was in fact the same skunk, perhaps the critter had already exhausted his current supply of perfume. I made a mental note to check up on the recharge time for skunks once this was all over.

My informant told me that the animal was lying under the sink, just inside the door of the men's side of the building. When last observed, he appeared to be ready to take a nap. Since skunks are nocturnal animals this was probably true, which meant this critter likely had no intention of coming out on his own before nightfall. Not cheering news, but not a surprise.

My plan was possible largely due to the foresight of the architect of this comfort station. The shower and restroom areas were designed to allow relatively easy cleaning, with a concrete floor that sloped slightly to a drain near the center of the room. Armed with this knowledge and my bucket filled with the world's strongest concentration of pine flavored water, I carefully approached my quarry.

Easing up to the doorway, I quietly placed my bucket on the walkway and peered cautiously around the doorframe. My intelligence source was good, and Mr. (or Mrs.?) Polecat was curled up comfortably under the sink, on the opposite side of the room from the doorway. From all appearances, the little rascal was settled down for a long day's nap, head resting comfortably on his front paws. Sensing my presence, he opened his eyes, glanced briefly in my direction, and then calmly went back to his nap. Obviously feeling in control of the situation, his message was clearly, "Go away, don't bother me."

Well, it was decision time, make or break it, so I took the five-gallon bucket, tipped it around the corner of the doorway, and quickly dumped the entire contents onto the concrete floor in the direction of the skunk. I waited only long enough to see that a small tidal wave of the smelly stuff was sloshing across the concrete floor in the direction of the animal.

When I was receiving weapons training during my stint in the Army, the sergeant in charge of the firing range had a favorite expression to get us to move from place to place in a safe but timely manner: "There will be no running on the range, but there's no speed limit on walking." In the campaign against the skunk I knew that I had just fired my best shot in what I hoped was a short battle, which meant it was time to apply that sergeant's advice and make as hasty a retreat as possible while still retaining my rangerly dignity.

As I strode briskly away from the building, I didn't forget that axiom about dealing with a crowd—you've always got to speak with confidence. "Okay, folks, stand back now. He'll be coming out in just a little bit."

An expectant hush fell over the now sizeable throng.

And proving once again that Heaven has mercy on the needy, that skunk did just that! Shaking his wet feet indignantly as he ran, he scurried out the door, across the open lawn, and headed at high speed for the nearby river.

A cheer once again went up from the crowd, and the front of the line headed for the comfort station.

"Ah, hang on, folks, I've got a little more to do before you go in."

The first camper had almost reached the doorway when he got a whiff of the interior of the room. "Man, what IS that stuff? It smells almost as bad as that skunk!"

With all due respect to the good folks who make that pine product, it really doesn't smell bad when mixed as directed, but the fumes from my special anti-skunk formula were probably already starting to peel the paint off of the walls.

"Just our patented skunk repellent," I replied. "Give me a few minutes and this place will be all yours."

I returned the now empty mop bucket to the chase, hooked up the garden hose, and began to rinse down the floor. It actually took more than a few minutes, and I had to work mostly from outside for a while. The room eventually aired out, but I'm told the maintenance staff didn't have to use anything but water on that floor for quite a while!

So, the next time you're visiting a park and are accosted by a "cute" critter looking for a snack, do everybody a favor and "just say no." Above all, please don't feed the skunks!

"Thousands of Chickens"

One of the major attractions for visitors to "the Buffalo" is a canoe trip, and protecting the river's clean, clear water is a job the rangers take seriously. There are only four major highway crossings along the river's entire 150 mile length, adding to the sense of serene isolation for visitors to the park. However, those four highway bridges provide more than enough excitement for the rangers from time to time.

Because the Buffalo has carved its path hundreds of feet deep into the limestone rock of the Ozarks, all of these highways must negotiate a series of sharp switchback curves as they wind their way down into the depths of the Buffalo's valley, which is really more like a canyon in many places. Those long, steep grades can present a challenge for any driver, but the real test is for the brakes of the big eighteen-wheelers.

At the crossing over the Lower Buffalo, so many drivers have failed that test on Highway 14's switchbacks that the name "Dead Man's Curve" has long been applied to one sharp turn—even though none of the old-timers could actually relate a story where the driver didn't live to tell the tale. There were, however, plenty of cases where the driver survived only by virtue of a desperate leap from the cab of his runaway truck, just before the big rig made contact with a world-class guardrail at this particular curve. The most harrowing wreck I had the dubious opportunity to see at that location involved a tanker loaded with about 8,500 gallons of gasoline—but that's another story.

A similar situation prevails where U.S. Highway 65 crosses the middle section of the river. This is by far the most heavily traveled of the highways that bisect the Buffalo, and the road carries plenty of big trucks making the trip from I-40 and Little Rock up to Missour. beyond. The state highway department finally spent a bunch of tax do. lars to widen and realign this crossing of the Buffalo, thereby eliminating many of the sharp curves and reducing the steep grade as well. For one driver back in the 1980s, however, those improvements came a little bit too late.

I was enjoying that best part of a good night's sleep that comes just before sunup, when the park's two-way radio in our house crackled into life. It was the ranger who lived about thirty miles upstream from us, along the Middle Buffalo, and not far from the Highway 65 bridge. He was calling to let me know that there had been yet another truck accident at that location. After reassuring me that the driver had joined the ranks of those who made a lucky, last-second leap from the cab, he passed on the really good news—the truck had overturned on the bridge, taken out part of the guardrail, and spilled all of its cargo into the river, some fifty feet below. I was being requested to put our boat in the water and head upstream to help with the cleanup.

Before I continue this little saga, perhaps I should issue a gentle warning to any readers who are members of groups such as C.L.U.C.K (**C**oalition **L**obbying for **U**nderstanding **C**hicken **K**arma), P. E. C. K. (**Pe**ople **E**steeming **C**hickens **K**indly) or anyone else who has an unusually soft spot in their hearts for chickens. You may wish to skip ahead to the next chapter. Meanwhile, back to my radio conversation.

"What was he carrying?" I had visions of previous truck wrecks, where the loads had ranged from charcoal to frozen chickens, and wooden table legs to chicken fat. (You may have noticed that this list tends to be heavy in the chicken category. In case you've not spent much time in the Ozarks, raising chickens and turkeys is a major industry in that part of the world.)

The ranger on the other end of this radio conversation had the answer about our current situation.

"Chickens." There was a brief pause. "One of those flatbed trailers that haul cages carrying live chickens.

"How many chickens are we talking about?" I countered. I was still optimistic that this wasn't going to be all that bad, although the prospects of a big chicken roundup along the riverbank didn't sound like my idea of a good way to start the day.

There was another brief pause. "Ah, we're talking about THOUSANDS of chickens!" The worst was yet to come. "And, it looks like the cages all broke open and they're all in the water."

"How many survivors?" I asked. I presumed that by the time I got on the scene, any need for CPR on chickens would be long past, but I was still less than enthused at the prospect of chasing a bunch of Rhode Island Reds through the brush in the river bottoms.

"Only seen one so far. She's sitting on a rock out in the middle of the river, looking a little befuddled. The rest are headed your way downriver, and we've got a pretty good current. It would be good if we could keep them upstream from the Point."

Buffalo Point, in my district, was the park's largest developed area, with a big campground, cabins, and a major launching point for river trips. I had to agree that a river full of chickens, dead or alive, wouldn't be a real strong point for local tourism promotion efforts.

I signed off the radio, got on the phone, and roused one of my fellow rangers out of bed. After telling Mike to meet me at the ranger station and start loading up the boat, I suggested that he would want to take a lunch, because this was probably shaping up to be a long day. I also commented that a chicken salad sandwich would probably not be a great choice for the day's menu.

Early morning can be a great time for a boat trip on the Buffalo River. This one had lots going for it—blue skies and not a hint of a

The steep grades and sharp curves leading to the Highway 65 bridge over the Buffalo River created a challenge for plenty of drivers before it was replaced in recent years with a new and safer crossing. The old bridge in this photo was the launching pad for the truckload of chickens described in this chapter. (National Park Service, Buffalo National River)

breeze, so the surface of the water was like a mirror, reflecting
of the great bluffs and mighty trees lining the river. It hadn't ra
some time, so the water was crystal clear. It was the kind of day
prompts lots of well-meaning citizens to say something like, "Man,
sure wish I had your job. Nothing to do but ride up and down the river and enjoy the great outdoors!" Occasionally (well, rarely) that's actually true. For some strange reason, however, scanning the river for a flotilla of chickens "took a little of the shine off the apple," as they like to say in these parts.

We made good time in our flat-bottom johnboat, still not entirely sure what to expect. About twenty miles upstream we got a quick education in the hydraulics of chickens. To fully understand what I'm about to describe, you need to be aware of several things.

First, the river was flowing downstream at a speed of about four miles per hour. (For you non-athletic types, that's faster than most normal people can walk, more like the speed that a lot of people jog).

Second, if you'll think back to that science class in school, you might recall that because light beams passing through water don't travel in a perfectly straight line, an object a couple or three feet under the water is not exactly where it appears to be if you're looking at it from above the water. I believe the word from science class was refraction, or the bending of those light rays as they pass through the water. Trust me, that information will be important in a moment.

Finally, to make any progress and maintain steering control against a four-mile-per-hour downstream current, our johnboat had to be traveling upstream at a speed greater than four miles per hour.

So, you ask, what's the point of all that? Remember those great word problems we had back in about sixth grade math? They usually went something like this: "If one train leaves Chicago at 9 a.m. and travels west at 45 m.p.h., and a second train leaves Sioux City at 11 a.m. traveling east at 55 m.p.h., where will they meet?" Remember how your teacher always said something like, "Some day you'll thank me for making you learn this?"

Well, maybe she was right. Here's the application: Suppose you are on the Buffalo River, which is flowing east at four m.p.h., and you are in a boat traveling west at six m.p.h., and your mission, if you choose to accept it, is to capture any and all chickens you encounter in the water. To solve the problem, compute the effective speed of a submerged chicken that is moving downstream. Don't forget that the river always flows downstream, which means that in this case, so do the chickens.

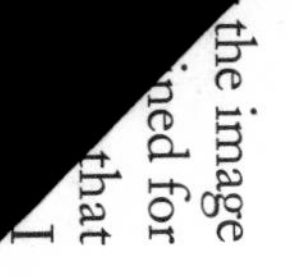

ne answer in the back of the book (whatever it
wrong, if you are actually trying to catch that
that moving boat. The reason is good ol' refrac-
call we reviewed just a little bit earlier. Simply
en you look at one of those chickens under two
f you try to grab him (or her) by plunging your
ace where he appears to be, you will come up
empty handed 100 percent of the time—even if you are a very fast plunger.

In short, folks, things in this situation aren't what they appear to be to the naked eye. (For you guys and gals who think your hand-eye coordination is pretty sharp, I challenge you to try fishing for chickens this way someday.) To make it more interesting, while you are busy trying to corral one of those rascals, about umpteen dozen more are merrily sailing by all around you, and the goal is to catch as many as possible in the shortest length of time. It was truly "chickens to the right of them, chickens to the left of them."

We quickly learned some other basic principles about chickens: (1) they are apparently terrible swimmers; (2) even if they could swim, they have a dismally low survival rate when placed into a cage that is then dropped into a river from a fifty-foot-high bridge; and (3) therefore, based on principles number one and two, these chickens were absolutely no help to us whatsoever in our efforts to rescue them from the river, especially since their cages had broken open upon reaching the river, and the birds were all taking their own individual paths to the great chicken house in the sky.

We also soon learned that due to some previously unknown law of chicken aerodynamics, a submerged chicken in a moving river will always assume a posture resembling a white torpedo that will always zoom along exactly twelve inches off of the river bottom. That's all well and good, except that the depth of this particular river bottom varies quite a bit, so we found we had a moving target that was always changing in depth in relation to the surface of the water. (Bet even that sonar guy tracking the *Red October* would have a challenge with this one).

Finally, we added to the world's store of knowledge by quickly confirming the following scientific principle: "A dead, wet chicken is a whole lot heavier than a live, dry chicken," and its corollary, "A dead, wet chicken takes up a whole lot less space than a live, dry chicken." (This is due to the fluff factor, which becomes non-existent in the case of the wet chickens in question.) The application of that principle is that a boatload of the wet variety weighs a lot more than you'd think, so you have to be careful not to overload your craft the next time you go fishing for chickens.

People sometimes ask me why the NPS requires their rangers to complete a four-year college degree before going on to specialized on-the-job training. It was days like the great chicken roundup that made me wonder the same thing, because I can assure you that nothing I had been taught in either the undergrad or graduate level in one of America's finest institutions of higher learning had done anything to prepare me for the task at hand. One of my regrets after the fact was that we didn't have someone on hand with a video camera, because I'd bet we would be in contention for a prize winner for "America's Funniest Home Videos."

Actually, we had come about as well prepared as possible, given the fact that I'm not personally aware of a large body of knowledge about the recommended equipment for this particular job. Mike and I had brought along the tools we had at hand that looked useful, so we experimented with several techniques.

We had one of those metal poles about four feet long with a little spring-loaded, claw-like device on one end and a trigger on the other end that people sometimes use to pick up cans and other stuff along the side of a road. Pull the trigger and the claw snaps shut on your prey. I can verify that this approach is absolutely worthless for snagging chicken torpedoes in a moving current.

Next, we tried a net on the end of a pole—the kind fishermen use to land a trophy trout once they have the fish on the end of their line. That worked only a little better, but it was still too hard to control underwater, especially with the current.

Confirming once again that the design of the human body is a true work of supernatural genius, we quickly found that the only really good approach was to just let one of us drive the boat while the other leaned over the side, stuck one arm under the water, and grabbed 'em as they came by. Since our primary objective was to corral as many of the fowl as possible, we concluded that an age-old proverb was applicable, with just a minor variation: A bird in the hand was definitely worth two in the river.

Because the water temperature of that beautiful, sparkling clear, spring-fed Ozark river was somewhere in the fifties, it was pretty hard to keep your catching arm warmed up in this game. For that reason, Mike and I were mighty glad that we live in the good ol' USA, where the free enterprise system soon came to our rescue. While we had been hard at work out on the river, my associate onshore who had gotten me into this situation in the first place had also been busy. His calls to the insurance company for the truck in question had finally gotten approval to hire any and all available boaters to join us on the river. It didn't take long for the grapevine to spring into action. Before long, the local folks started showing up in their own johnboats to join the battle, and eventually the odds shifted in our favor.

Oh, and that one surviving hen who was stranded on the rock in the middle of the river? She was a star on that evening's news broadcast from one of the Little Rock stations. A local family rescued her and took her home to their farm to join some of her kinfolks out in the barnyard, where I trust she contributed many an egg to an Ozark Mountain breakfast.

One moral to this story is that the next time you feel a touch of envy for that park ranger who has "nothing to do but ride up and down the river and enjoy the great outdoors," just keep in mind that there's sometimes more to the job than meets the eye. Oh, yeah, for those of you who aspire to one of those great jobs—don't forget those lessons from sixth grade math and science classes. You never know when some of that stuff actually will come in handy.

13

"Ranger, We Lost, We Lost!"

It had been a nice, quiet, early spring day on the Buffalo River in the Arkansas Ozarks. It was still too chilly for most campers or canoers, the spring break crowds wouldn't show up for another month, and I was looking forward to a relaxing evening at home.

I had just pulled out of my parking space across from the ranger station when I saw a big, 16-passenger van and a small sedan drive up to the station and stop. In good, rangerly fashion, I paused and looked back to see if there might be a problem. Almost immediately, a crowd emerged from both vehicles, and, being an alert observer, I realized these weren't our typical visitors in this part of the country. Many were wearing turbans on their heads, several were wearing Middle Eastern–style robes, and a vigorous discussion had immediately broken out among various members of the group.

Most rangers subscribe to the theory, developed over many years of dealing with park visitors, that you can sometimes get lucky and nip a problem in the bud—if you can just catch it early enough. This one looked like it had potential, so I backed into my parking space, climbed out of my truck, and eased over toward the group. There were about six conversations underway at the same time, and none of them we[illegible] English. After a few seconds one of the group noticed my arrival and soon got the attention of the crowd. Silence descended as we sized each other up. The numerical odds were about nineteen to one, but at least they looked friendly.

I know the essential phrase in several languages. For example, I can say, "no parlez vous Francais," "no sprechen Sie Deutsch," and "no habla Español" to let folks know right up front that I don't speak French, German, and Spanish. (Actually, I can get by with the basics in Spanish, but it's a lot easier to avoid getting in over your head right from the get-go.) However, my experience in what sounded like Middle Eastern languages was sadly lacking. That being the case, I just gave it my best shot.

"Hi! Can I help you folks?" Nothing ventured, nothing gained.

After a brief silence, I realized it was my lucky day. Well, maybe not, but at least I had an interpreter. One of the group stepped forward and responded in heavily accented but passable English. By the time this story sees the light of day my readers will probably find it interesting that I learned that they were all from Afghanistan.

These folks now lived down in Little Rock and wanted to camp for a few days and take a river trip. I gave my interpreter some basic information and directions to the campground and said I would stop by their campsite in the morning and tell them what they needed to know about the river trip. This was repeated in rapid-fire fashion to the rest of the group, who responded with smiles and much excited conversation. The group then piled quickly into their van and car, and roared off down the road to the campground.

The road from the ranger station to the campground at Buffalo Point winds down a fairly steep grade for about a mile, ending at the boat ramp and campground on the banks of the Buffalo River. I could hear the loud squeal of tires as the van took each sharp curve at a speed that was obviously a lot faster than the posted or realistic speed limit. During the interval between squeals, I could catch snatches of loud music from the van's stereo. Still operating optimistically under the "nip it in the bud theory," I locked up my personal vehicle, climbed into my government truck, and eased down the hill to check on things.

I knew from my earlier patrol of the campground that there was only one other group in the area, a middle-aged man and his wife. They had been there for several days, were camped at one end of the only section of the campground that was open at that time, and had a very large German shepherd dog. Fortunately, they had been good about keeping the dog on a leash. I had directed the latest arrivals to a site at the opposite end of the campground loop, to allow plenty of space between the two groups.

I reached the campground just in time to realize that my international group had missed the entrance to the campground and had ended up in the adjacent parking lot for the boat launch area. This put their vehicle only about fifty feet from the occupied campsite and about a hundred yards from the spot I had in mind for them. Before I could catch up, they parked both vehicles, piled out, and headed by the most direct route from their parking spot to the camping area. That took them right through the middle of the campsite occupied by the couple and their dog.

If that German shepherd had not been tied up with a really good chain, I'd probably still be filling out the paperwork for the resulting international incident. As it was, the whole group of new arrivals trooped cheerfully through these people's campsite, apparently oblivious to the man who was screaming, "Stay back, he'll bite," and to the dog, which was in an absolute frenzy, barking, leaping, and straining against his chain. Apparently, this dog didn't bark in a universal language because this canine's message had absolutely no discernable effect on this little caravan. The good news was that their route took them just out of range of those snapping jaws, and everyone passed safely by and headed on to look for a campsite.

By the time I reached the scene of this near-disaster, the man and his wife were standing there in open-jawed amazement, unsure about whether to be mad or worried. I let them get through the expected, "Hey, ranger, who are those guys?" before I apologized for the inconvenience and thanked them again for keeping their dog properly tied up. I then assured them I'd go have a talk with the new arrivals.

The good news is that I did arrive in time to steer the group toward my originally intended destination, a site as far as possible from the other campers. After sending the drivers around to retrieve their vehicles, I did my best to explain the basic rules of campground etiquette. Darkness was quickly settling over the area, and after waiting to make sure they were successfully started on setting up camp, I finally headed for home.

As I mentioned in an earlier chapter, one of the fringe benefits of being a park ranger is that sometimes you get to have your home phone number listed under the heading, "In case of emergency call . . ." This gives you a wonderful opportunity to engage in a lot of interesting conversations at all hours of the day and night. Occasionally, they actually involve a real emergency. Most of the time, they run more along the line of "Is it going to rain tomorrow?" or "Are the fish biting today?" or if you happen to be working in Arkansas, "Is this the number to reserve a campsite at the Grand Canyon?"

On this particular night I had only been home for about an hour when the phone rang. It was the campers who owned the German shepherd, calling from the pay phone in the campground. The gist of the excited conversation was that I needed to "get back down here *right now*." As best I could tell, no one was hurt and the campground was still intact, but I was assured that there was *trouble*. I asked the man to remain calm and stay away from the other group, and assured him that I was on the way.

It was really dark as I headed down that steep grade to the river, and a couple of sharp curves before getting to the bottom of the hill, I began to see an ominous orange glow in the vicinity of the campground. My worst fears weren't realized and I arrived to find that the whole campground wasn't ablaze, but it didn't miss it by much. The new group of campers had proven to be exceptionally efficient at picking up loose firewood in the area. In fact, I later found that they had collected the vast majority of downed limbs, branches and twigs in at least a quarter-mile radius, and had turned most of this fuel into a truly gigantic campfire. It was a conflagration that almost any school would be proud to claim for their homecoming game bonfire!

I was at least lucky on two counts. Due to the size of their group, I had put them in an unusually large campsite, one that had no trees overhanging the campfire grate. As a result, their fire had not yet ignited the surrounding forest. Lucky news number two was that the weather had been very damp for several days, and so the flying embers from the fire had not yet caused a problem. At any time, however, this could change, and definitely for the worse.

Try to picture this scene from the perspective of the middle-aged campers in the other campsite: Here's a huge fire, surrounded by what looks like a crowd and a half of bearded guys wearing turbans and long robes. To complete this tableau, the group had the stereo in their van cranked up to the maximum level, playing what I'm sure was a favorite tune in a distant land, but one which sounded pretty weird to American ears. During rare pauses in the music, multiple animated conversations could be heard in a dialect probably never before spoken in the Arkansas Ozarks.

Before heading over to talk to the group, I stopped to check in with the two local campers, and found them sitting in their truck, motor running, with eyes about the size of ping-pong balls. The dog was in the back of their pickup, evidently suffering from serious laryngitis after barking non-stop for the previous hour or so and looking somewhat confused by the whole situation. If I had walked up behind them and said "boo," I'm sure they would have gunned the motor of their truck and headed up the hill, leaving tent and gear behind.

After confirming that they had not had any actual contact or trouble with the group, I assured them I'd try to calm things down and headed over to the scene of the action. I was greeted warmly by my friendly interpreter and managed to explain over the din that they needed to turn the music way, way down. After it became possible to carry on a conversation, I was able to discuss the problem with the fire. It took some doing, but we were finally able to use a long-handled rake from my truck and spread the pile of burning wood far enough apart to get things back under a reasonable semblance of control. I made the most headway by reminding them that it was going to get pretty chilly at night, and they needed to save what was left of their wood for a much smaller fire that would last until they were ready for bed (which I hoped would be soon). In an effort to reinforce that idea, I reminded them that they would need a good night's sleep before spending the next day on the river.

When it looked like order had been restored and they were actually working at getting ready for bed, I used the standard ranger ploy of driving away, parking out of sight up the road, and then slipping back down on foot to observe for a while. Lo and behold, all looked calm and peaceful, so after touching base with the other camping couple one more time, I headed home.

In a burst of optimism, I decided that the tide had turned when I got through the whole night without any more phone calls. The next morning I headed down the hill to the campground and located my interpreter to discuss the group's planned river trip. I viewed this expedition with some trepidation, even though I was assured that several in their party were "very experienced." Only a couple of the local canoe rental outfitters were going to be open that early spring weekday, so I called and gave them a "heads-up" about their unusual potential customers.

The rest of the day was uneventful, and even the couple in the campground seemed satisfied that peaceful coexistence was possible.

Another family group had arrived and taken a spot between the two groups, so the original duo seemed to take some comfort from the presence of local reinforcements. As the end of the day neared, I made the usual round of the campground, and was flagged down by a man in the campsite of the latest arrivals.

The gist of his message was that I might want to "go check on the river for those guys with the robes." He went on to explain that his family had just come off the river and the last time he had seen the big group, they had been on a gravel bar a long way upriver, trying to start a fire. His impression was that all of them had capsized their canoes and gone for an unplanned dip shortly after leaving the launch ramp. They had seemed "Okay, just wet, but we haven't seen them come back off the river yet."

With a strong sense that this would be another long day, I headed across the loop to the group's campsite. There I discovered the possibility of both good news and bad news. The bad news was that the whole group was obviously not back from their trip. The good news was that there were at least a couple of guys in camp, so maybe they were just the first arrivals, with the rest coming along any minute now.

A conversation of sorts followed, since my main interpreter didn't prove to be one of those at the campsite. One of them did speak enough English for me to determine that yes, the rest of the group had gone on the river, but the two in camp had stayed behind; no, the boaters weren't back yet; and, not to worry, they would return "very soon, very soon."

I checked my watch and glanced up at the tall, rocky bluffs above the river, noting that they were entirely in shadow, the sun having already sunk behind the ridgeline. I got on the radio and contacted Mike, the other ranger on duty, asking him to pick up the boat and bring it down to the launch area. We might as well get started while we had at least a little bit of daylight left. Meanwhile, I'd check with the outfitter where the group had rented their canoes and see if they had heard anything from the group. I'd also check the only other takeout point on the river between their starting point and Buffalo Point, which was located at the Highway 14 bridge, only a mile or so upstream from the campground.

As a contingency, I also left instructions with people at all three of the occupied campsites at Buffalo Point to telephone the park's emergency number right away if the group returned on their own. That would hopefully avoid a lengthy and unnecessary search for someone who didn't need to be "found."

The Buffalo is a beautiful river, its clear, cold water flowing over a rocky bottom and its channel winding back and forth below dramatic bluffs that can tower hundreds of feet above the river. Depending on the time of year and how much rain has fallen in recent weeks, its depth can vary from many feet in deep pools to less than a foot if you get out of the main channel in riffles and rapids. Much of the year there is enough current along most of its length that paddling upriver for any distance can vary from a good workout to impossible. Those same qualities—sharp bends, a good current, occasional rapids, and sometimes shallow water—can make for a really challenging trip in the dark. As a result, I didn't want to wait until nightfall to get started on what was beginning to look like a search for an overdue group.

While most of the river traffic on the Buffalo is by canoe, flat-bottomed "johnboats" with small outboard motors are also used occasionally, especially by the locals. These provide the ability to travel both up and down river, as long as you are knowledgeable about the location of the channel in the shallow areas and rapids. Rangers at the park use both canoes and johnboats, and sometimes even inflatable rafts for their patrols, depending upon the job at hand and the water levels. On the lower end of the river, where I was working, the motorized johnboat was normally the preferred craft since it allowed us to carry a lot more gear, cover more river miles in a short time, and provided room for a couple of passengers in event of a rescue. Unless you were both careful and river-savvy, however, that rocky river bottom could spell an untimely end for an outboard motor's prop, or even the whole lower unit of the motor.

The best news in this situation was that my fellow ranger Mike Holmes was a great hand on the river, and he had the skills needed to give us a safe and efficient run upstream. The fact that there was a pretty good current that evening helped us in one regard: We could be fairly sure that our overdue group couldn't have gotten confused and gone *up*stream from their starting point. That gave us three possibilities.

Most likely, they would be on the river somewhere between the campground at Buffalo Point and the spot where they started their trip. That was a river access point named Maumee, eleven miles upstream from the Point.

Second, it was always possible that they might have cut their trip short, abandoned their canoes, and tried to get back to camp overland. This was unlikely, since there was virtually no sign of "civilization" between their starting and planned ending points, except for a takeout point where State Highway 14 crossed the river a mile or so upriver from Buffalo Point. Even if that had happened, we should at least be able to spot their canoes at the place where they had been abandoned along the edge of the river.

Finally, and worst of all, they could have overshot their takeout point at the campground and continued on downriver. If so, their next possible access point was at a place called Rush Landing, about seven miles downstream. However, given what we suspected about their skills and the information from the other boaters, it was unlikely that they had made it as far as Buffalo Point.

With all those factors in mind, Mike and I launched our boat and headed upstream in the fading light. Mike was in the back of the boat, handling the motor and keeping a close eye on the river ahead, picking his route to stay in the deepest water. My job from the front seat in the boat was to help keep an eye out for any obstructions in the water such as partially submerged logs, and to scan both shorelines for any sign of our group. It was already getting chilly, but the skies were clear and it would have been a nice evening for a slow, relaxing ride on the river. In this case, however, we weren't interested in going slow, and we weren't exactly relaxed. We just hoped we'd be home by bedtime.

For the first couple of miles we made good time, but soon Mike had to slow our speed as the twilight faded into a very dark night. There was no moon, and only the stars provided the slightest hint of light. While we could have used a battery-powered spotlight, we chose so far to rely on Mike's knowledge of the river and our night vision, which would have been ruined for an extended period of time if we used artificial light for even a second or two. At frequent intervals, Mike would kill the outboard, and we would give a yell, to try to avoid the possibility that we might miss the group if they had pulled up on the bank of the river.

When you start one of these search missions you're never quite sure what to expect. Fortunately, this one didn't make us wait too long for an answer. As we eased around one bend in the river, I thought I spotted the tiniest glimmer of light ahead on the water. I strained to see if I could pick it up again, and all at once, there it was. I turned and yelled at Mike over the sound of the outboard. He immediately cut the engine and we both peered ahead into the darkness as the boat quickly began to lose its forward speed. The sound of our motor would have been heard for quite some distance upriver.

Cupping my hands around my mouth, I let forth a long, loud (and hopeful) "Hellooooo."

Almost instantly, we were rewarded with a returned "Helloooo." Did we detect a hint of an accent? Hopefully an Afghani accent?

I responded with a loud, drawn out, "Park rangers."

After the briefest of pauses, we heard a distinctly accented, "Hey, park ranger, we lost, we lost!"

I couldn't resist. "We know, we know," I hollered in reply. "Wait right where you are, we're coming." What we didn't want was a game of bumper cars on a dark river with a bunch of inexperienced canoeists.

Mike started the outboard, and we eased upriver. We were soon alongside the first of six canoes, most with three passengers. In an inspired bit of planning the group had taken along what they described later as a survival kit, which consisted of some matches, long since used up in attempts to start a warming fire on the bank, and a single penlight flashlight. It was this light, carried by the man in front of the lead canoe, that we had spotted. To their credit, even those meager supplies were more than were carried by a lot of people who were making what was intended to be a short, easy day-trip on the river.

We managed to gather the group on a nearby sandbar, counted noses, and confirmed that everyone was accounted for. Thankfully, everyone was, and through a babble of excited conversation we were able to determine what had been happening through our helpful interpreter. After starting their trip, everyone had managed to capsize his canoe within the first half-mile or so of river. Thankfully, the shallow water made it easy for them to wade to shore and start again. After repeating this process several times, they had stopped and tried to build a fire to dry out. This was unsuccessful, so after using up their supply of matches, they set out again downriver. During the course of the day, they had eventually gained enough experience with their canoes that everyone had been able to stay upright and dry for the past several hours.

Mike and I weighed our options. I could wait with part of the group while Mike shuttled them, three at a time, back to the nearest road access at Highway 14. That would take a good part of the night, so we quizzed the group about their collective ability to finish the trip by canoe. The remaining stretch of river was basically "flat water" (with no rapids to contend with). They were eager to get back as quickly as possible, so after making sure everyone was wearing his life jacket, we set out again.

Our little flotilla must have resembled a mother duck and family of ducklings, with our boat puttering along in front, barely above idle speed, six canoes trailing along in our slight wake. We called ahead by radio and arranged for the canoe rental company to meet us at the Highway 14 launch ramp with their vans and canoe trailers, and, sooner than we had originally dared hope, everybody was safely back in camp.

As a result of the previous night's bonfire, firewood was in pretty scant supply, but the remainder of the group in camp had managed to scrounge the rest of what was left in this end of the county and had a small fire and a hot supper waiting for their reunion. Mike and I had only one chore left before putting away the boat and gear—the inevitable, official United States Department of the Interior Case Incident Report. I intended to keep it as simple as possible, but decided to at least try to get the names, addresses, and ages of our rescuees.

Our translator understood what I needed and helpfully called each man over to be introduced. He was willing to help with the spelling of names. I was quickly reminded of the meaning of "extended family." (It's been a while since this incident back in the late 1980s, so I'm using fictitious last names, but you'll get the idea.)

"Okay," I told my interpreter. "Who's first?"

My friend flashed a quick smile and gestured to the nearest man. "This is my cousin, Mr. Azir."

I jotted that down, along with his age and an apartment address in Little Rock.

"Now, who's next?" I asked.

"This is my cousin, Mr. Azir." He had the same address.

"Next?"

"This is my brother, Mr. Azir."

After repeating this process a couple of more times, I decided to cut to the chase. "Anybody here have a different address and name?"

As it turned out, they did come up with two apartment numbers for the whole group, and a couple of them did have different names, but we quickly decided in view of the successful outcome, we'd just list the interpreter and "sixteen others at same address" on the report. I was about to wrap it up and wish them a good night's rest when one of the group tugged on the arm of our assistant and rattled off a quick question. Our go-between then turned back to me.

"Oh, ranger, my cousin reminds me that he lost his camera when he tipped over his boat on the river. He would like for you to take him back and find it."

I think the correct adjective for my reaction would be incredulous.

"*Tonight?*" I asked. "Does he know where he lost it, and was it in any kind of waterproof bag or box?"

After a brief inquiry, our interpreter turned back, nodding his head and smiling. "Oh, yes, he says it was at a place where the water was very, very fast and very, very deep. It was not in anything because he was trying to take pictures of the fast water."

"How long after you started your trip?" I asked.

Another consultation. "He's not sure, he did not take his watch. He didn't want to get it wet, but it was before you found us."

I quickly determined that this description could cover several spots up and down the ten miles of river they had navigated, and was not exactly optimistic about the condition of the camera even if we succeeded in finding it and then fishing it out of the river. "Tell you what, it would be pretty hard to spot in the water in the dark. How about if we go look for it in the morning?"

The interpreter relayed this to his cousin, who agreed that this was a fine idea, and who pointed out, "Not to worry, we have insurance." At least these guys had quickly picked up on some of the essential points of life in the USA!

The best news of all came the next morning. I headed down to the campground to try again to get a better idea of the location of the elusive camera and found the group breaking camp. After discussing the virtues of American insurance over supper, they had decided to write off looking for the camera and were ready to head for home. I wished them a safe trip.

When all was said and done, they had not been a whole lot different from many other visitors. Proving that there is almost always a silver lining in any situation, I knew of at least one person who would be really glad they had come. After the visit by this group, the guy who sold firewood to campers during the summer was bound to have a banner year!

At the End of Their Rope

It began as a typical warm and sunny August afternoon along the Buffalo River. On a gravel bar near the campground at Buffalo Point, several children splashed in the cool water, while their parents relaxed in the shade nearby. Occasionally a canoe would drift into sight, the paddlers steering over to the shoreline to end their trip. The sound of their aluminum canoe being dragged across the smooth stones on the gravel beach would briefly drown out the kids' gleeful laughter, which echoed off the sheer bluffs across the narrow river.

Nearby, a common formula for calamity was starting to unfold: Two 18-year-old guys had spotted a couple of cute teenage girls sunbathing on the "beach," and the game was on. The challenge for the boys was how to meet and really impress the girls, and this duo had just the answer. They'd brought along some basic mountaineering equipment, and the rocky bluff right across from the gravel bar looked like just the place for an impressive rappelling demonstration. Unfortunately, along with their limited gear, they'd also brought along even less know-how.

One of these days, medical science will confirm the theory that for a significant percentage of males between the ages of fourteen and twenty-three, the effects of a particular hormone cancel out seventy-two percent of the brain's reasoning capacity. The old saying about people who toss caution to the wind can be traced to this syndrome, recently dubbed T.O.S.S. (**T**estosterone **O**verrides **S**ensible **S**chemes). This is a concept long understood by the auto insurance industry—a fact that you can confirm if you've ever had to pay the policy premiums for a driver in that age category. Also known as Macho Mania, T.O.S.S.

was a major factor in the events that were unfolding that afternoon along the tranquil shores of the Buffalo River.

For those of you who aren't into climbing, rappelling is simply a quick way to get from the top of something to the bottom. You've probably seen this on TV: mountaineers rappelling off of sheer cliffs, fireman rappelling over the sides of tall buildings, or Army Rangers rappelling out of helicopters. In very basic terms, a rope is secured at the top of the bluff, the climber straps on a harness, and attaches the harness to the rope with some special pieces of hardware. The climber then slides down the rope in a (hopefully) controlled descent. It looks fun and easy. It is—if you know what you're doing and have the right equipment.

The English writer Robert Burton made an observation way back in 1621 that was later repeated by Albert Einstein: "Imagination is more important than knowledge." That may be true in the search for new ideas, but it can get you into some serious trouble at times in the real world! In the case at hand, our two teenaged climbers had an abundant supply of imagination about how they were going to impress those girls by rappelling from the top of that rocky bluff. Unfortunately, their knowledge and equipment to actually do that successfully were definitely in short supply. To use a somewhat more modern expression, these guys knew just enough to be dangerous.

As we pieced the story together later, it developed something like this: About mid-afternoon, our intrepid mountaineers headed across the gravel bar, carrying their rope and a small bag containing their other gear. Their route was carefully calculated to take them directly past the two sunbathers, at which point they stopped to "check their gear" and managed to strike up a conversation about their plans. The gist of the discussion was, "Wait here and we'll show you some really cool stuff." As part of the plan, it was also apparently important for the guys to show off their great summer tans and impressive physiques, because they set out on their mountaineering adventure wearing only their bathing suits and tennis shoes.

The girls could look across the river to a rocky bluff, which is about 300 feet high. The cliff is more or less straight up and down, but gradually slopes back away from the river in an occasional stair-step fashion. At intervals there are horizontal ledges that run part of the way across the face of the bluff. Most importantly, there is a distinct outward bulge in the lower part of the cliff face, creating a definite overhang. This is critical because it means that someone standing above that overhang cannot look down and see the bottom of the cliff.

Since even these two guys realized they weren't Spider Man, they had to find a route up the almost sheer bluff before they could rappel back down. They understood enough about the topography of the area to know that at intervals the vertical cliffs were interrupted by side canyons—narrow valleys carved by streams that flowed into the Buffalo River. Many of these tributaries were dry except after a rain, but they all provided a much less vertical route to the rim of the main river canyon.

Armed with this knowledge, our duo struck out down the bank of the river, looking for a good place to cross to the opposite side. Once out of sight of their audience, they realized that the river is deeper than they thought, but, hey, no problem, they were only wearing their bathing suits anyway, so a short swim got them safely to the other side, right at the foot of a promising side canyon. The water was a good bit colder than they expected, too, but they would soon work up a sweat during their climb and warm up.

In addition to a possible route to the top, those side canyons also provide a great place for plants to grow, and grow they do. The ravine proved to be absolutely choked with trees large and small, shrubs, vines, and assorted other greenery. As they say, "It's a jungle out there," and progress up the steep ravine was surprisingly slow. It probably didn't take long for the idea to develop that some long pants, socks, and a shirt would be really useful, but it was too late to turn back now—wasn't it?

"Man, where did all those thorns come from, and say, do you remember what poison ivy looks like? This @*%$ rope is really bad about getting hung up in the branches, too! Oh, well, it's all for a good cause, and let's hurry up, before those babes get tired of waiting and leave!"

About four hours later, our adventurers had made it part of the way up the ravine and had located a promising ledge that leads out across the face of the bluff. The ledge varies from about two to four feet in width and is sometimes partially blocked by rocks or small trees, but finally they were almost there. It took them another half-hour or so to pick their way across the rocky face to a point where they are more or less directly across from the gravel bar where they started. Are the girls still there? It's hard to tell, because from about 150 feet up, those people on the opposite shore look pretty small, and you know what, it's going to be dark before long.

Before they can rappel down, the first order of business is to find a good anchor point at the top for their rope. A tree growing in the skimpy soil on the ledge looks promising—and also happens to be the only possible anchor in sight, so they tie one end of the rope to the tree and toss the remainder over the side. Oops, one small detail has just dawned on our pair: After they get to the bottom, they'll have to return to their perch on the cliff to retrieve their rope. Well, they'll deal with that later. Now it's time for the fun to begin!

Another look across the river confirms that a small crowd is starting to form. "That kinda looks like the girls, doesn't it? Hey, maybe this is going to work out after all! Aw, man, is that a ranger truck pulling up down there? Well, no big deal, he can't get to where we are, and besides, there isn't any law against this—is there? We'll be at the bottom before he even figures out what's going on."

Back on the other side of the river, our seasonal ranger has fortunately arrived on the scene just in time to try to save the day. The two girls proved to have more sense than their would-be heroes and after failing to see the climbers for several hours had gone back to camp and told their parents what was going on. The parents wisely decided to Contact the Proper Authorities, which led to one of those, "Hey, ranger, maybe you'd better check on . . ." conversations.

As soon as he arrived on the scene, a quick look at the situation with the ranger's binoculars revealed one really important point. Even though our would-be stars couldn't see this because of the overhang in the cliff face, their rope wasn't long enough to reach the bottom of the bluff!

This meant one of two things would happen when the first rappeller got to the end of his rope: Depending on his skill level and how they set up their equipment, he'd either slide right off the end of the rope and fall onto the rocks below, or he'd be stranded fifty feet or so above the ground, with no way to climb back up to the top. While on option was definitely a lot worse than the other, even the better of t two left them in a Definitely Melancholy Situation.

The good news is that even our dynamic duo, or at least o f them, still had a little common sense. At first they thought the d across the river was shouting to cheer them on, but it was h to tell because several people were yelling at the same time. Th ger was able to quiet the crowd and then used the P.A. syste his truck to finally get the message across. The news must not have been well received up on that bluff: "Don't climb down, your rope is too short!" Finally the boys yelled back that they understood.

A few more shouted messages got some more details, and it was time for the seasonal ranger to get on the radio and call his supervisor, known in park lingo as the District Ranger. Hey, that's why I got paid the big bucks, right?

Daylight was fading fast when I got the call at home. The bottom line was that the two kids had no food or water, no lights, minimal clothing and equipment, and no idea what to do next. They were at least willing to sit tight and wait for somebody who had a better idea.

The ranger assigned to Buffalo Point at that time was Scott Pfeninger, who was already enroute down to the vantage point on the edge of the river. After driving to the rescue cache to pick up our equipment, I met Scott at the gravel bar to size up the problem. We then loaded our packs with the necessary gear, borrowed a canoe to get to the other side of the river, and beached our boat at the foot of the same ravine the boys had used for their climb. By then, it was after 9 p.m. and really dark. As we thrashed our way through the thick bamboo along the bank of the river, I decided it was best to just not think about the big snakes that really like to hang out in those thickets!

Our main challenge was to find the same ledge where the two boys were perched. The face of the bluff was cut with a number of ledges, and as we made our way up the side canyon, we were completely out of sight of the face of the main bluff. We solved that problem by having the seasonal ranger on the opposite side of the river keep the spotlight on his truck trained on the bluff just to the right of the boy's location. That kept them from being blinded by the light, but provided a reference point for their location.

Scott and I were able to follow the path the boys had beat through the brush for most of their route and found that they had made several "false starts" in trying to find a ledge that provided a good route. As we followed each possible lead from the side canyon out to the edge of the luff itself, our partner on the other shore could see our headlamps. He uld then radio back to us where we were in relation to the boys.

It took several tries to locate the correct level, but by about midt we had reached the location of our would-be stars. They apparrealized that any fame at this point would probably not portray as they had hoped, because their first question was, "We're not o be on TV, are we?" I assured them that no news people were on hand to record their "escape," and we got down to more serious business.

By this time our intrepid pair was pretty cooperative because they were tired, hungry, and thirsty, as well as scratched, scraped, and starting to get chilly. They were initially ready to head for home right away, but Scott and I explained that everybody was safe right where we were and there wasn't any reason for a risky nighttime descent. We rigged up a safety line, got everybody into a climbing harness and clipped to the rope, passed out some warm clothes and a midnight snack, and settled down for something that passed for a nap on our rocky perch.

As soon as we had enough light to retrace our steps, we headed down to safety. Except for a couple of early morning fishermen, the humbling return of the pair was unwitnessed, and when we last saw them they were headed for home in Fayetteville, ninety miles away. The two girls who helped inspire this little saga? At that moment they were probably still sound asleep back in their campsite, but when I talked to them later, let's just say that they were less than impressed by the boys' performance.

True to my word, the pair escaped fame on TV. Their little exploit did make the headlines in the local newspaper, but at least for the sake of their egos I suspect the *Mountain Echo* didn't get much distribution back in their hometown. It likely would have been hard to talk these guys out of their adventure before they started, but as the Roman poet Horace noted a long time ago, "A good scare is worth more than good advice." If nothing else, I hope their experience helped reduce their T.O.S.S. level.

15

Sometimes, Chicken Soup Is Not Good for the Ranger's Soul

Arkansas Highway 21 is a scenic delight as it winds its way through the northern Arkansas Ozarks. Just south of the little community of Boxley, the two-lane road twists and turns around a series of sharp curves as it drops down toward the Boxley Valley and crosses the cool, clear waters of the Buffalo River. The headwaters of the Buffalo are not far to the west of Highway 21, up in the rocky slopes below Turner Ward Knob and Devil's Den Canyon. This is a beautiful and often rugged landscape, with miles of green forest broken occasionally by family farms and small, crossroads communities. The modern world can seem far away when you're making a leisurely drive up and down the hills along Highway 21.

There are only four highway crossings over the Buffalo as the river makes its way from west to east across 150 miles of the Land of Opportunity. As a result, there are more large trucks using these winding mountain highways than you might expect. Growing and processing chickens and turkeys is big business in this part of the country, and a lot of those big rigs are connected with that industry. Sometimes the combination of those mountain roads and big trucks provide an unwelcome opportunity for excitement for the truckers and for the rangers working at the Buffalo National River.

It wasn't a dark and stormy night, but it was definitely a cold and wet winter's day in the Ozarks. I was assigned to the Lower Buffalo district, about a hundred miles downstream from that pastoral scene in the Boxley Valley. We had only about a dozen full-time rangers assigned to the entire park back in the late 1980s, so allowing for days off during the week and two shifts on busy weekends, there were many times when only a handful of us were on duty. When a serious emergency arose, rangers from all up and down the river had to pitch in and help.

We got the call from the Upper Buffalo District late in the morning. A truck driver had either lost his brakes or taken one of those curves too fast for the rainy conditions. The initial report from a passerby included both good news and bad news.

The good news was that the driver was reported to be okay. The bad news was that it was a tanker truck of some kind. It was said to be on its side in the ditch and leaking an unknown substance from the ruptured tank. The even worse news was that the wreck site was near the top of a short, steep ravine that led directly down to the river, and the combination of gravity and a steady rain would help carry the spill down to the river. The nearest ranger was headed up the mountain to investigate. In the meantime, two of us from the Lower Buffalo District were requested to load up our hazmat gear and "expedite" our response.

So many similar situations had occurred over the years that each of the three district offices in the park kept a cache of supplies to help contain hazardous materials spills. Because the park is located in a pretty rural area it could take quite a few hours for a commercial hazmat crew to respond to accidents in our area. My fellow rangers and I had seen spills of gasoline, diesel, and millions of tiny plastic beads destined for a nearby boat manufacturing plant. We'd handled truck wrecks involving loads of charcoal, lumber, and furniture legs. A truck en route to a fish hatchery overturned and dumped hundreds of live catfish on the road. We'd seen spilled loads of frozen chickens, live chickens, and chicken feed. I thought we'd seen most of the weird cargos associated with chickens, but on this day, we were all in for a surprise.

When you're en route to an emergency response you want as much information as possible so you can start developing a plan and preparing yourself mentally for what lies ahead. Occasionally, however, you almost wish in retrospect that you didn't know in advance what you're facing. This was going to be one of those days.

The first ranger to reach the scene called us on the radio with an update shortly after his arrival. We were advised to continue our response, but we could "back off" on the speed a bit. He had more good news and bad news. It seems the leaking material was in fact headed down the slope toward the river, but it was moving very slowly. That was the good news.

The bad news was that the reason it was moving so slowly is that liquefied chicken fat doesn't move very fast when the air temperature is about 35°. Yep, this had been a whole tanker truck full of chicken fat. The only estimate was that the truck had been carrying several thousand gallons of the stuff, very little of which was still in the tank. That's news that will definitely bless your heart.

The chicken processing industry has apparently copied a page from their counterparts in the pork business, which is said to use "everything except the oink." Chicken fat is a by-product of the chicken processing business, and the substance is liquefied by a process probably classified top secret by the industry. This allows it to be piped into tanker trucks and hauled away to points unknown, where it is used for a variety of purposes. (Don't ponder this information too deeply, unless you and your cats intend to become vegetarians.)

My partner and I arrived at the scene after adjusting our speed to take due care on the wet roads—and hoping that for once a cleanup crew hired by the trucking company would beat us there. No such luck. Since we were on the turf of the upper district ranger, he had the responsibility of being the IC or Incident Commander. We were simply there to follow his directions, which were really pretty simple: take whatever you've got to work with and keep that "stuff" contained in the ravine as close to the road as possible.

We took a quick inventory of our hazmat supplies, which consisted mainly of some pads that look a little like oversized pampers and some long booms of the same material that resemble pampers rolled into giant, six-foot-long sausages. These are all made from a special fabric that is mainly designed to absorb petroleum products. Hey, if they would work on gasoline, why not chicken fat? Plan number one was to just deploy some pads and booms in front of the advancing ooze and contain it until the pros arrived to take over the clean-up.

Actually, plan number one wasn't a bad one, except that the ravine was filled with a thick layer of leaves, and the goop had a strange tendency to run under and through the leaves instead of on top of them. That meant that we had to rake and shovel most of the leaves out of the way before we could place the pads and booms. In the process of raking and shoveling, we just had to be sure we didn't spread the "stuff" around.

Plan number two, to just build some low earthen dams in the ravine and contain the flow sounded great, but it, too, was quickly discarded. There's a good reason there aren't many farms on these rocky Ozark slopes—loose dirt is a very scarce commodity in those parts, whether you want it for a garden or for damming up a gully to contain chicken fat—and a dam built from the abundance of rocks was too porous. We finally settled on a combination of low rock dams lined with sheets of plastic and absorbent pads.

To get the full picture, try to recall that it's about 35º and a steady rain is now falling. Runoff from the rain was carrying our adversary down the hill, although thankfully rather slowly. Whatever process is used to liquefy this stuff apparently prefers an ambient temperature somewhat higher than 35º. If you are looking for a path to fame and fortune, I'd suggest you unlock the hidden secret about how to turn partially liquefied chicken fat into industrial-strength adhesive. I can testify from first-hand experience that under the conditions described above, it will really, really, stick to almost anything, with a decided preference for boots and pants legs. Somewhat to our surprise, the cold temperature didn't do much to reduce the aromatic qualities of the substance and as an added bonus a distinctive odor hung heavily in the air.

Well, once again sheer persistence triumphed over evil; we contained the enemy, saved the Buffalo once again, and eventually turned the rest of the cleanup job over to pros. It was about dark when I made it back home, cold, wet and suspecting that I was hungry, but not entirely sure. I had already changed clothes back at the ranger station, consigning my uniform for the day to a well-sealed trash bag and wondering whether it was worth washing. I won't blame you for thinking the end of this story is too good to be true, but it is.

I had asked that a message be relayed to my family that I had been working a truck wreck and might be a little late getting home, so those were all the details they had to work with. I opened the door to be greeted by a loving wife, who welcomed me home with the cheerful news that she knew I'd be ready for a nice supper, so she had prepared a great meal. It was just coming off the stove, so all I had to do was wash up and sit down at the table.

Yep, you guessed it—fried chicken, mashed potatoes, and cream gravy made right from those tasty chicken drippings! Velma was a really good sport when she found out why I said I'd just wait outside until the smell of freshly cooked chicken was aired out as much as possible, and for once the rest of the family didn't have to try to beat Dad to the best pieces! Time eventually restored my appetite for a good drumstick, and chicken is now back on the menu for our household. On that particular evening, however, a cheese sandwich sure tasted a whole lot better!

Unusual incidents involving trucks are certainly not limited to the Buffalo National River. As evidence I offer a situation at the Big South Fork National River & Recreation Area in Kentucky and Tennessee. According to a report from the park, "rangers found themselves in a real 'pickle'" on March 15, 2004, when they received a call about a tractor-trailer stuck along a road in the park. When they arrived on the scene rangers found that the tractor was gone, but the trailer had been abandoned—with a full load of cucumbers.

This case initially proved to be a real dilly, since there were no license plates or other identifying marks on the trailer, but good rangers relish a challenge. Success is sweet, however, and the owner was located after investigation determined that the rig had been stolen from a truck stop the previous weekend. Incidentally, this situation occurred on a Monday, so you can keep it in mind the next time you think your week is off to a weird start!

16

Setting the Stage: Glacier National Park

Straddling the Continental Divide along the Canadian border in northwestern Montana, Glacier National Park contains some of the most spectacular mountain scenery in the United States. It doesn't take most people who visit this park long to understand why Glacier was one of the early additions to the National Park System in 1910. In 1932, Glacier and the adjoining Waterton Lakes National Park in Canada were designated Waterton-Glacier International Peace Park in recognition of the longstanding peace and friendship between the two nations. This designation is largely symbolic and the parks are managed separately, although their staffs cooperate closely on items of mutual concern.

The park's official website notes that Glacier "preserves over 1,000,000 acres of forests, alpine meadows, and lakes. Its diverse habitats are home to over 70 species of mammals and over 260 species of birds. The spectacular glaciated landscape is a hiker's paradise containing 700 miles of maintained trails that lead deep into one of the largest intact ecosystems in the lower 48 states." This is also definitely "pretty as a postcard" country, and scenes from the park have graced many a calendar, magazine cover, and computer screensaver.

Like many of the large western parks, Glacier can seem very crowded or offer plenty of solitude—depending upon when you visit and how far you're willing to venture off of the road. The park receives about 1.8 million visits a year, which may not sound like much compared to the Blue Ridge Parkway's 21.5 million, until you consider that the vast majority of Glacier's activity is compressed into about a 10-week period in the

Mountain goats are often seen by visitors along the trail to Hidden Lake, near the Continental Divide in Glacier National Park. Enjoy them from a distance, and for their sake and yours, don't attempt to feed them. (Jim Burnett)

middle of the summer. Late July at popular destinations in this park can be pretty hectic.

The reason for that short season is simple—this part of the northern Rockies is serious winter country, and snow comes early and stays late. Most visitor facilities open in mid-May and are closed by mid-September. One of the most magnificent scenic highways in the world is the Going-to-the-Sun Road, which allows visitors to drive through the heart of the park from one side to the other. Based upon the amount of snow received each winter, this road usually opens for the season sometime during the first two weeks in June, but that date can be earlier or later by several weeks, depending on the weather. The gates are swung shut again for the year in about the third week of October—unless earlier snowfall forces an earlier closure.

The following stories set in Glacier focus primarily on life during the winter, since that is a season most visitors don't have a chance to experience first-hand. As you'll see, winter in this park also provides ample opportunity for some rather unusual adventures.

For additional information, check the park's website at www.nps.gov/glac or write to Glacier National Park, P.O. Box 128, West Glacier, Montana 59936.

17

"Mister, It's Not Too Late"

One of the widely held myths among the general public about the ranger life is that most of us live in a spacious, but cozy, log cabin, set in a secluded, scenic site with a postcard view of a mountain lake. In the ranger ranks we sometimes referred to this as the "hunt, trap and fish" concept, which is what some people think describes our day-to-day activities out in the "wilderness." I often said during my career that if I had a dollar for every person who said with unmistakable envy, "Man, I wish I had your job," I could have retired a whole lot earlier! While it's true that some rangers do have a rugged existence in some very remote locales, the reality is that the majority of areas in the National Park System are east of the Mississippi River and log cabins are in short supply.

Like a fair number of my colleagues, I did look forward to a chance to work in one of those mountain "crown jewel" parks, and that opportunity finally came in the winter of 1978, when I was offered a transfer to Glacier National Park in Montana.

Despite the dire predictions of friends and casual bystanders, the first day of our February cross-country move from southern Indiana to the Northwest had proceeded without mishap. Since our collection of houseplants couldn't go with the movers, we had squeezed them into the back of the family Blazer, along with our four-year-old and her essential toys. Because of the cold weather, all of the plants had to be unloaded for each night's stop. This task provided yet another opportunity for unsolicited advice from well-meaning strangers.

It was the first night of our journey, and I was on my third trip through the lobby of a St. Louis motel with yet another armful of potted plants while a heavy snowstorm raged outside. Another guest had been sitting in the lobby, trying to pretend he was reading a newspaper rather than watching my activities. Finally, his curiosity got the best of him.

"Moving, huh?" he observed astutely.

"Yes, to Montana," I replied through the branches of a Norfolk Pine.

"Montana?!" The man glanced out the nearby window at a scene that looked more like Alaska than Missouri. "What's the matter? Not cold enough for you around here?"

I cheerfully assured him that we were really looking forward to the move. After all, we were old hands at winter, after surviving two of the worst ones ever recorded in the Midwest. Or so we thought.

Five days, 2,000 miles, and lots of snow later, we got the first hint that maybe we hadn't experienced everything that winter has to offer. The last day's journey across the open plains had been over clear, dry roads, with only patches of snow covering the stubble of last year's wheat harvest or the straggling stalks of grass in a rancher's pasture. A few miles west of Cut Bank, Montana, the Rocky Mountains appear to rise abruptly from the open, rolling prairie, and the snow pack increased just as dramatically in the space of only a few miles. It was suddenly a real winter wonderland.

Those of you who are fans of the Weather Channel may recognize the name "Cut Bank"—usually in the context of a shockingly low winter temperature reading. (East Glacier, or St. Mary, or Browning, closer to the park where the REALLY cold air is located, don't make the TV maps because there isn't a daily weather report from those tiny communities.)

Our new home was East Glacier, a mountain village of 300 hardy, self-sufficient souls on the edge of Glacier National Park. We had promised our daughter that we were going to live in a "really neat house in the mountains," and as we entered town, a huge, rustic hotel came into sight. The Glacier Park Lodge is a legacy of the Great Northern Railroad's efforts to bring the majesty of the great European chalets to the new national parks in the early days of the twentieth century. It commanded a view worthy of any chamber of commerce calendar.

Our four-year-old looked out the car window at the grand old lodge. "Is that our new house, Daddy?" I felt a brief stirring of sympathy for her future husband and wondered if the child was destined to marry into the moneyed class. Somewhere in her bloodline there must be a previously unknown touch of royalty.

Explaining that the majestic log hotel was just one of our neighbors, we continued a short distance down the road to the realm of the common folk. The setting was still remarkable for a trio of flatlanders. Nestled into a stand of lodgepole pine, the dark brown house with the green metal roof looked like a mountain house ought to look. The majestic Rocky Mountains rose right at the edge of town, while at the opposite edge of the village, the Great Plains swept away to the eastern horizon. In between, in what I supposed was our yard, lay the remnants of the Great Ice Age, which, contrary to published reports, was apparently still underway.

We parked the car at the edge of the road and after some searching located a narrow path through the deep snowbank to the door. The key had been left with the neighbors in the other half of our duplex as promised, and a quick inspection of our 1920s vintage home revealed that it was what we would later describe to friends as "snug."

"This is a lot smaller than our other house, Daddy. Where are we going to put all our things?" Our daughter's royal bloodline apparently omitted a sense of appreciation for cozy historic structures.

I quickly looked for a chance to change the subject before my wife could ask the same question. No problem. She was busy looking in amazement at the snow which was piled up outside above the tops of the first-floor windows, giving the house something of a cave-like feel. The reason for the house's steeply pitched metal roof became apparent: The snow slid off the roof and simply piled up around the perimeter of the building, all winter long. I thought it gave the place a kind of nice, secure, bunker effect. If the question of bears came up, I could jokingly point out that the snow piles would keep them from looking into the windows, just in case any of them came out of hibernation ahead of schedule. However, I decided not to raise the question of various wild critters at this point.

"Look at it this way," I tried gallantly. "At least we won't have to worry about curtains until the van gets here." Fortunately, I was saved by the timely arrival of our next door neighbor, who assured us that, no, the van driver hadn't called yet to tell us when he might appear. We gratefully accepted an invitation for supper, and I went out to unload the sleeping bags—and the house plants.

Two days later the van driver finally phoned. A resident of southern Florida, he had warned us before we left our previous home that he had never driven "up north," but he was sure it would be no problem. I later concluded that "up north" must have meant anywhere on the map above North Carolina. The driver was calling to inform us that he was stuck in a "blizzard" 200 miles away in Great Falls, but would "try to get through as soon as the storm let up." The single channel on our neighbor's TV set had mentioned a two-inch snowfall overnight at Great Falls in the context of an unusual, pleasant break in the normal winter weather. Hoping we would see our furniture before the 4th of July, I was curious about the driver's reaction when he finally made it up into some real snow in our mountain village.

We were pleasantly surprised when two days later, the van did actually arrive, creeping to a halt outside our private snowbank. The driver climbed out into the 5° air and sank to his knees in the snow alongside the road. Looking in absolute disbelief at the winter scene, he waded through the snow to where I was standing.

"You know, mister," he said hopefully, "it's not too late. Just give me the word, and I'll turn this rig around and take you good folks right back where you came from!" The thought that we might actually volunteer to stay in such an inhospitable location was totally beyond his comprehension.

After the driver was assured that we really weren't being held here at gunpoint, he turned reluctantly toward the truck and yelled to his helper. "Go ahead and open 'er up, Harry. They said they're gonna stay." Shaking his head in amazement, the driver then followed us into the house to size up the job. His first words sounded strangely like my four-year-old's question a few days earlier. "Say, where are you folks gonna put all your stuff?"

Amazingly, it all did go into our 850-square-foot home. Well, almost. The narrow stairs to the second floor proved to be too tight for a few items, like our dresser and double bed, so a downstairs room suddenly became the master bedroom, and the kid's things went upstairs. Other "stuff" went into the single car garage. Some of it eventually made it back into the house before we moved again.

A previous occupant of the same house stopped by one day and informed me cheerfully that we could get the larger items into the upstairs bedroom simply by taking out a large window and hauling the furniture up to the second floor and through the window space with a couple of ropes. That project, however, waited until somewhat more moderate temperatures arrived. Unfortunately, when we eventually moved on, we departed in December, making the reverse of that process a bit more interesting.

After sending our van crew back to the sunny south, we enjoyed a good night's sleep on real beds and woke up to a beautiful, sunny morning, visible at least from the upstairs windows in our daughter's room. I got dressed, opened the door to savor the crisp, mountain air, and hastily retreated back inside. The thermometer tacked outside the kitchen window read –23°. I was glad for his sake that the van driver had come the day before.

My wife suggested, from somewhere behind a wall of packing cartons, that if I would just hook up the washer, she would tackle the week's accumulation of laundry. Eager to confirm my wisdom in not paying the van driver to handle such trivia, I rapidly completed the job and summoned the lady of the house to the utility room, which was actually a converted screened porch only slightly larger than a telephone booth. She loaded the machine and pulled the knob to christen our first load to be washed with honest-to-goodness pure Rocky Mountain spring water. Nothing happened.

It is a tribute to her diplomacy that Velma failed to cast any aspersions on my mechanical aptitude. Still, I was puzzled since even I felt competent to connect a pair of washing machine hoses to the faucets. My deliberation was interrupted by a knock on the back door. Before I could negotiate the obstacle course through the packing boxes, the door opened and a cheery face peeked inside.

"Hi! I'll bet your pipes are frozen too," ventured our next-door neighbor.

Four hours later, I was intimately acquainted with the art of thawing frozen water pipes, as well as with that new chamber of horrors, the narrow, uninsulated crawl space under our sixty-year-old, almost uninsulated house. This was an experience I would later rank right up there with trying to put tire chains on my pickup in a blizzard while parked on glare ice on a steep mountain road. For now, however, all was well; the laundry sloshed merrily around in the washer, and a chinook (a warm wind) arrived later in the day to raise the temperature by an incredible fifty degrees before nightfall. Surely, spring must be right around the corner. After all, it *was* almost March!

Just another winter morning in Glacier National Park, and the author has a bit of work to do before hitting the road in his truck! (Jim Burnett)

The photo was taken in the parking lot behind our house after a typical snowfall, just to give you a little peek at a Montana winter.

On Memorial Day weekend, I stood ankle deep in fresh snow, trying to focus my camera with slightly numb fingers. I wanted the photo to prove to the folks back home that it really does snow someplace in the lower 48 during the last week in May. Since we lived at an elevation of only 4,600 feet, even I was a little surprised to see six inches of the white stuff this late in the season. Surely spring must be right around the corner. After all, it was almost June!

Spring, we found, did come suddenly in June, and it was worth the wait. It exceeded our wildest dreams: bright, sunny days, crystal blue skies, wildflowers as far as the eye could see, pleasant temperatures, air so clean it actually tasted good—and possibly the world's hungriest mosquitoes. Their appetites were exceeded only by those of our houseguests. Our announcement about our upcoming move to friends and family brought a record bounty of guests that following summer. Since we were living on the border of a world-famous national park, we soon surmised that all of the major travel guides had rushed out a special, revised edition just to include our guest room. Our "resort location" put us back in touch with people we hadn't heard from in decades, along with a few we couldn't really remember ever having met before and probably never would in less sublime locations.

Actually, we loved every minute of it, despite the fact that ten sets of company in twelve weeks came close on the heels of the birth of our son on June 1st. We quickly developed the one-hour, one-day, and one-week guided tour options for our guests, and our newborn spent so much time in the car his first three months on earth that he's still a great traveler to this day. My wife also learned how to politely rush one set of company out the back door and then change the beds in record time, while I cheerfully stalled the incoming company on the front porch. If you think you have a future in the bed-and-breakfast business, I'd suggest you first try renting a place in a popular vacation spot for a summer and then spread the word among your acquaintances that the welcome mat is out!

As the locals promised, summer really does follow spring in the mountains of northern Montana, and we were actually home that day in July, so we didn't miss it! (Fall began the following morning.) With a growing season of less than thirty frost-free days, it wasn't worth trying to get tomatoes to ripen in the garden, but there were lots of other compensations. Check out a subalpine meadow full of wildflowers in

Keeping the roads open in and around Glacier National Park can often be a challenge in the winter. In this photo, a rotary plow works to clear a snowdrift near the East Glacier Ranger Station. (Jim Burnett)

July, and you'll see what I mean. We were also introduced to huckleberries, a wild relative of the blueberry that makes the world's best ice-cream, pancakes, and jelly.

By late August the bugs were gone, along with the summer crowds, and September's aspen groves brought the kind of gold that no bank vault could ever hope to contain. During those great autumn days, it didn't matter that the next winter would bring a night of −48° and almost a month with frozen water mains. Hey, no place is perfect all the time, right?

If the spot you think is your dream location is in a totally different kind of environment than you're accustomed to, go for it if you get a chance, but expect to have some adventures and adjustments along the way. The grass may be greener outside your new home, but you may also have to wait for the snow to melt to be sure! Even if your next move isn't to your Shangri-La, any place you live has the potential for fun and adventure, if you'll just keep the oft-quoted proverb in mind: "Blessed are the flexible, for they shall not be bent out of shape!"

"Okay now, does anybody remember which packing box has the . . . ?"

18

Lions and Tigers and Bears, Oh My!

National parks in this country are not known to contain any tigers, but bears and an occasional mountain lion do add extra interest to a number of locations. Several parks, including Yosemite, have a very active program to reduce bear problems in developed areas such as campgrounds—and for good reason. As recently as 1998, black bears broke into about 1,100 vehicles in Yosemite, causing more than $630,000 in damage. I suspect some of those car owners had interesting conversations with their big-city insurance agents when they turned in a claim for repairs due to a break-in by a bear.

Thanks to aggressive measures, including strict regulations on the storage of food in vehicles, that damage figure had been reduced to about $30,000 by 2001. If you plan to visit a park where bears (or mountain lions) are residents, be sure to get the latest information on both regulations and safety tips. That could be important for your well-being—and save you a potential hassle with your insurance company.

Considering the number of visitors each year to places like Yellowstone, Glacier, and Great Smoky Mountains National Parks, the small number of actual confrontations between bears and people is testimony to the success of the parks' bear management programs. Actually, those programs are often more about managing people and their activities, since as far as I can determine, the bruins (**B**ears **R**esolutely **U**ninterested **I**n **N**on-edible **S**olutions) haven't ever officially signed on as participants.

One of the basic principles of avoiding bear problems is careful storage of food and garbage. Bears are a lot like people—if there's a free supply of food to be had, they'll take it, and our garbage seems to be high on a bear's list of delicacies. As a result, parks have made stringent efforts in recent years to keep garbage and any other type of people food away from bears. This includes the use of various kinds of "bear-proof" containers for both food and trash, although the long-term success of anything designed by humans as being "bear-proof" is somewhat speculative.

During my tour at Glacier National Park, we lived at the East Glacier Ranger Station, a cluster of aging rustic buildings that housed four families, a small office, and some space for storage of maintenance and emergency equipment. This complex was in the village of East Glacier, which claimed about 300 year-round residents and was actually on the Blackfeet Indian Reservation, which adjoins the eastern boundary of the park.

Part of our contribution to keeping bears out of town involved depositing all of our household garbage into a single dumpster centrally located behind our little housing area. As long as the heavy lid to that big metal box was kept closed, it would be very difficult for a bear to get to the goodies (from a bear's viewpoint) inside.

Late one spring, word got around that a poacher had shot, but not killed, a grizzly not far from town. No further details were known except that a wounded, and therefore probably very ill-tempered, bear could be roaming the area. This created a definite sense of unease around our little community—people no longer let their kids walk to and from school, and the locals were more inclined to drive rather than walk the several blocks to one of the town's two mom-and-pop grocery stores. Rumors were rampant, of course, and false sighting reports kept various authorities scurrying around in hope of capturing the injured animal.

It was against this backdrop that just before bedtime one night my wife Velma made one of those classic household requests: "Honey, before you go to bed, could you take out the trash?" I was almost ready for my shower and it was an unusually mild night, so I just pulled on a pair of jeans and tennis shoes, grabbed the bag from the kitchen, and headed out the back door into the dark. Several streetlights around the edge of the complex provided just enough light that I could make my way to the dumpster without needing a flashlight.

The heavy lid on our "bear-proof" dumpster required both hands to lift. The usual technique was to raise the cover far enough to make a "deposit," then hold it in position with one hand while using the other to toss your offering into the dumpster. You could then leap back and

Grizzly bears are one of the most dramatic species of wildlife found in parks like Glacier and Yellowstone, but they command caution and respect. When visiting areas in bear country, always get current information from rangers about safety and regulations regarding bears and other wildlife. (National Park Service, Yellowstone National Park)

let the lid drop with a loud bang that reassured everyone within a block or so that at least the rangers were holding up their end of the discourage-the-bears campaign. This also meant, of course, that in order to avoid a reprimand from Miss Manners we tried to limit our trash deposits to reasonable hours. I had almost completed raising the lid when that elusive sixth sense told me that I was not alone in that dark parking lot.

The following events took place in a lot less time than it takes to tell them. Before I had time to really react to that rather ominous information, some of my other senses came into play, and I simultaneously heard and felt a whoosh of warm air as a breath from an unknown lifeform was exhaled onto my bare back. I'm a reasonably tall person, so the fact that the breath was felt above my waist was a pretty good indication that my unexpected companion was not Ricky the Raccoon. Given the recent bear scare, this immediately fell into the category of a potentially Very Melancholy Situation.

I can't tell you in retrospect exactly what went through my mind in the next few microseconds, but I did know that my options were somewhat limited, since I was pretty well pinned between an unknown, warm-blooded companion and that very solid dumpster. Ironically, I was also in something of an "I surrender" position, with both hands over my head holding the lid open. A reasonable course of action seemed to be to turn my head very slowly to size up the situation, while hoping for divine inspiration for a solution.

When I turned, I was just able to make out in the faint light the very large St. Bernard dog that belonged to a family down the road! I don't know how you spell "relief," but for just a few moments that night, I cast my vote for "d-o-g." The reported wounded bear was never seen or heard from, at least not via any official channels, and life in town gradually returned to normal.

Plenty of bear stories have been told in other books, so I'll share only one recent one with you here. My pick for the winner of the Cool Head under Fire Award, Bear Encounter Category, is a woman named Abigail Thomas. According to a report from Yellowstone National Park, Ms. Thomas "was jogging on a trail in the Lake Lodge area of Yellowstone on June 4, 2002, when she encountered a male sub-adult grizzly bear approximately fifteen yards to her right." Following proper grizzly bear protocol, "Ms. Thomas immediately stopped and stood perfectly still; she did not make eye contact with the bear, and continuously reassured the bear that she was not a threat." [Editorial comment: the report did not elaborate, so I unfortunately can't enlighten you on exactly how she "continuously reassured the bear." I presume the choice of words and her tone of voice may come into play, but you're free to use your imagination on those details.]

The report continues, "The bear stood up on its back legs and sniffed the air, then dropped to the ground and slowly approached Ms. Thomas on her right side. When it reached her, it began sniffing her from the waist down, then opened its mouth and—very gently—closed its mouth around her right upper thigh." [Again, the report doesn't enlighten us about whether or not the lady continued to reassure the bear that she was not a threat. At that point, of course, her options were somewhat limited, and I would rate this as a Seriously Potentially Melancholy Situation.]

Well, back to the official account: "The bear applied a small amount of pressure, then released her leg. Ms. Thomas received no injuries, other than some very minor contusions; her skin was not broken from the bite. After she felt the bear release her leg, she reached for her water bottle and squirted the bear between the eyes. The bear immediately ran from the area. Park officials praised Ms. Thomas for how well she handled the potentially life-threatening bear encounter, remaining calm and focused throughout the ordeal." Fortunately, it ended well for all concerned, and I certainly salute this lady for a remarkably composed response to the situation.

Occasionally an encounter with a bear will motivate a person to try to expand the boundaries of technology. Some of these efforts have been recognized by the awarding of an Ig Noble Prize, bestowed by the Annals of Improbable Research and several groups at Harvard to "celebrate the unusual, honor the imaginative—and spur people's interest in science, medicine, and technology."

In 1998 the winner in the Ig Noble category of Safety Engineering was Mr. Troy Hurtubise, who was inspired to develop a bear-proof suit after a narrow escape from a close encounter with a grizzly while hiking in British Columbia. Although this didn't occur in an American national park, it has enough bearing on park bruin encounters to be worthy of mention.

Mr. Hurtubise has spent more than fifteen years and a small fortune on his project. The latest version of his protective suit, the Ursus Mark VII, is fabricated from titanium, stainless steel, and heavy-gauge aluminum, and contains a cooling and ventilation system, advanced protective airbags, a built-in video screen, and a two-way communications system. A finger-activated trigger in the left arm can activate a can of bear repellent stored in the arm.

In order to test his invention, he has worn the suit while being subjected to an amazing range of "attacks," in addition to close encounters with bears. He's been hit by trucks, cut by industrial saws, and assaulted by three bikers armed with an axe, planks, and a baseball bat. While it's not intended for use by the average park visitor, maybe his invention would be useful for people who live in bear country to wear while taking out the garbage late at night! It also has potential serious applications for uses such as protecting bomb squad members. His website, projecttroy.com.nexx.com/ has all the details if you'd like to know more.

Although they are less common than bear encounters, visitors and employees in parks occasionally come into contact with mountain lions, and there have been a few tragic incidents. As is the case with bears, your risk of coming to harm from a lion is a lot smaller than being struck by lightning. Even so, if you're in lion country it is exceedingly prudent to get some basic safety instructions from the local authorities before venturing out on a hike.

In the spring of 2002, rangers at Pinnacles National Monument in California noticed an "increase in mountain lion sign and vocalizations" along the Old Pinnacles Trail. In plain English, vocalizations means sounds had been heard that seemed to be spoken in the lion dialect. My ancient version of *A Field Guide to the Mammals* says that a mountain lion has a "voice like ordinary tomcat, but much magnified." I take this to mean it sounds something like a neighbour's annoying cat under your bedroom window at midnight, except that it is being played over their teenager's boom box.

"Mountain lion sign" would include things like tracks and scratching in the dirt made when the lions, like all felines, tried to cover their exhaust emissions, otherwise politely known as droppings or scat. In this usage of the term, "scat" is not what you say to a lion if you see one at close range, although in contrast to the official advice about how to deal with bears, reassuring a lion that you are not a threat is not proper protocol. In the case of lions, most experts say you should do everything possible to make the lion think you *are* a threat, so I suppose yelling "scat" with enough vigor might qualify.

When situations such as increased lion sign and vocalizations arise, rangers are often called upon to make special patrols at times when lion activity is most likely to occur—which includes the dark of night. Those tasks probably fall under the infamous category in the ranger's job description: "Other Duties as Assigned." Unfortunately, limited staffing sometimes requires that they make these patrols alone, which is one reason that specially trained rangers—and not visitors—are allowed to carry firearms in parks.

On the night of March 31, 2002, a ranger was patrolling the trail in question at Pinnacles and heard movement on the hillside above him, followed by the sound of a large animal running down the hillside in his direction. Turning his flashlight on, he saw that the animal was a medium-sized mountain lion. The ranger's flashlight then faded and died. (Where is that Energizer Bunny when you need him?) This may be further proof that the government's policy of buying supplies from the supposed lowest bidder isn't necessarily the best idea.

Confirming that just when you think things can't get any worse, they can, the ranger tried to yell to frighten away the animal. Unfortunately he was hoarse from a cold and could barely speak above a whisper, and so he was unable to yell "scat" or any other appropriate word at the approaching lion. This definitely qualifies as a Positively Melancholy Situation and also confirms that most rangers are far too dedicated to their jobs, reporting for work even when they have good reason to call in sick. At that point, having exhausted his other options, the ranger drew his pistol and, when the lion closed to within five yards, fired a round into the hillside between them.

The lion fortunately received the intended message, and the animal veered off and continued across the trail ahead of the ranger into the brush of a creek bottom. The ranger backed down the trail, covering the area where he could hear the cat moving along the creek bed. The report does not mention any vocalizations by the lion at that point, which was probably just fine with the ranger. The cat followed the ranger for about 300 yards, then disappeared. An intensive educational and safety information campaign regarding mountain lions was undertaken at the park to make visitors aware of the situation, and no further incidents occurred.

Sometimes it's hard to get solid information from visitors about wildlife incidents, since most people can be understandably excited about their experience. This problem is illustrated by a report from Bryce Canyon National Park about a hiker's encounter with a mountain lion a few years ago. The man reported that the lion followed him on a trail, then approached and growled. The animal left only after the hiker waved a stick, then threw it at the lion. The ranger's report noted that "it's not known if the mountain lion was a juvenile or an adult, since the size description given by the hiker would more nearly fit the size of a saber-tooth tiger." (I started this chapter with the claim that national parks in this country don't harbor any tigers, but . . . .)

Wildlife adventures aren't limited to dry land. On September 27, 2000, Nanette K. and Michael C. rented a boat from a local business near Jean Lafitte National Historical Park and Preserve in Louisiana and went canoeing in the park.

Sometimes once a situation starts to deteriorate it just keeps on getting worse. The pair's troubles started when they attempted to return by a different route and became lost, but the situation really became interesting when their canoe was almost swamped by a large alligator! In the midst of that near-miss Michael, who is a diabetic, managed to break his glasses and lose his cell phone. The report doesn't mention any specific comments by the visitors, but under the circumstances it would be understandable if they had later described that alligator as being larger than a saber-tooth tiger.

The boaters were due back at 6 p.m. and were reported overdue at 9:15 p.m. Rangers Leigh Zahm and Eric Ulitalo began a search of the waterway and found the couple at 11 p.m. By then they had been lost in the darkness for several hours, and after their encounter with the 'gator, I can only imagine their reactions every time they heard a splash somewhere nearby. If you've never spent any time at night in the deep, dark woods (or swamp), you'd likely be amazed at how many mysterious noises there can be in places that are highly touted for their "peace and quiet." The two canoeists were guided safely back to their starting point, tired and hungry but otherwise unscathed.

Wildlife hazards aren't limited to the obvious carnivores such as lions and bears, or even alligators. Yellowstone National Park has advisories posted warning that bison can weigh up to a ton and sprint at speeds of up to thirty miles per hour and that it's against the law to approach within one-hundred yards of bears or within twenty-five yards of all other wildlife. Even so, it's a rare year without one or more incidents involving bison (which—thanks mainly to Hollywood—are often referred to incorrectly as buffalo).

Many problems with wildlife occur when people ignore information, advice, warnings, regulations, and a multitude of other efforts made at taxpayer expense and either get too close to animals or try to feed them. Often these actions are the result of attempts to get a good photograph, which can sometimes prove that a picture is not worth a thousand stitches. People who are determined to get up close and personal with wild animals have often been found to suffer from a malady known appropriately as C.U.B.S. (**C**onstitutionally **U**nable to **B**ehave **S**ensibly).

An example occurred on the morning of July 11, 2001, when 19-year-old Hyun J. of Los Angeles and a group of several friends left Lake Lodge and spotted a bison grazing in an open meadow directly in front of the lodge. The group jogged to within a few feet of the animal and, compounding their error, surrounded it on three sides. This was not a great plan, since virtually every animal (including people) tends to get uncomfortable if it feels cornered. This astute group then remained in their position around the bison for the next five minutes, while the animal continued to graze and move slowly closer to Ms. J. As it got even nearer, the woman turned to run, but the bison butted her and knocked her to the ground. She was taken to Lake Hospital for treatment and was fortunate to escape without serious injury.

You don't have to be in the heart of the wilderness to get into trouble by breaking the rules concerning wildlife. On a July afternoon, 50-

It's a bison, not a buffalo, despite what you've read in all those Westerns. By any name, these animals are an enduring symbol of the American West, but enjoy them from a safe distance. Bulls such as this one in Yellowstone can weigh upwards of 1,800 pounds and can charge with surprising speed if approached too closely by people. (National Park Service, Yellowstone National Park)

year-old Garry B. from Florida spotted a bison near the Madison off-ramp at the Old Faithful interchange in Yellowstone. (The description of that location unfortunately doesn't sound much like a national park, but that's the reality of heavy traffic in some of our more popular areas.) Mr. B apparently couldn't resist getting a closer look, so he approached to within two feet of the animal! The bison charged and gored the man in the left shoulder and right thigh. Mr. B. was taken by ambulance to a hospital in Jackson, where he was treated and released—another example of a fortunate if somewhat painful escape.

Other animal adventures can have an even more unusual cast of characters. On September 16, 2002, two visitors made a cell phone call to the Harpers Ferry National Historical Park in West Virginia and reported that they were being attacked by a group of pigs in the Maryland Heights section of the park. Ranger Ryan Levins responded to the area and found the two visitors, who were uninjured but shaken up. Investigation revealed that they'd avoided a noisy charge by six pigs by moving to cover and throwing a rock at them. In this case, the visitors had unusually good powers of observation, and they were able to provide accurate descriptions of their assailants, including length, color, and types of snouts and tails.

Ranger Levins located two of the assailants on an adjacent property owner's land, returned them to their pens, and left a note for the owner asking that he repair his fence. At the time of the report, the other four animals were still at large, but an All Points Bulletin had been issued for their capture.

If a weird situation can occur, sooner or later it will probably do so in a national park someplace in the country! Hopefully, you won't be the first person to spot those elusive tigers.

19

Water, Water, Everywhere, Nor Any Drop to Drink

Yes, I know that seems like a strange title for events that took place in the Rocky Mountains. Ironically, after spending almost three years in the desert in Arizona and Nevada with no big problems with water, we had the greatest challenges with the wet stuff in the midst of the evergreen forests of Montana. It wasn't that the water wasn't there—it's just that for much of the year it was tied up in the form of ice or snow, which isn't as convenient to use for most household tasks on a day-to-day basis. Because of the extreme cold, getting useable water to successfully survive the trip through the pipes was also sometimes a bit of a task.

The chapter on our move to Glacier mentions some of our adventures with frozen water pipes in our house, but the water mains themselves posed their own special challenges. We arrived in East Glacier in February, and a couple of months later, as the "spring thaw" approached, we suddenly had a new experience. We turned on the faucet in the house one day and got—coffee!

Well, it looked like coffee, but it didn't smell like it, and fortunately we didn't give it the taste test. Our next-door neighbors, veterans of previous springs here on the frontier, soon solved the mystery. It seems that our water supply came right out of a creek up in the mountains, and once the snow melt started in earnest, the silt washed down the slopes by the thaw turned the creek into something other than "pure, Rocky Mountain spring water."

We soon learned that this problem would last for a couple of weeks or so, and then the situation would return to normal. In the meantime, we hauled water for drinking and cooking purposes in five-gallon containers from the next closest ranger station at St. Mary or sometimes from the house of friends twelve miles away in the town of Browning. Since St. Mary was about a two-hour round-trip in the winter, we learned to be very conservative in our use of water.

The real fun with water came our second winter at East Glacier. Water mains in this village are buried really deep—something like eight feet or more—to try to keep them from freezing. Even so, the key during the winter is to keep some water moving through the pipes at least occasionally. One day in early spring, the village water folks had to shut down the whole system due to a problem of some kind. By the time service was restored, mains and pipes were frozen all over town.

Just to prove that American ingenuity is alive and well, I soon found that there is a solution of sorts for this problem. A couple of local residents had some big, truck-mounted electric welding machines, which were hooked up to the water mains at various points. As it was explained to me, this in effect made the metal water pipes part of the "circuit" for the welder, and the resulting heat in the pipes thawed them enough to let the flow of water resume. I gather this was a somewhat delicate operation, since there seemed to be a fine line between too much and too little current, but the system worked for most people in town.

The bad news was that it didn't work for the four families living in the ranger compound. Something about the type of pipe used for the water main serving those houses or the distance between points where the welder could hook on kept this thawing system from working for us. The worse news was that it was impossible to dig up several hundred feet of waterline buried under many feet of solidly frozen ground until the soil thawed. We were looking at many, many weeks of hauling water. Even coffee-colored water sounded fairly good at that point!

Once again, ingenuity saved the day, although it led to its own comic routine. If a video camera had just been available back then, I feel confident we would have won some serious money on "America's Funniest Home Videos." Here's how our temporary water system worked.

The four families living at the ranger station compound occupied three buildings. The Burnetts and Blairs shared a duplex on one end; the center building was the actual ranger office, with living quarters upstairs for a volunteer biologist and her husband. The house on the other end of the compound was occupied by the Ries family. The closest point with running water was a fire hydrant located about 250 feet behind all three houses. The plan was to run a fire hose from the hydrant toward the houses, then use a fitting called a reducer to split off three sections of garden hose, one for each house. The garden hose for each house was then connected to an outside faucet, allowing the water to run backwards from the outside faucet into the house itself.

This was actually a pretty good system, except for one small challenge—it was cold, and I'm talking about way below zero at night and barely above that in the daytime. As a result, water in the fire hose and especially in the smaller garden hoses had a tendency to freeze unless a pretty good flow was kept up continuously through those hoses. This meant leaving at least one faucet in each house running continuously.

We knew that snow is a fairly good insulator and snow was something we had in abundance, so we covered the hoses with a good layer of snow to help protect them. During the daytime, when temperatures were a little more moderate (at least by Montana standards), all was well. The fun started late at night, when the temperatures really began to drop.

Maybe you've accidentally left a garden hose outside your house in cold weather and you forgot to drain all the water out of the hose. Remember how stiff it got? If it wasn't split and ruined, you had to wait for a warm spell before you could even think about rolling it up. That gives you an idea of what we'd be facing with several hundred feet of fire hose and garden hose if they froze solid in –20° weather (or worse). That (along with the prospect of hauling all our water for weeks and weeks) gave us an incentive to keep things flowing.

An incentive was definitely needed, because here's what happened if we heard the flow of water start to diminish. The key was to find the point in the hose network where the freeze-up was starting to occur. We did this by starting at a point fairly close to the hydrant, uncoupling the hose, and seeing if water was still flowing. If so, we'd reconnect the hose at that point, move further down the line, and repeat the process. Once we found the section where the water was starting to freeze, we resorted to all kinds of tricks to get it moving again from that point on to the houses. Some of those techniques have since been adopted by our military in event of hostilities at the North Pole, so they are classified and you'll just have to use your imagination.

It's amazing how your mind can adapt fairly quickly to a new challenge. In this case, the goal was to be able to get a good night's sleep with the sound of water running continuously in the kitchen or bathroom. At the same time, the brain had to send a quick alarm in case the sound of that running water changed—as in slowing down or worse still, stopping. If the water stopped moving for even a couple of minutes, those hoses would freeze solid and we were out of the water business. This is where the comedy routine came in, although at the time I don't think we saw a whole lot of humor in it!

There was an unspoken rule that all four households were responsible for keeping their "ear to the ground," so to speak, on the alert twenty-four hours a day for the sound of slowing water flow. When that happened, we immediately sounded the alarm by phone to our neighbors to make sure they were on the ball. The men of the households then dashed outside as quickly as possible and started uncoupling and reconnecting hoses. Words truly can't do justice at this point, but maybe you can picture some of this in your mind.

It's about 2 a.m. on a clear, cold night. The temperature is diving past –20°, and there is a brisk wind off the mountains to the west. The scene is surprisingly bright, with the moonlight reflecting off the snow-covered ground. Suddenly, four men, apparently escaped maniacs from some institution, burst out of the back doors of the nearby houses, pulling on jacket and caps as they stumble through the snow, bootlaces dragging and shirt tails flapping. Shouting to each other, they dash toward the edge of the parking lot and begin digging frantically in the snow.

In short order they uncover several lengths of fire hose, and one of them loosens the connection between two sections of hose. Water gushes everywhere in the numbing cold, and these guys actually seem glad that they are in danger of becoming instant ice cubes! Rapidly numbing fingers fumble to reconnect the hose as water continues to spray all around, while a second man repeats the process nearby. He lets out a shout to the others that it's okay there, and they wade through eight inches of new snow to the next spot, where they repeat their antics. Finally, a woman's voice is heard from one of the houses, yelling something like "Okay!"

This must be good news, because the men decide to stop playing in the snow and head back indoors. It's time to try to thaw out frozen bodies and get back to sleep, but only while keeping one ear on the sound of running water!

Somebody once asked me, "What in the world do you find to do out there in the middle of nowhere, all winter long?" If I told them, they probably wouldn't believe it!

Setting the Stage: Colonial National Historical Park

Colonial National Historical Park (NHP) is located in the Tidewater region of southeastern Virginia, and includes two of the most historically significant sites in our nation: Yorktown, site of the final major battle of the American Revolutionary War in 1781; and Jamestown, where the first permanent English settlement in North America was established in 1607. Jamestown will really be in the spotlight in 2007, when the site celebrates its 400th anniversary.

The park's Yorktown and Jamestown units are linked by the Colonial Parkway, a twenty-three-mile scenic roadway that is worth a drive for its own sake, especially in the spring and fall. Near its midpoint, the Parkway passes via a tunnel under the heart of another of the nation's premier historic sites, the privately managed Colonial Williamsburg. The Colonial Parkway was the first roadway in the national park system built for the purpose of joining separate sites into a single, cohesive park and was intended to link those areas via a scenic drive that was to remain free of any commercial development.

For the most part, that concept has been successful, although the planners in 1930 would probably be amazed at the population explosion in the surrounding area over the past seventy-five years. That growth poses one of the greatest challenges for the Colonial Parkway—and the park staff—since this scenic road also serves one other unintended function: for many local residents, it's also the shortest route between home and work—or school—or shopping or just about anywhere else.

The Yorktown Victory Monument at Colonial National Historical Park in Virginia commemorates the decisive battle of the American Revolution—and the winning of our independence. (National Park Service, Colonial National Historical Park)

Many people are surprised to learn that with more than 3.3 million recreation visits, Colonial NHP was ranked number fourteen in visitations out of 349 units in the national park system in 2003, ahead of such notables as Yellowstone and Rocky Mountain National Parks. Some of those visitors are simply local residents who enjoy driving on the Colonial Parkway and you'll rarely encounter enough of a crowd to be an inconvenience at the park's primary attractions.

If you have even a passing interest in our nation's history, this is definitely an area worth a visit. For more information about the park, check its website at www.nps.gov/colo/. You can also write to Colonial National Historical Park, P.O. Box 210, Yorktown, VA 23690. If you need information on short notice about Yorktown, phone 757-898-2410, or about Jamestown, call 757-229-1733.

"Excuses, Excuses"

The Colonial Parkway is beautifully designed to allow for a leisurely scenic drive between the park's two main units at Yorktown and Jamestown, but as it winds gently up hill and down dale for twenty-three miles, the road's many curves leave relatively few places to safely pass slower-moving vehicles. Since a key purpose of the Parkway is to let visitors enjoy the view, mixing in some impatient commuters who want to drive a lot faster than the 45-mile-per-hour limit can be a definite safety concern. As a result, the rangers really do have the best interests of everyone in mind when they enforce those traffic laws.

I guess it's just human nature to try to rationalize our actions, good or bad, but for many people some previously untapped reservoir of creativity suddenly wells to the surface when they hear those dreaded words, "May I see your driver's license and vehicle registration, please?" Perhaps there's something here that teachers of creative writing have overlooked, because unique ideas that just won't come in the classroom suddenly blossom forth when those flashing lights appear in some people's rear view mirror. These inspirations are usually known as alibis (**A** **L**ively **I**magination **B**egets **I**ncredible **S**tories). If it's an excuse for speeding, the rangers on the Colonial Parkway have probably heard it. The following are a few of my favorites from several parks around the country.

One of the least effective alibis was offered by a teenage driver who was stopped near the spot where there is an access point from the Parkway to Colonial Williamsburg. This is often a fairly busy place, and as a result the Parkway speed limit drops in that area from 45 to 35 miles per hour. A ranger was both amazed and understandably rather annoyed to clock the vehicle in question at over 90 miles per hour. This obviously presented a serious risk to everybody else on the road and is a good example of how traffic enforcement is an important tool for the safety of park visitors.

Thankfully, the driver pulled over promptly when the ranger signaled for him to do so. Proving that in such situations it's best to just be polite, say as little as possible, and take your medicine like a man, this driver made the mistake of choosing denial in place of discretion. The conversation as I later heard about it went something like this:

Ranger: "Sir, do you know why I stopped you?"

Driver: "Well, I might have been going just a little fast."

Ranger: "Do you realize how fast you were going?"

Driver: "No, not really."

Ranger: "You were clocked on my radar at ninety-two miles per hour."

Driver: (With righteous indignation). "Well, that can't be right! I wasn't going a mile over eighty!"

On a rating scale for successful alibis, I'd have to rate that one well on the negative side of zero.

Another driver didn't do much better when he was stopped for speeding just before sunset. After obtaining the usual items of identification, the ranger explained the reason for his stop and also pointed out that the vehicle's safety inspection sticker was expired.

Driver: "Yeah, I know I was driving a little too fast. I'm in a hurry to get home.

Ranger: "Is there a problem of some kind at home?"

Driver: "Well, not exactly. The headlights on my car don't work, so I thought it was a good idea to get home before it got dark. That's why the sticker is expired, because my car won't pass inspection."

This conversation confirms that advice given by George Washington in a letter to a niece way back in 1791 is still pretty good today: "It is better to offer no excuse than a bad one."

Another unusual incident also involved headlights, but for a different reason. The hour was late and although the night was very dark, it was fortunately not stormy. A ranger had pulled his car just off the Parkway where he could monitor a straight stretch of road for a few minutes. The area seemed to be totally deserted until suddenly the display on the ranger's radar unit began to register an approaching vehicle. That was not especially unusual, except for one detail—there was absolutely nothing in sight. Furthermore, the numbers on the radar display quickly jumped to 50, 55, 60, 65.

The ranger said later he did a proverbial double-take and looked down the road again. Still he couldn't see a thing—not even the slightest glimmer of light or activity. All at once, he sensed more than he saw something flash past his location. Being a prudent ranger and not putting much stock in UFOs or apparitions, he made haste to follow in the wake of the not-so-visible object. Almost as soon as the ranger turned on his lights and pulled onto the Parkway, he had a much better view of his mysterious visitor. The flash of brake lights on the car ahead was followed by headlights coming on as the driver pulled his car to the side of the road.

The young man's explanation, if you could call it one, was that a friend had dared him to see how fast he could drive on the Parkway at night—without using any lights. This is further proof that many teenagers often find themselves in Melancholy Situations because they couldn't say "no" to dares (**D**angers **A**dolescents **R**eally **E**xpect to **S**urvive). Thankfully, the road was virtually deserted that night and this midnight ride that was not revered came to a safe conclusion almost as soon as it had begun.

Another loser in the bad alibi sweepstakes was yet another speeder, and since there seems to be a pattern here, I'll point out that people who insist on ignoring the speed limit sooner or later learn that driving "fast" refers to **F**olks **A**cquiring **S**peeding **T**ickets. I concluded long ago that being a fast driver doesn't necessarily correlate with being a fast learner. As the English poet John Pomfret observed about such folks, "We live and learn, but not the wiser grow."

We'll join the following conversation in progress, after the usual preliminaries have been completed, and see if you agree.

Ranger: "Ma'am, the reason I stopped you is that you were going sixty-five in a forty-five-mile-per-hour zone."

Driver: "Really? I didn't realize I was going quite that fast, but I *am* running late. Couldn't you just give me a warning this time, so the judge won't be mad at me again?"

Ranger (sensing there was probably a good story here): "Why would the judge be mad at you?"

Driver: "Well, I'm supposed to be in court in just about five minutes, and I was late for court the last time, too, and the judge said I'd better not let that happen again."

Ranger: "Do you mind telling me why you have to go to court?"

Driver: "I forgot to pay my last two speeding tickets."

I rest my case!

Pomp and Circumstances

Parks are often selected as the site of all kinds of celebrations and special events. It would be a Herculean task to try to compile a list of all such activities that occur during the course of a year in national parks all across the country. Undoubtedly, the clear winner for the sheer number and scope of such events is what's known as National Capital Parks (NCP), a designation that includes all of the areas administered by the National Park Service in and around Washington, D.C.

If it's your job to help manage places like the Washington Monument and the National Mall, major celebrations like the Cherry Blossom Festival and the 4th of July go with the territory. Many proposals are for less ambitious undertakings and can often tell you how much the person knows about the area. I heard about one phone call to the NCP office from a lady in a distant state. Her high school choir was planning a trip to Washington, D.C., and wanted to perform a free concert of patriotic music at the National Mall. Such requests are not uncommon, but when asked if she had a specific spot in mind, she immediately replied, "Yes, anywhere between the Food Court and the entrance to Macy's would be fine."

Just for the record, the National Mall doesn't offer much in the way of shopping. That's the name for the open space that stretches for about two miles from the Lincoln Memorial to the U.S. Capitol, and includes sites such as the Vietnam Memorial and the Washington Monument.

Sponsors of a proposed event have to be prepared to develop an appropriate plan and present it to the park before a final decision is made. In many cases, there are a lot more things to consider than the average citizen realizes. In the early 1990s, a local housewife called my office at Colonial National Historical Park to discuss her idea for an event that had the potential to attract a huge crowd to the Yorktown Battlefield.

Her concept wasn't bad but there were quite a few details to discuss. A fellow ranger at Colonial named Dick Young had been involved in countless such activities for many years and was widely considered the park service's expert on such matters. He immediately thought of a number of practical considerations: how many people might attend, where they would park their cars, which dignitaries would be invited, what kind of extra security would be needed, and so forth.

Dick and I got on the phone with this lady, and after some preliminary discussion he politely asked a key question: "Have you ever had any experience in planning or organizing a big event?" There was a moment's pause before she replied cheerfully, "Well, I had a multi-family garage sale last year." Dick and I exchanged glances and knew we had a big job ahead! Work on the event did go forward, but somewhat to our relief a competing activity elsewhere in the area that same day stole most of the attention—and the crowd.

Plenty of events in parks around the country have their share of pomp, pageantry, and ceremony. Some recognize a unique moment in history, such as the recent dedication of the World War II Memorial in Washington, D.C. Others are an annual tradition: Fourth of July celebrations all across the country, including some major ones in several national parks, are a good example.

One such recurring event occurs on October 19 every year in Yorktown, Virginia. In case it's been a year or two since your history class, I'll refresh your memory about several happenings of note on that date. Back in 1873, that was the day when four Northeastern universities agreed on the first set of rules for American football, thereby changing life in this country on autumn weekends in ways they probably couldn't even imagine. October 19 is also celebrated in Russia for the defeat of Napoleon I of France and the date that his army began its disastrous retreat from Moscow in 1812. So what, you may ask? I'll bet the answer will surprise most of you.

As part of the commemoration of that victory, the Russian composer Tchaikovsky was commissioned in 1880 to write a piece of music that he called the 1812 Overture. With its booming cannons and pealing bells, that composition has become a tradition at many 4th of July events

Members of the United States Army's elite "Old Guard" participate in the annual Yorktown Day ceremony at Colonial National Historical Park. Held each October 19th, the event commemorates the victory that secured American independence in 1781. (National Park Service, Colonial National Historical Park)

in the United States—despite the irony that some of the most popular sections of the piece are based on the national anthems of France and Russia. This either proves that we are a nation of people graciously willing to embrace the contributions of other cultures or that most of us don't have a clue about the background of that music, but we do know a tune that goes well with a fireworks show when we hear one.

The real reason for celebrating October 19 in Yorktown, Virginia, however, is that on that date in 1781, British General Charles Lord Cornwallis surrendered his army to American and French forces under the command of General George Washington and the Count de

Rochambeau. That surrender effectively ended the American Revolutionary War and years later gave the Boston Pops and countless other orchestras across the country the opportunity to play the 1812 Overture on Independence Day. Now, don't you wish your history teacher had explained to you that clearly how all those seemingly unrelated historical events really do fit together so neatly?

It didn't take long for the idea of an appropriate commemoration of the victory at Yorktown to develop. Only ten days after the British surrender in 1781, a resolution of the Continental Congress called for a "Yorktown Monument to the Alliance and Victory." Another tradition may have been born that day, which is the fact that translating a resolution by Congress into tangible results can require quite some time. In this case, it was almost exactly one hundred years later—October 18, 1881—that the site was secured and the cornerstone was finally laid for the Yorktown Victory Monument.

By the time Congress authorized the establishment of Colonial National Monument on July 3, 1930, the Yorktown Victory Monument had long since been completed. That monument was included in the new park, along with key portions of the Yorktown Battlefield. The park also included Jamestown, where the first successful British colony in North America had been established in 1607. It was certainly very considerate of the English to begin and end their American empire at locations that are only a few miles apart, so the sites of those momentous events could be conveniently administered in later years by a single national park.

It may have taken a hundred years to get work on the Victory Monument underway, but once a piece of public property big enough for a major event was available, things kicked into high gear. Just a little over a year after Colonial National Monument (later renamed Colonial National Historical Park) was established, there was quite a stir in October 1931 for the Yorktown Sesquicentennial. That's a big word for a 150th anniversary of anything and such milestones have a tendency to inspire big celebrations.

Those big celebrations have a tendency to attract politicians and other celebrities, most of whom feel the need to make a speech or two to inspire and enlighten those in attendance. That may explain why one of the definitions of the word "sesquipedalian," which is closely related to "sesquicentennial," means "long and ponderous."

The Yorktown Sesquicentennial *was* rather long, beginning on October 16 and lasting through the 19th, but I won't presume to speculate on whether or not those present found it to be ponderous. Given the number of dignitaries who were invited to address the crowd, spreading the event over four days was probably a good thing.

The opening day, for example, was designated as "Colonial Day," and the program began "promptly at 10 a.m." Following speeches or other remarks by fifteen separate people, including the governors of ten states, the event mercifully adjourned at noon for a two-hour lunch break. It resumed at 2 p.m. for speeches by four more luminaries. The official report of the event doesn't list what time those remarks ended, but other activities continued well past dark. By almost any standard, this celebration qualified as a Big Deal for a village of about 300 people and according to an official report, attracted an estimated 150,000 visitors on the final day alone! The U.S. Navy sent a fleet of forty-one ships, including a battleship, five heavy cruisers, eight light cruisers, and seventeen destroyers. This armada anchored in the York River immediately adjacent to the village of Yorktown and the battlefield, and additional craft from the French Navy and U.S. Coast Guard were also present.

Planning an event of this magnitude always requires lots of meetings, and plenty of suggestions for activities are debated and accepted or rejected before everything is finalized. In what probably seemed like a really good idea at the time, the arrival in Yorktown of President Hoover aboard the Battleship *Arkansas* was marked by the firing of a twenty-one-gun salute by almost thirty of the naval and Coast Guard vessels present. That must have been a spectacular tribute, but one which also had the unfortunate result of breaking a number of windows in town. This is a good example of the "Oops factor" (**O**utcome **O**utside of **P**lanned **S**cenario), and to the best of my knowledge, battleships or similar vessels weren't invited to fire their large guns at subsequent events in Yorktown.

Back in those days, it was also very popular for people to purchase commemorative postage stamps issued in honor of a major event. It's safe to say that the two-cent Yorktown Sesquicentennial commemorative stamp was a success. An official report says that 221,037 of the stamps were sold at the Yorktown Post Office on the first day alone and ultimately more than 1.5 million of the stamps were purchased in Yorktown. And you probably complain that the lines at your post office are too long right before Christmas!

Another major commemoration was held in 1981 to mark the Bicentennial of the British surrender at Yorktown, but in all other years an appropriate but much less ambitious celebration is held. This is understandably still a big deal in Yorktown, and the busy day is filled with the laying of wreaths at various sites, a wonderful example of an all-American, small-town parade, and the highlight of the day, the Patriotic Exercises and Memorial Wreath-Laying Ceremony.

This formal observance is held at the Victory Monument and is a classic example of tradition, decorum, and protocol. The event is sponsored by the Yorktown Day Association, a group whose thirteen members include such diverse organizations as the York County Board of Supervisors, the local chapter of the Daughters of the American Revolution, the Association for the Preservation of Virginia Antiquities, and Colonial National Historical Park. The nearby area includes a number of major military installations and given the fact that the day celebrates a historic military victory, it's appropriate that personnel from those facilities have a major role in the day as well.

I've given you a few more details than some of you may want to know, because it's important for you to sense the tone of the ceremony to fully appreciate the following story. Civility, dignity, and protocol are the order of the day, and because of the important role of the French naval and land forces in the American victory at Yorktown, there is always a significant French presence at this event.

At the conclusion of the parade down Main Street, members of the Official Party take their places on a stage erected in front of the Victory Monument. Other dignitaries and spectators from the general public take seats on folding chairs set up on the monument grounds or find a spot on the lawn for the ceremony. Following a colorful parade of flags, appropriate music, speeches and remarks, an enormous wreath five feet in diameter is hung on the monument in honor of those who fought and died in the battle. A memorial prayer is then offered, and the ceremony concludes with a solemn playing of Taps by a military bugler.

All of the above is thoroughly planned, meticulously scripted, and carefully rehearsed, right down to the final detail. That's the case for almost any formal ceremony of this type, and there's a certain amount of pressure on those involved to be sure everything runs according to plan. It was against that backdrop that I reported to my new assignment as Chief Ranger at Colonial National Historical Park, barely a week before the 1990 Yorktown Day event.

By then, all the planning had long since been completed, and my role was actually pretty straightforward. At the appointed time near the end of the ceremony, it was traditionally the role of the park's Chief

Ranger and Chief Historian to carry the Memorial Wreath down a long walkway leading to the monument, climb several steps up to the platform, and hand it up to a pair of rangers who were already positioned on a ledge that runs around the base of the monument, several feet above the ground. Those rangers then hung the wreath on two metal hooks permanently installed just for that purpose in the face of the stone.

Once the wreath was hung, my fellow wreath-bearer and I walked with appropriate dignity to our respective corners of the monument, where we stood behind the platform during the closing prayer and the playing of Taps. So far, so good, and everything had gone exactly as planned. I hadn't dropped the Memorial Wreath, tripped going up the steps, or committed any similar indiscretion. It looked as if my first Yorktown Day was going to be a success.

The Memorial Prayer was to be voiced by a popular local minister, and as I waited for him to make his way to the podium, my position just above the base of the Victory Monument provided a nice view of the crowd. My new boss stood a few feet away on the platform, along with an admiral and general or two and various other officials, dignitaries, and politicians. The crowd spread out on the grounds included a number of other high-ranking military officers, most of my fellow residents of the village of Yorktown, and several hundred other citizens. The media was well represented, and a camera crew captured the whole event for later broadcast on the local government cable channel. I couldn't ask for a better opportunity to make a good, if minor, impression on most of the people I'd work closely with in my new job.

As the reverend began his prayer, the military bugler slipped quietly into his position directly in front of me. He had been waiting out of sight, behind the monument, until this point in the program. According to the script, he would begin playing Taps as soon as the prayer was concluded. My last remaining assignment, if for any reason it became necessary, was to cue the bugler when it was time for him to play.

The prayer was eloquent and being nicely delivered when suddenly, at the end of one sentence, the pastor simply stopped speaking.

At first, I thought he had merely paused for effect, to let us ponder his words. After a few seconds, I wondered if he was considering his next thought, since he didn't seem to be reading a prepared text. The crowd remained still, heads respectfully bowed. Except for a soft rustle of fabric as the flags posted around the platform stirred in the gentle breeze, there was hardly a sound to interrupt the dignity of the moment.

Several more seconds passed, and I decided to chance a discreet glance toward the podium. Perhaps the speaker needed to clear his throat and was taking a sip from a glass of water? All at once a terrible thought crossed my mind. Perhaps he was finished and I hadn't realized it? I'd expected that he'd end his benediction with a good, hearty "Amen," giving a clear signal to the bugler. What if that wasn't the case in his particular denomination?

Maybe you've had a similar experience somewhere along the road of life, when some situation causes you to lose all sense of perspective about the passing of time. I'm sure this unexpected moment of silence was fairly brief, but it suddenly felt like an eternity. The French philosopher Voltaire expressed this concept quite nicely when he posed the question: "What, of all things in the world, is the longest and the shortest, the swiftest and the slowest?" His answer was "time," but before I had much opportunity to ponder such deep mysteries of the universe, a whispered question reached my ears.

"Sir! Is he finished?" It was the Army bugler, standing in front of me.

Asking this question discreetly was not an easy task, since the soldier didn't want to attract any attention by turning his head very far, just in case anyone in the audience who was supposed to have his or her head bowed happened to be stealing an irreverent glance in his direction. At the same time, he couldn't speak too loudly, since he was standing almost directly behind the members of the Official Party on our end of the platform. I'm sure some of them couldn't avoid hearing his whispered question, but they politely showed no sign of having done so. They were probably wondering the same thing and thanking their lucky stars the question wasn't directed at them!

For the same reasons, my reply also had to be unobtrusive, but at the moment I was a lot more concerned with giving the correct answer. This seemed as good a time as any to apply the time-honored principle that honesty is the best policy, so I whispered back, "I don't know."

Proving that the switch from the draft to an all-volunteer Army years ago has indeed resulted in a high caliber of personnel in the military, the young soldier astutely tossed the ball right back into my court. "Sir! Should I start playing?" I may have been a civilian, but in this case I represented the closest source of higher authority available to him in his moment of need, and he wisely seized the opportunity to pass the buck instead of the bugle.

In retrospect, I realize that the bugler probably felt he had a lot more at stake than I did in the outcome of this little dilemma. Somewhere out there in the crowd stood not only his immediate superior, but probably the entire chain of command from his nearby Army post, all the way up to the commanding general. They all knew that Taps was supposed to begin when the prayer was finished, certainly not before, but also without undue delay.

However, this little drama was being played out within earshot of several of the platform guests, and it was obvious to them that whatever happened next would be determined by my answer. It was a rather uncomfortable situation, and the young musician and I were unquestionably facing a Truly Melancholy Situation.

Well, it was obviously my call, and as the saying goes, that's why I get paid the "big bucks" (another example of the concept that everything is relative). After stalling for as long as I felt I could, which was probably about another 3.5 seconds, I was right on the brink of giving the bugler the go-ahead. Once again, however, merciful Providence showered undeserved favor upon me—and the Memorial Prayer resumed, just in the nick of time.

The minister came quickly to a close and best of all ended with a nice, clear "Amen." I believe I heard an audible sigh of relief from the bugler—or maybe it was from me! Taps was played skillfully, the program ended as scheduled, and only a handful of people present that day knew (until now) how close I had come to introducing the "Oops factor" into an otherwise textbook example of a flawless Yorktown Day event!

As the crowd was breaking up after the ceremony, a number of people were heard to comment about how "perfectly" everything had gone. Ah, if only they knew how close we'd come to starting a new tradition: the case of the bungled bugler! I'd be willing to bet that if the truth were known, almost every event of any complexity has one or more similar behind-the-scenes mishaps—or near misses. If the people in charge are lucky, the close calls outnumber the calamities, and more often than not the difference is one of just a few seconds. The Greek poet Hesiod understood this fact centuries before Yorktown, Virginia, ever existed, and he gave excellent advice for anyone in a similar situation: "Observe due measure, for right timing is in all things the most important!"

To that, I can only add a hearty "Amen!"

Setting the Stage: Grand Canyon National Park

The Grand Canyon requires little introduction to most people, so I'll limit this introduction to just a few key facts. A frequent question is "How big is it?" A common answer is that the Grand Canyon extends from a place called Lees Ferry, just below Glen Canyon Dam and the Arizona–Utah border, to the Grand Wash Cliffs, near the upper end of Lake Mead in northwest Arizona. If you measure that distance by the miles of Colorado River that twist and turn through the canyon, it's about 277 miles long.

From Grand Canyon Village on the South Rim, it's about a vertical mile from the rim down to the river. At that same point, it's about ten miles across to the opposite rim, although in places the canyon is as much as eighteen miles wide. No matter how you measure it, this is a big park, covering more than a million acres. Much of that area, however, is virtually inaccessible, so the developed areas, especially the South Rim, can often be pretty crowded—about four million people a year visit the park.

Someone who would be astounded by that fact if he were still alive today would be Army Lt. Joseph Christmas Ives, who completed an exploration of areas on the south side of the Grand Canyon in 1858.

This is Arizona? The Grand Canyon is no stranger to winter, and a blanket of snow on the South Rim provides a striking contrast to the colorful rocks in the canyon. (Jim Burnett)

At that point in our nation's history, there wasn't much interest in tourism, and the concept of national parks was still in the future. In that context, Lt. Ives was apparently not especially impressed by his visit, since he wrote, "Ours has been the first, and will doubtless be the last, party of whites to visit this profitless locality. It seems intended by nature that the Colorado River, along the greater portion of its lonely and majestic way, shall be forever unvisited and undisturbed."

Lt. Ives' talents obviously lay in exploring, not prophecy, so if you plan to visit the park yourself, keep in mind that reservations for overnight lodging or camping need to be made well in advance, especially for the summer months. Park officials note that the least crowded time is November through February, but winter weather is a major consideration when planning a trip during these months.

Most important, be aware that there are two major developed areas in the park, on the South and North rims. It's most of a day's drive between those points, so if you're making reservations, be sure you specify the correct side of the canyon. The South Rim is open all year, but can have some serious winter weather at times. The North Rim, which is much less developed, is open only from about mid-May to mid-October each year.

The elevation on the North Rim is more than 8,000 feet above sea level, or about a thousand feet higher than the South Rim. The altitude on both sides of the park is a big factor and makes any kind of physical activity more strenuous than you might expect. If you're planning to do any hiking, especially into the canyon itself, it's absolutely essential that you are in good physical condition and that you get accurate information before making your trip. The park has excellent information on its website at www.nps.gov/grca/, or you can write to Grand Canyon National Park, P.O. Box 129, Grand Canyon, AZ 86023, or phone 928-638-7888.

24

"You Can See It All When We Get Home"

In the early 1970s, a motorcycle rider named Evel Knievel got a lot of publicity out of a proposal to jump from one side of the Grand Canyon to the other on his motorcycle. Although the stunt was never actually attempted in the park itself, one spot he may have initially had in mind was on the extreme upper end of the canyon, in an almost inaccessible area called Marble Canyon. There, the distance between the two canyon rims is much, much shorter than in the main part of the Grand Canyon itself. The vast majority of visitors come to the developed area of the park known as the South Rim, where they can gaze across an immense expanse of canyon to the North Rim. This is the mental picture most people have when they think about the Grand Canyon.

During the summer of 1971, an older couple approached me at one of the canyon overlooks and asked a common question:

"Hey, ranger, how far is it over to the other side?"

At that particular location the answer was, "About ten miles."

The gentleman thanked me for the information, and he and his wife wandered a few feet over to the edge of the rim. They leaned on the top of the guardrail and solemnly contemplated the view to the distant North Rim. After a long pause, the man turned to his wife, and in a distinct drawl, commented, "You know, Ma, I just don't think that Knievel feller is gonna make it!"

One of the most interesting aspects of a ranger's job is observing human nature. While recognizing that everyone has his or her own reasons for visiting a national park, I suppose it would be possible to classify many visitors into one or more general groups, such as campers, hikers, photographers, history buffs, and those who just enjoy the beauty of the out-of-doors. One such group might be called the "park collectors."

Now, don't get me wrong. Park collectors can be great folks, and I probably fall into that category myself at times. These are the people who just enjoy visiting as many different parks as possible. The NPS even encourages this activity by selling park passports, which you can buy in the book and gift shops found in most park visitor centers. Once you have your passport, you can get it stamped at each park you visit. The difference in my own value system comes when you see whether or not the person has any interest at all in the park other than simply checking yet another one off their lifetime list of places they've "seen." The following story is a classic example of the "been there, done that" variety of park collectors.

Most visitors approach the Grand Canyon from the south, via either Flagstaff or Williams, Arizona. As you entered the park back in the 1970s, the first place you could stop and actually see the canyon is called Mather Overlook. As this story was told to me by a fellow ranger, a family pulled into a parking spot at that overlook, and the doors of the family station wagon all flew open. (You can date this story

"Hey, Dad, look at this!" These visitors to the South Rim of the Grand Canyon will hopefully take a little time to enjoy the view. (Grand Canyon National Park)

by the vehicle, since today they would arrive in an SUV or a minivan.) Mom and three kids jumped out of the car and rushed over to the safety railing that follows the edge of the canyon rim. They were suitably impressed, exclaiming about one part or another of the spectacular view.

In the meantime, Dad was busy with his cameras. This was before the days of digital cameras and video recorders, so he had an 8mm movie camera and a 35mm camera slung around his neck. He stood at the edge of the overlook, and panned back and forth across the view with the movie camera until that roll of film was apparently exhausted. He then switched to the 35mm camera and fired off a quick series of shots. After one more scan of the horizon to be sure he hadn't missed any possible photographic targets he turned around and headed at a brisk pace for the family wagon.

"Okay, everybody back in the car," Dad shouted, glancing no doubt at his wristwatch. Total elapsed time was probably under five minutes, which, based on Dad's tone, was presumably a little behind schedule.

"But Dad," one of the kids protested. "We just got here!"

"That's no problem," came the reply, "I've got it all on film, and you can see it when we get home!"

I'm told that mom added the clarifying information that they needed to "keep moving," because they had "two more parks to see that day."

I hope Dad had lots of film!

25

"I Can't Find the Bridge"

At times during my first summer at the Grand Canyon, I helped out at the information desk in the main park visitor center. That job is the perfect chance to experience human nature, up close and personal, in all of its possible variations. The experience tended to get more interesting as the day wore on, and by late afternoon we were usually dealing with people who had been on the road for most of the day. Recognizing that mom and dad had probably suffered through several hours of "are we there yet?" we tried to be patient when visitors got a little testy while waiting their turn to talk to a ranger.

It was also important to remind ourselves that most of the people we were dealing with were city folks, with little or no experience in the wild, wild West. As a result, they often had no real comprehension of the distance between places out here. This was their big adventure, so we tried to make it a special visit for them. Even so, it was sometimes hard to keep a straight face.

Some of the questions dealt with the famous mule trips from the rim down to the bottom of the canyon (and hopefully back). One of my all-time favorites was from a nice older lady, who asked very primly, "Ranger, can you tell me if there is a dining car on the mule train?"

Every park has its own quota of similar questions, especially if an area doesn't meet the visitor's expectations. My wife and I were on vacation ourselves one year in Olympic National Park in the state of Washington. One of the unique areas in that park is the Hoh Rain Forest, perhaps the wettest place in the lower forty-eight states. At the time of our visit, however, it was a spectacular early summer day, with clear, blue skies and perfect temperatures.

Shortly after our arrival at Hoh, a tour bus with a group of senior citizens pulled into the parking lot. The passengers unloaded, and a spry older lady marched straight into the lobby of the visitor center. She spotted a young ranger on duty behind the information desk and zeroed in on him right away.

"Young man," she said in a commanding voice as she reached the desk.

"Yes, ma'am?"

"I thought this was supposed to be a rain forest!"

The young ranger proudly had his facts in order. "Yes, ma'am, it is. We get an average of 140 inches of rainfall here each year. If that rain fell all at once, the water would be deep enough to fill this room to the top of the ceiling, and . . . ."

The lady wasn't interested in any additional facts. Rapping her umbrella smartly on the counter in front of her, she glared directly at the ranger, and snapped, "Then why isn't it *raining*?"

Probably the people I had the most sympathy for were those who didn't pay really close attention to their maps. To understand this story, you need to know that the Grand Canyon is more than 200 miles long, and there are places to stay overnight on both the North and South Rims of the Canyon. As the crow flies, it's about ten miles from the Bright Angel Lodge on the South Rim to the Grand Canyon Lodge on the North Rim. However, there is only one spot where vehicles can cross the Canyon, many miles to the east near Page, Arizona. The trip by car from one rim to the other, via Page, covers more than 200 miles and takes at least five hours.

Back in my years at the park, some highway maps also showed a bridge across the Colorado River, just below the main visitor facilities on both rims of the canyon. A dashed or dotted line on the map ran from this bridge up to both the North and South Rims of the park. Based on the scale of the map, it looked like a short hop from one side of the canyon to the other. This is one time when it really pays to read the fine print on your map. We always knew when someone hadn't done so.

The conversation at the visitor center information desk usually started something like this, at the same time that the person was laying his trusty road map down on the counter, folded to show the vicinity of the park.

"Hey, ranger, we've been driving around for a while, and I can't find the bridge that goes over to the North Rim." This statement was often accompanied by vigorous pointing at the "bridge" shown on the map, which was apparently intended to convince us that the crossing really did exist. The implied problem was that there obviously weren't enough signs to point the way to the elusive bridge.

At this point we got to see human nature at its best or its worst, because we had to tactfully explain that we had good news and bad news. The good news was that yes, there is in fact a bridge right there. However, the bad news was that the fine print on the map said something like "foot bridge only," and the dashed line connecting the south and north rims of the canyon was not a road, but a very steep and narrow trail for hikers and mules. The really bad news was that it was more than 200 miles by car from where we stood to their room for the night over on the North Rim.

Be sure to read the fine print on your map! There is a bridge over the Colorado River at the bottom of the Grand Canyon, but it can be reached only by hikers and mules, not by cars! (Jim Burnett)

As the expression goes, what we had here was definitely a Melancholy Situation. Some people took it pretty well, whereas others . . . By the time these folks were headed back to the parking lot, we usually knew who in the group was responsible for trip planning. The moral to this story is when you plan a trip to a place you haven't been before, get a good map and study it carefully. This is one case where it really does pay to read the fine print!

26

"Let It Down Slowly"

Park rangers have a well-deserved reputation with most people for being friendly and willing to help out people in distress. The familiar wide, flat-brimmed "Smokey the Bear hat" is a widely recognized ranger symbol, even though Smokey is actually the official "spokesbear" for a different agency, the U.S. Forest Service. Sometimes, however, the polite part of that ranger image can be put to a serious test.

A ranger worked at an outlying station at the Grand Canyon and was on his way to an important meeting at park headquarters. He was all dressed up in his best "Class A" uniform, shoes shined and pants creased. About fifteen miles from headquarters, he came upon a pickup truck with a big slide-in camper mounted in its bed, parked partially off the side of the road. A young woman was standing alongside, peering sadly at a flat tire on the left rear wheel. A small child peered out of the open window of the truck cab. The woman looked up, spotted the ranger's truck, and frantically waved him over.

Well, what's a good patriotic ranger to do? He pulled over, sized up the situation, and learned that the poor woman had no idea how to change the tire. Assuring her that he'd get some help, he called on his radio to the dispatcher, to see if another ranger might be nearby and available to help. No such luck. A second request for the wrecker service at the Fred Harvey garage determined that they were out on another call and wouldn't be available for at least an hour or more.

They don't get a whole lot of rain at the Grand Canyon, but when they do, it can be a dandy. In the best Hollywood fashion, a line of ugly, dark clouds began to drift into view. Rumbles of thunder were clearly heard in the distance and it was obvious a storm was brewing. The woman looked increasingly distraught and, right on cue, the child began to cry. The ranger suppressed a sigh, took off his dress coat, radioed dispatch that he would be late for his meeting, rolled up his sleeves and went to work.

As is usually the case, the spare tire for the pickup was stowed underneath the bed of the truck, where it eventually picks up a good layer of everything thrown up off the road. After a couple of years of travel, such tires provide a good archeological record of every place the truck has been, especially if the vehicle has done any traveling off of paved roads. This one was a classic example, with several year's accumulation of caked and baked dirt and gravel, plus a generous sampling of thoroughly dried weeds that had been stuck to the tire before the mud dried to the general consistency of concrete. It's possible to date trees by counting the growth rings in the trunk. I'm told that it would have been possible to chronicle the travels of this camper by analyzing the numerous layers of dirt coating that spare tire.

Getting a tire in this condition freed from the underside of the truck usually required that some lucky soul crawl part-way under the truck and loosen up enough of the petrified grime to allow the spare to be removed from the chassis of the truck. The trick was to position your body so that you could reach the tire, but avoid having all the stuff you dislodged fall directly onto your face.

Fortunately for modern truck owners, some auto company engineer from Detroit must have had this experience, because most recent models of trucks and even some vans and SUVs use a little winch cable to make this job a lot easier. You just put the end of the tire tool through a hole somewhere near the back bumper, line it up just right, and rotate the tool to lower the tire to the ground. (That assumes you can locate the tire tool and jack, which are cleverly tucked away in hiding places Detroit engineers have ingeniously designed to store those tools, but that's another matter.)

Unfortunately for the ranger in this particular story, this was back in the good ol' days when a truck was a real truck and the spare was bolted right to the frame of the truck, held in place with a big wing nut. This meant that considerable persuasion was required to remove the nut, along with most of that accumulated dirt from the tire. Perseverance was finally rewarded, the spare was freed from its prison, the flat tire was removed, and the spare was installed in its place. The now thoroughly sweaty and very dirty hero was ready to lower the truck back to the ground and put his hand on the jack handle. The timing was providential, as the first big drops of rain were just starting to fall.

The driver of the truck spoke up. "Please be careful, now, and let it down slowly."

The ranger was a little puzzled, since the woman had already asked him to "be careful" several times, and he thought he'd done so throughout the whole process. He thought it was at least considerate of her to be concerned that he not get hurt in the process.

"Sure, I'll be careful."

"Good," the woman replied, "I wouldn't want the truck to bump too hard when you let it down. That might wake up my husband. He was tired after our long drive, and he's taking a nap inside the camper!"

27

Setting the Stage: Lincoln Boyhood National Memorial

Just in case you end up as a contestant on a quiz show someday, here's a little history brain-teaser for you: In what state did Abraham Lincoln spend the majority of his life before he became an adult? I'll give you a break and make it multiple choice:

A. Kentucky
B. Illinois
C. Indiana
D. Ohio

If you guessed Illinois, you're in good company—but, sorry, you're wrong. Most people associate Lincoln with Illinois, since that's where he was living as an adult when he entered politics and became well-known. You can tour his house at Lincoln Home National Historic Site in Springfield, Illinois. Lincoln's family migrated to Illinois when he was twenty-one years old; soon afterwards he left home and struck out on his own. So, no adolescent Abe years in Illinois.

The second most popular choice for many people is Kentucky. Yes, you can tour a log cabin that is preserved at Abraham Lincoln

Birthplace National Historic Site near Hodgenville, Kentucky. However, the Lincoln family left Kentucky when little Abe was seven years old and moved to Indiana. If you got this one the first time, you're a better than average history buff and probably paid closer attention that most in your American history class.

Abraham Lincoln lived on the family farm in southern Indiana for about fourteen years. If you recall those stories about young Abe doing his homework in front of the fireplace in a log cabin, here's the actual farm where that took place. You can visit a reconstruction of the family log cabin, which is located on a working living history farm. During the summer months, park employees in historic costume continue to operate the farm using tools and methods from the early nineteenth century. A beautiful visitor center of native limestone has a film and exhibits and is open all year with the exception of New Years Day, Thanksgiving Day, and Christmas Day.

Lincoln Boyhood National Memorial is just a few miles south of Interstate 64, near the town of Dale in southwestern Indiana. It's definitely worth a visit, and the area is especially pretty in the spring and fall.

The Lincoln Living Historical Farm at Lincoln Boyhood National Memorial allows visitors to see activities that were part of the Lincoln family's daily life in the early 1800s. (National Park Service)

If you want more information, you can write to the park at Lincoln Boyhood National Memorial, P.O. Box 1816, Lincoln City, IN 47552, check their website at www.nps.gov/libo, or phone them at 812-937-4541. The adjoining Lincoln State Park has a campground, cabins, and a 1,500-seat covered outdoor amphitheater where a drama about Lincoln's life as a youth is presented during the summer. For more information, you can contact that park at Box 216, Lincoln City, IN 47552, or phone 812-937-4710.

28

Hockey Pucks in the Chicken Coop

Perhaps you've visited a park with a living history program or an area such as Colonial Williamsburg where employees in period costume depict life in a bygone era. If so, maybe you've wondered where those people learned how to do all of that stuff the old-fashioned way. Well, I can give you at least a little insight based on my two years at Lincoln Boyhood National Memorial.

Those folks in historic costume are often referred to as "interpreters," as are their counterparts who take you on tours or hikes in parks all around the country. Their job is to interpret the facts and figures about that site in a way that helps you enjoy and understand the subject. Some of those rangers are permanent employees and have degrees in history or biology or whatever subject is appropriate to their assignment. Others are seasonal or part-time employees, working only during the park's busier months.

Even those with academic training, however, usually need hands-on instruction in most of the skills used decades or even centuries ago. Few of us today know how to milk a cow, cook a full meal over an open fire, or plow with a team of oxen. In that respect, training a living history interpreter is not unlike an apprenticeship program in past generations. Most parks are fortunate enough to have a few employees with years of skills in those lost arts and training of the occasional new hand is done by passing on the necessary knowledge one-on-one. Sometimes this has unexpected and amusing results.

During my days at Lincoln Boyhood National Memorial, we were blessed with a great but small staff of talented men and women. Most of them had grown up in the local area, many of them were second or third generation farmers, and several had worked for the NPS for quite a few years. The majority were employed for three to six months per year, with only a small permanent staff on duty all year. My second year at the park, one of our most experienced women retired, and we hired a local schoolteacher to take her place for the summer.

Current attitudes notwithstanding, most aspects of life on the American frontier were definitely divided into "men's" work and "women's" work. While the men and boys were outside plowing and splitting rails for fences, the women and girls were often back at the cabin, preparing a meal, tending the garden, or washing laundry in a big tub using lye soap they had made themselves.

It's fun for visitors to stroll around a living history farm and see all of those steps taking place. Just as on a real farm, the activities on any given day are determined by what needs to be done at that time. In spring, the fields are being plowed; during the summer, the garden needs to be weeded; and fall brings harvesting of crops and preparation of food for winter storage. This is a great way for kids to see history come to life and such spots are popular destinations for school field trips.

One of the constants on the farm was lunchtime, and every day the interpreter playing the role of the "lady of the house" was busy preparing a meal. As far as possible, the items used were grown right on the farm, whether it was ham from the smokehouse or eggs from the chicken coop. Cooking was done over the open fire in the cabin's fireplace, using tools of the trade such as an iron skillet and Dutch oven. If you've never tried that, it's a whole lot harder than grilling steaks on your gas grill!

Any of you readers who are sensitive to good use of tax dollars will also be glad to know that all profits from the farm go into a special account that is used to help cover the cost of operations. When last year's "crop" of lambs is ready to be sold, for example, that money may help buy a new harness for the horse. As for those lunches cooked over the cabin fire and served at noon, the menu is pretty limited, and preparing it can be quite a challenge.

Have you ever been working on a project at home or work and found that it was hard to make progress because of interruptions? Just about the time you reached a critical step, the phone rang, or somebody knocked on the door, or your second-grader just had to have your attention right now! If so, you can appreciate the plight of the living history interpreter. Although he needs to finish mending that fence and she needs to get lunch ready in the cabin, their primary job is to talk to visitors and help them understand what they are doing, along with the why and how. Sometimes, if the task allows, they might even let you try a little hands-on participation. The tradeoff, of course, is a lot less efficiency in getting the chores done, and concentration on the current task can be difficult.

My supervisory duties at the park covered many different areas, so my chances to work on the farm in costume were limited to times when we were shorthanded for a day or two. One of those occasions gave me the chance to experience an unusual result of on-the-job training for our new interpreter. She was a local schoolteacher in her early thirties, intelligent, hardworking, and great with the public and would work for us during the summer and some weekends in the fall. As you'd expect, her skills in fireplace cooking needed a little fine-tuning, but she learned quickly from another experienced woman on the staff.

A couple of weeks into her summer, it was time for her first solo assignment at the cabin, which meant that she was responsible for preparing the meal from start to finish, all the while talking with visitors and tending to other chores. As it turned out, this was also one of the rare days when I was filling in at the farm. The fact that the boss was there probably didn't make the lady's day any more relaxing. Even so, things seemed to be running smoothly and the dinner bell was sounded right on time.

The other "farmer" and I headed for the cabin, washed up in the bucket outside the door, and were careful to wipe the mud off our boots before we stepped inside. Lunch was set out on the table and the three of us grabbed places on the two wooden benches. I was glad to see hot biscuits on the table—I've been known to eat more than my share—and my compadre grabbed a couple as well. Our "housewife" was trying to hide her curiosity, but she was naturally a little anxious about how her first meal would be received. For our part, the "men of the family" wanted to be sure to encourage her efforts. As soon as those biscuits hit our plates, I realized diplomacy was going to get a serious workout.

We got a little help when the lady picked up a biscuit, looked at it with some skepticism, took a small bite, and promptly (but delicately, of course) returned it to her plate. With a look of absolute horror, she cast a baleful eye at the plate of bread, then looked tentatively at the two of us seated across the table.

"Ah, you really don't have to eat these if you don't want to," she offered.

"Oh, no, I'm sure they'll be fine. You did a great job with lunch," I replied gallantly. To prove the point, I managed to break off a tiny bite, chewed it enough to swallow, and then washed it down with a more than generous gulp of water. My fellow farmer was doing his best to follow my lead.

You have to keep in mind that this meal was being conducted in an on-again, off-again fashion as visitors trooped into the cabin and we stopped to chat with them. After a couple of lengthy breaks in our meal, our cook finally had a chance to offer an explanation. She admitted that she had a lot of interruptions during the biscuit preparations and had lost track of where she was in adding ingredients to the dough. In retrospect, she realized that she had apparently forgotten to add the baking powder. To make matters worse, it was quite obvious that she had at least doubled the amount of salt required. The resulting product had a distinct resemblance to a nice, golden brown hockey puck.

The day was saved, from the diplomatic standpoint, when a whole busload of visitors showed up at the cabin. Lunch was put on hold as we all helped welcome the group and show them around the farm. It was during this interruption that my fellow farmer managed to grab the remaining biscuits and spirit them out of the cabin. Once a semblance of calm was restored and we returned to the table, the plate that had held the bread was nice and bare. In an approach that I'm sure "Miss Manners" would endorse, the subject of the missing biscuits was not broached by any of us around the table, and the rest of the meal was declared a success.

It wasn't until later in the day that I had a chance to inquire about the disposition of the biscuits. My co-worker grinned and pointed over to the fence around the chicken coop. I peered through the wooden poles and sure enough, there they were: a half dozen or so nice, brown nuggets. As far as I could tell, they had been untouched from the moment they hit the ground.

The chickens were busy scratching away at the dirt, and studiously ignoring the latest offering. I think those baked hockey pucks survived pretty much intact for several days despite a good rain shower or two and were eventually removed and consigned to the compost pile. Perhaps in centuries to come an archeologist will do a dig at this site and puzzle for a while on those mysterious objects from the late twentieth century. I suspect they'll survive in their original form for quite a long time!

29

Serious Basketball Country

It was immortalized in the movie *Hoosiers*, and the state of Indiana's passion for basketball rivals the love of football in my native Texas. This was confirmed several times during my assignment at Lincoln Boyhood National Memorial. Our first clue came shortly after our arrival on a February afternoon. After several years in some pretty remote corners of Arizona and Nevada, we were looking forward to being a little closer to civilization for a while. Even the small town of Dale, only four miles up the road, had a real grocery store, hardware store, a couple of restaurants and other "city" conveniences.

Among the amenities we were looking forward to was the chance to choose from more than a couple of radio stations, so one of the first things we unpacked was our stereo and FM tuner. I hooked up the antenna, powered up the set, and started scanning the dial to see what was available. The fact that almost every station on the air was broadcasting a high school basketball game gave me my first clue about how serious these folks were about the game.

We soon had further confirmation about the passion for "roundball" when we learned that the high school gyms in a couple of nearby towns had seating capacities that exceeded the population of the whole town! The fascination with the game starts at a young age in Indiana. My wife taught a children's Sunday school class in the church we attended in the area. One morning, the scripture passage for the lesson included the term the "fowls of the air." Velma noticed a couple of blank expressions and paused to ask if anyone knew what that term meant. After a moment of silence, one boy raised a tentative hand.

"Does it have anything to do with basketball?" he inquired.

Velma managed to keep a straight face as she explained that the fouls in a basketball game were different from those with wings.

I also found that basketball fever extended to the highest levels of state government, especially as the season begins to approach the play-offs. Each year in February, Lincoln Boyhood National Memorial made an understandable fuss over Lincoln's birthday with a "Lincoln Day" event. Part of the day's activities included a speech by some notable individual, and one year we were pleased to learn that the governor had accepted our invitation to attend. In the interest of discretion, I'll be vague about the year this event took place.

The auditorium in the park's visitor center was filled to the brim, and the audience included many folks from the area anxious to see and hear the governor. The park superintendent was all set with the appropriate introductory remarks, and seating had been carefully assigned for various political figures from the local area. As the park's only commissioned law enforcement ranger, one of my jobs was to assist the State Police with security arrangements, which back in those calmer days were actually pretty minimal. My primary job that day was to be the gopher (as in "go for this" and "go for that") for the park superintendent.

The governor had a State Police officer assigned as his driver and security guard, and we knew he would be arriving by car. A second officer from our local area was on-site to assist for the event. As time drew near for the program to start, there was no sign of the governor, and my boss grew increasingly anxious. At the appointed hour, with the guest of honor still missing in action, I was sent out to the curb to check with the state policeman once again and told to come back inside as soon as I had any news. In those days before cell phones, such coordination was not quite as simple as it is today, but the trooper waiting with me outside the building did have two-way radio contact with the governor's driver.

In retrospect, I realize that the governor was well aware that there was a plethora of other politicians, along with the ladies from the local Lincoln Club, on hand for the event, and each one needed the opportunity to make a few appropriate remarks. As a result, there was certainly a little extra time built into the program before the main address. Even I was getting a little nervous as preliminaries got underway without the featured speaker on hand. After I had checked with the beleaguered state trooper one more time, he finally decided he could take me into his confidence. It turned out the governor had been attending a basketball game at the University of Indiana, and the game had gone into overtime, causing an unexpected delay in his schedule.

I immediately recognized that our crowd of 300 or so paled in comparison to the thousands at that ballgame, and it would unquestionably be a serious affront to those fans if the governor had left his prominent VIP seat before the outcome of the big game was determined! Besides, I'm sure the governor was enjoying a good game.

Stalling tactics for our program worked out, and the governor did arrive in time to give his speech. I don't recall if he explained to the crowd the reason for his slightly tardy arrival, but if he did, I'll bet they would have understood. If the truth were known, most of them probably didn't leave their houses until the game was over, either—they just had a lot shorter drive to get to the park for our event than the governor did!

Where There's Smoke

In recent years, it has become almost a staple on the evening news: scenes of firefighters, all decked out in their helmets and bright yellow Nomex fire-resistant shirts as they head into the woods to attack yet another wildland fire. In general terms, fires are classified either as structural (buildings) or wildland (forest, brush, grass, etc.). Rangers and other park employees sometimes get more chances than they really want to hone their skills in one or both varieties of fire fighting. No matter how exciting it may look on TV, this is hot, dirty, and dangerous work and those men and women must pass a rigorous annual physical fitness exam in addition to completing classroom and hands-on training before they are assigned to a fire. As the saying goes, "These are professionals—don't try this at home!"

Because of those tough standards, only a limited number of qualified firefighters are available either in each park or on the national level. There are actually very few personnel assigned full-time to fire duties, and those fire helmets are simply one of many hats worn by some park employees. During major wildland fire emergencies, park employees join their counterparts from other federal, state, and local agencies to provide the large numbers of personnel needed. Fortunately, according to a very reliable source, the National Interagency Fire Center, 99 percent of wildland fires are controlled while they are still small, using personnel from the local area during what is dubbed the "initial attack." That's a good thing, because fighting wildfires is a costly proposition. In the last year for which statistics were available, federal agencies alone spent more than $1.6 billion on those activities.

I'll make a very brief detour to note that there is considerable controversy these days among some politicians, various government agency officials, a host of special interest groups, their designated experts, and even a few interested citizens about whether fires are good or bad for the environment. The answer to that complex question is far beyond the scope of this book, so I'll simply say that in my humble but well-informed opinion: it depends. Rest assured I won't be chasing that rabbit much further—he's a smart bunny and has already run far away to keep from getting his fur singed in the heated political debate. For purposes of this little epistle, this chapter will touch only on a few aspects of fire suppression, which is what you do when you decide, for better or worse, to try to control a wildfire.

The importance of taking quick action against an unwanted fire was recognized long, long ago. A character in Shakespeare's *King Henry the Sixth* noted, "A little fire is quickly trodden out; Which, being suffer'd, rivers cannot quench." Truth to be told, that statement was uttered in a context fairly far removed from forests and fields, but it makes a valid point: If your goal is to put out a wildfire, you'd best get about the business of doing so with reasonable haste, whether you plan to trod it out or employ some slightly more sophisticated techniques.

It's the process of trying to keep those fires small that can make a ranger's life interesting at times.

Since qualified personnel are limited, a "fire callout" often means rounding up personnel who are off-duty at the time. This gets to be a case of good news and bad news. The bad news is that during certain times of the year in some parks, it can be really hard to get a day off. The good news is that if you are called in to work, you'll at least get paid overtime for your trouble. At the pay levels for most rangers, especially the younger folks just starting out, that's not inconsequential. Yes, rangers are an especially dedicated lot, but it's also nice to be able to pay the bills.

I mentioned that by way of background for the following story. Especially in parts of the rural South, there is a long-standing tradition among the local population that "a little fire in the woods is a good thing." I've already said that's a complicated topic, but if your goal is to keep open fields from being invaded by brush and trees or if you want to keep hardwoods from moving into a pine forest, to cite a couple of examples, fire can be a very useful tool. Native Americans successfully used fire this way long before the Europeans showed up in North America. In some locales, you can even muster up a pretty good discussion on the pros and cons of fire as a way to control ticks and chiggers and a host of other stimulating ecological issues.

This is definitely a situation where the devil is in the details. A lot of people have learned to their sadness that a "good" fire on one day can become a disaster the next if weather or other conditions change and the fire gets out of hand. This is especially true in much of the United States today, where homes and businesses have moved into formerly unsettled terrain. There's even an official term for this trend in the fire business: the wildland-urban interface, and this has become a big, and expensive, concern. A website, www.firewise.org/, provides tips for landowners to reduce the risk of wildland fire to their property.

There are also other elements in the "let's burn the woods today" philosophy. In addition to all of those noble reasons mentioned above, fire can also become a political statement of sorts. If the federal government, for example, happens to be a big landowner in your neck of the woods, and you don't hold that institution in high regard, you might choose to extract your "pound of flesh" by trying to burn down some of Uncle Sam's woods. (Well, yes, I realize that *you* wouldn't do that, but some people would.) If nothing else, some people with this mindset derive a certain amount of satisfaction from getting their local representatives of the U.S. Government (also known as the rangers) out of bed so they can spend the rest of the night—or day—putting out a fire in the woods.

Depending on how many times this has occurred lately, the rangers may or may not feel especially charitable towards their firebug neighbors under these circumstances. Now that you've completed this lesson in backwoods politics, you're in a position to understand why the following bit of country psychology worked for one of my fellow rangers. For obvious reasons, I'll be a little vague about the exact location of this discussion.

One of the real facts of life in rural areas and small towns is that the grapevine is alive and well, and the local coffee shop is still a key link in spreading the word. In this particular location, there had been an epidemic of "let's burn the woods" fever, and even the most ambitious young rangers had earned about all the overtime they wanted for that month in the process of chasing fire up and down hill and dale. Sensing that it was time to put a damper on the local enthusiasm for starting fires, the wise old ranger made his traditional stop for a morning cup of coffee in the local café. During the course of conversation, somebody just had to ask him "how things were goin'?"

His reply was that things were "going great." This came as a little disappointment for a couple of local denizens, who happened to know for a fact that the ranger and his associates had been out every day and night for a couple of weeks fighting fire. Surely they were getting a little tired?

"Yep," the ranger went on, "this has been a super month for me. Why, I've gotten called out so much and made so much overtime pay with all these fires that I figure I'll be able to pay off my pickup at least six months early. Heck, another week or two like we've had, and I might just go out and buy me a new one. Sure hope this dry weather lasts for a while longer."

This response was reported to have been met with some dismayed expressions at a nearby stool or two along the café's counter.

After a little more conversation, the ranger noted it was time to get to work, and eased on down the road. The strangest thing happened right after that—for some mysterious reason, the fires suddenly stopped in that neck of the woods for quite a while!

On the other end of the scale from the coffee shop grapevine, high tech has also arrived in the world of fire protection. Computers have been a part of the world of wildland fire for quite a while and can be very useful in predicting things such as how much risk there is that fires will occur and how fast a fire will spread if one starts in a given area. If you've traveled much in either national parks or national forests, you've probably seen those Smokey the Bear signs at key locations, with Smokey's hand pointing to the fire danger for the day. Fire personnel use computers to help determine if that degree of risk is low, moderate, high, or extreme. Computers are great at this kind of work, because those fire danger calculations involve analyzing bunches of data, such as how much rain has fallen over the past several months, how hard the wind is blowing, temperature and humidity readings, and lots more stuff than you want to read about.

Computer programmers are obviously very bright people, but I discovered quite by accident that at least some of them also have a good sense of humor. Early in my career, I was learning how to enter daily weather observations into a computer to determine the fire danger rating for that day. My instructor explained that the computer program was designed to catch obvious errors, such as forgetting to enter a decimal point in the right place. To prove his point, he had me enter the number 50 in the space for "inches of rain the past 24 hours," instead of the correct number of 0.50. While 50 inches of rain in a day instead of one-half inch of rain is obviously not likely unless you live down the road from a guy named Noah, the program responded with a lot more originality than the usual "invalid input" message.

As soon as I hit the return key after entering my record deluge, the computer promptly came back with this message: "Make thee an ark and gather the animals two by two!" Who says computers can't be fun, even if you work for the government!

Creativity, occasionally a little fun, and sometimes a touch of irony also turn up in the process of assigning names to fires. Fire names, you might ask? Yep, this is the government, and since an unusual happenstance like a fire certainly requires a report, it must follow that a system is required to distinguish one fire from the other.

It would be possible, and maybe even logical, to simply use a sequence of numbers rather than a name. To some extent that's the case, since a fire is assigned a numerical account number that is used by the budget folks for tracking costs associated with the fire. However, if several fires occur in the same area at the same time, they may all use the same account number. For that and several much better reasons, a name has a lot of advantages over a number for all other purposes. (Just for the record, all of the fire names in the following discussion are from real fires in the past several years.)

For starters, a major fire becomes a media event. You've likely seen some of that TV news footage of a reporter standing on a ridgetop with an impressive scene of smoke and flames visible in the background. With an appropriately somber expression, the journalist says something like, "I'm here on the scene of the Storm Creek Fire." Somehow, that same story would seem to lose a little pizzazz if the news anchor had to say, "Let's go now to our live coverage from Fire Number 4299-04-0751."

For a very similar reason, the lack of fire names would be bad for the economy as well as for firefighter lore and legends. Really, really big fires such as the ones in Yellowstone back in the late 1980s generate their own mystique and business spin-offs. In such situations, thousands of firefighters are housed in makeshift camps, complete with field kitchens, first-aid stations, supply depots, and even mementos.

Being part of the monumental effort to conquer one of those major conflagrations is a memorable experience. Fire assignments are normally dirty, dangerous, exhausting, hot, occasionally exciting, and sometimes downright dull. Ironically, I've rarely felt colder than I did sleeping on the ground in a fire camp in northern Wyoming in

Think you want to be a firefighter? It may sound exciting, but in reality it's a grueling and often dangerous job. This fire crew is hard at work in Yellowstone National Park. (National Park Service, Yellowstone National Park)

September—and finding the water in our canteens frozen solid the next morning! Fire fighting is very much like a military fighter pilot once described his job: "Days of boredom punctuated by occasional moments of sheer terror."

If you're going to put up with all that for days (or often weeks) at a time, you've got to at least come away with some war stories to swap with fellow firefighters in years to come. How can you not have at least one great tale if you were part of the Hell Roaring Fire in Yellowstone back in 1988? Hey, we're talking about legends in the making here, and using a number in place of a name for such epics just won't cut it!

A lot of firefighters, especially those who don't do this on a regular basis, like to take home an item like a t-shirt or baseball cap showing the name of the fire and an appropriate graphic. Proving that the free enterprise system is alive and well, most large fire camps will have one or more vendors who have risen to the occasion and quickly cranked out some of those mementos, often complete with some pretty impressive art work. Again, a t-shirt from the Wolf Lake Fire leaves a lot more room for such creativity than would "Fire 2003-516."

So, you might wonder, how does a fire get its name? I'm glad you asked.

Fire names are normally chosen by one of the supervisors on the fire and are often taken from a nearby geographical feature or other place name, such as the Piñon Canyon and Phillips Ranch fires. Sometimes, however, even those rather straightforward choices can sound a little ironic. For example, the "Green Swamp Complex" in Florida or the "Oasis" Fire in Washington State don't exactly conjure up images of smoke and flames or a charred landscape.

Creeks are often prominent landmarks but when their names are applied to a fire the results can sometimes present interesting contrasts, as evidenced by the Muddy Creek, Clear Creek and Hot Creek fires. Edible terms aren't overlooked, so you can also find fire names such as Cherry, Strawberry, and Plum Creek. Animal and bird names also play a big role, so the files include a veritable zoo, such as the Goat, Cougar Creek, Mourning Dove, Pony, Beaver Creek, Crow, Panther, Grizzly, and Moose fires. I'm not sure everybody was anxious to rush to the scene of the Rattlesnake Fire, but I'd give the prize in this category to the Dragon Fire at Grand Canyon.

Fires can conjure up quite a range of emotions, but I don't think those were necessarily a factor in dubbing a blaze in Yellowstone the Unlucky Fire or one in Death Valley the Happy Fire. I don't know of many places that sound like they have less potential for a wildland fire than the classic desert country of Death Valley, but yes, fires can occur even there. That fire was located at elevations between 5,000 and 8,000 feet in the Panamint Mountains of the park, a roadless area so rugged that firefighters had to be deployed by helicopter.

The name notwithstanding, I'm sure the personnel assigned to that fire were far from happy to tackle that job. According to the report, the fire was located in "some of the most remote and hostile terrain in the United States," and with temperatures around 112° in the valleys and 90° on the fire line, the heat was described as "debilitating" to firefighters. Those men and women definitely earned every penny in the several days it took to control the 5,500-acre blaze.

Some names do seem downright appropriate, such as the Hell's Half Acre and the Rampage fires, but ironically the Giant Fire was not very large. It was located in Sequoia–Kings Canyon National Park, home of those giant trees. Other labels definitely sound foreboding. Zion National Park in Utah has a number of rock formations with interesting names, but I'm not sure I'd have been thrilled to be sent to the Altar of Sacrifice Fire!

One of my personal favorites is the Son of Kibble Fire, which was an "offspring" of an earlier, nearby fire named the Kibble. Fires are by their nature smoky and smelly, but some might wonder if the Old Rag Fire was especially pungent. (Actually, it was named for Old Rag Mountain in Shenandoah National Park.)

In some cases, the name comes from an event associated with the fire. At Carlsbad Caverns National Park, the "Voltage Fire" started next to the superintendent's office when some wiring fell into nearby vegetation, sparking a blaze, and undoubtedly creating some electrifying excitement. There are bound to be some interesting stories behind the Microwave Fire in Florida and the Lugnut Fire in Oregon, but I cast my vote for the most original fire name to one in the Big Thicket National Preserve in Texas.

One nice sunny afternoon, a man whose house was located on private property adjoining part of that park decided to burn some trash in his yard. The timing wasn't exactly auspicious since the weather had been fairly dry, which in that part of soggy southeast Texas meant it had been at least sixteen hours since the last rain. It wasn't long before the fire spread from the trash pile into the woods on park property.

The good news is that conditions weren't right for a major conflagration, and a small crew from the park was able to contain the fire before any major damage was done. Establishing how a wildland fire began can sometimes be a tricky proposition, especially if thousands of acres in a remote area have been burned. In this case, however, even a rookie investigator would have had a pretty easy time following the scorched area back to the still smoldering trash pile in the homeowner's front yard.

Operating under the principle of striking while the iron—or in this case the trash—is hot, an interview was promptly conducted with the neighbor. By this time sufficient time had passed for the man to ponder his options, and I'll have to give him some bonus points for creativity. He apparently realized that it was a waste of time to deny that his trash heap was the original source of the blaze, so he settled on a time-honored tactic: The best defense is a good offense.

The man sheepishly agreed that the fire had started in his mini-landfill, but he was adamant in his denial that he had any hand in setting off the blaze. He did, however, have a scientifically based theory. Taking the ranger over to the pile of ashes and embers, he pointed out a number of pieces of glass from an impressive variety of broken jars and bottles.

It was obvious, he explained, that the fire must have started when the rays of the afternoon sun, shining through a piece of inauspiciously positioned glass, had been miraculously focused at exactly the right angle to ignite a combustible item in the trash heap. Based on the size of the pile of ashes, there had clearly been an impressive volume of such items in that spot not many hours earlier.

Everybody, the man continued, had tried that experiment in school where a beam of light was focused through a magnifying glass onto a piece of paper, generating enough heat to set the paper on fire. It was therefore clear as day, according to the country's newest self-appointed arson investigator, that this was exactly how the blaze in question started.

If there had been any serious damage to park property or any significant expense in suppressing the fire, the park might have pursued the investigation with greater vigor. As it was, the rangers concluded that the man seemed to understand that he could be held liable for those costs and damages—since the fire started on his property and escaped into the park—regardless of how it started. In the end, the report was duly completed, and one more moniker was added to the long and distinguished line of fire names: The "Sun did it" fire was now a part of history.

31

Crime Still Doesn't Pay

Compared to many places in today's world, most national parks are still pretty safe spots, and the average visitor's chances of being a victim of crime are very low if some basic precautions are taken. However, if you leave cameras, purses, and other valuables unattended in vehicles or campsites, you're inviting a visit from the basic petty thief found virtually anywhere these days. (By the way, "hiding" those items under the front seat of your car isn't much protection, either—lock them in the trunk if you can or keep them with you.) It just pays to use common sense, whether you're visiting Grant's Tomb in downtown New York or the Grand Canyon.

From time to time, misdeeds committed in parks include an element of humor—at least for everybody except the perpetrator. While good work by alert rangers resulted in each of the following arrests, the good guys had some help from another factor at times. I believe that a little further investigation would confirm that many of these folks are members of D.U.M.B.O.S. (**D**esperados **U**nder-utilizing **M**ost **B**asic **O**rganizational **S**kills). Law-abiding citizens can be glad that's the case, since the apprehension of these people removes them from the general population for at least some period of time.

In a similar vein, I have another theory about why some perpetrators of mischief act in otherwise inexplicable ways: bozone. "Bozone" has been defined as "the substance surrounding stupid people, which stops bright ideas from penetrating. The bozone layer, unfortunately, shows little sign of breaking down in the near future." I'll let you be the judge about whether or not bozone was a factor in any of the following true stories.

On August 10, 2001, a visitor to Big Bend National Park in Texas named Eric called ranger Lance Mattson and reported that his car had been stolen the previous night. Eric admitted that he had consumed copious amounts of alcohol during the evening. When he woke up in the morning, he found his vehicle was gone.

Eric's situation provides yet further evidence that significant numbers of brain cells can be damaged in short order by binge drinking, or perhaps he was just not the sharpest knife in the drawer. Ranger Mattson and Brewster County deputies questioned Eric closely and eventually determined that he had stolen the car in question in Oklahoma and had driven it to the park. After his drinking binge, he lost track of where he had left the vehicle, so he called and reported the car that he had stolen had been—stolen!

Further investigation revealed that Eric had been a little short of cash and didn't have enough money to pay the park's entrance fee, so he had taken a cross-country route in order to bypass the park entrance station. The vehicle was eventually found about a half mile into the desert, where it ended up after plowing through the park's boundary fence.

Eric probably won't need another vehicle for quite a while. He was extradited to Oklahoma, where, in addition to state charges, federal charges for interstate transportation of a stolen vehicle were being considered.

A second incident at Big Bend occurred on June 24, 2001 (maybe it's the heat?). On that day, Ranger Gary Carver spotted a suspicious rental van in the Rio Grande Village area and kept an eye on it for most of the day. (Rio Grande Village is located on the U.S. side of the border with Mexico and sees its share of various border-related incidents.) The van headed northward from the village as Border Patrol agents were en route to assist Carver. The agents passed the van on the way and turned around to stop it. The driver quickly pulled into the main visitor center parking lot and four people got out and ran into the restroom to hide before the agents got there. Two nationals from Guatemala and two more from El Salvador were later found and arrested for entering the United States illegally. Due to radio communications problems, however, the Border Patrol officers had already released the driver and van, and the vehicle had disappeared.

The old adage about criminals returning to the scene of the crime apparently still holds true, and sometimes the forces of law and order do get a second chance. The following morning, the park dispatcher who had been unable to reach the Border Patrol agents the previous day was relating this story to another ranger. As they were talking, the dispatcher saw this same van drive back into the visitor center parking lot. The driver got out of the van and checked the restrooms, apparently to see if his four passengers were still there! The driver then left the area in the van, but this time was stopped only a few miles away, arrested, and turned over to the Border Patrol. Oh, one more thing about that van—further investigation determined that it had been stolen, so the driver was also being prosecuted on theft charges.

Because many parks are located in rural areas where local law enforcement resources are stretched thin, rangers are sometimes called upon to assist with emergencies adjacent to park boundaries. On August 29, 2001, rangers at the Buffalo National River in Arkansas received such a request from the county sheriff to assist with serving a drug lab search warrant on a residence immediately adjacent to the park. The residence was accessible only by crossing through park property, was located in very rough terrain, and the park radios were the only communication that worked in the area.

Ranger Ben Hansel initially served as a lookout and radio relay on the access road that passes through the park. As the sheriff and drug task force officers entered the front door of the house, a suspect named Jamey ran out the back door, where he was apprehended by Ranger Hansel. Jamey, along with six others in the residence, was arrested after the house was found to contain a working methamphetamine lab.

The fun part of this story came after the arrests. While officers were still processing evidence at the scene, two more people arrived at the house with the intention of purchasing drugs. (The following conversation is only conjecture on my part, but it's fun to imagine the dialogue when this duo arrived at the scene and contacted the officers): "Hey, dude, is this the place where we can buy some dope?" They were promptly arrested as well, one on a warrant from Louisiana and the other for possession of marijuana.

The next incident confirms that honesty is always the best policy. It also suggests that carrying a concealed weapon can create some unexpected hazards, especially if you carry it in the wrong place.

On the evening of July 21, 2001, rangers at Cape Lookout National Seashore in North Carolina received a 911 call reporting a shooting on Shackleford Banks. Ranger Richard Larrabee responded, meeting both the victim (whom I'll refer to as the shootee) and the suspected shooter at a local urgent care medical center.

Larrabee interviewed the two men, both of whom said that the shooting resulted from an accident. In a new twist on the axiom that "alcohol and guns don't mix," the alleged shooter was reportedly carrying a .22 caliber revolver in his front pocket, which fired accidentally when a beer keg he was helping to carry onto the island bounced off his leg. The round then ricocheted off the keg and grazed the shootee's leg, causing a superficial wound. All things considered, this is probably about as good an outcome as could be hoped for from this accidental discharge, given the location where the gun was being carried when it fired unexpectedly.

The shooter said that he then threw the weapon into the ocean and escorted the shootee by boat to the medical facility. Since he readily admitted to having the gun in his possession, the act of tossing a perfectly good gun into the surf raised some questions. The man told Larrabee and local officers that he didn't have a state driver's license (which was later found to be false) and provided them with what later proved to be a fictitious name and address. Since both parties said that the shooting was an accident, the shooter was released that evening after agreeing to return to the area the next morning to help search for the discarded weapon.

Strangely enough, the shooter fled the county before morning arrived and failed to appear as promised. Since such actions suggest about ten times out of ten that there is more to the story than meets the eye, Ranger Larrabee and Supervisory Ranger Jim Zahradka tracked down and interviewed the shooter. They seized the .22, which it turns out the shooter still had in his possession, and the shorts he was wearing when the gun fired in his pocket. The report didn't mention whether he was still wearing them at the time of the interview or whether he had decided to save them as a souvenir.

At last report, the shooter was scheduled for an appearance before the United States Magistrate to answer charges of possession of a weapon, providing false information, and disorderly conduct.

Occasionally, getting caught in a misdeed can be an expensive but life-changing lesson. On September 24, 2000, Ranger Mark Gorman spotted a group digging in a known fossil area near Sheep Mountain in South Dakota's Badlands National Park. Investigation determined that even though the group knew they were in the park and their activities were illegal, they had collected more than 1,700 fossil specimens by the time they were apprehended. All four were subsequently convicted of theft of government property and other charges. One of the group, Aaron K., was asked by the federal magistrate if he understood the seriousness of the violation. Aaron replied that he did and announced to the court that he was changing his major from geology to psychology!

Most rangers and other law enforcement officers probably share my amazement at how often people who know they are in trouble of some sort will do something that attracts the attentions of "the authorities." It is interesting, for example, to note how many people who are stopped for traffic violations such as speeding are also driving on a suspended driver's license.

On September 20, 2003, two individuals from Ajo, Arizona, were driving through Organ Pipe Cactus National Monument. Organ Pipe has some great desert scenery along the border between Arizona and Mexico. Unfortunately, it is also a very active area for illegal immigrants and drug smugglers, so rangers there are especially alert for suspicious activity.

On this particular day, the driver of a 2000 Chevy truck was stopped for speeding. I realize that this is not an especially unusual occurrence, but in this case it wasn't a very smart move for several reasons. First, the driver had no license, a situation which invariably leads the ranger to scrutinize the situation more closely, especially in a place like Organ Pipe. An appropriate citation was issued to the driver and during the course of the conversation the driver was asked for permission to search the vehicle.

Permission was granted, and the search soon produced a single bud of marijuana—hardly worthy of excitement in that area, where seizures of drugs are more often measured in bales and hundreds of pounds. Of somewhat greater interest was a shoebox found under the seat of the truck. The report of this incident contained only the basic details, so the following dialogue is simply conjecture based on my experience with similar situations.

Ranger: "What's inside this box, sir?"

Driver: "What box?"

Ranger: "This shoe box that was under the seat of your truck."

Driver: "Well, my sakes, where in the world did that come from?" Turning to his passenger, the driver asks, "Hey, Bubba, do you know anything about this box?"

Passenger: "Why, gosh no, I never saw it before."

Ranger: "Well, since you don't know how it got there or who it belongs to, you wouldn't mind if I had a look inside, would you?"

The box turned out to contain $26,635 in cash.

Both the driver and occupant continued to express amazement at this development and denied ownership or any knowledge of the money, so the ranger took the standard course of action. He determined that the cash was "abandoned property," issued the two individuals a property receipt confirming that he had taken possession of these mysterious funds for safekeeping, and sent them on their way with an additional citation for possession of marijuana. Further investigation concerning the money was being conducted by the U.S. Attorney's Office and NPS personnel.

If there's a moral to this story, I suppose it might be that if you (1) don't have a driver's license; and (2) have even small quantities of illegal drugs in your vehicle; and (3) have even the slightest guess that the tooth fairy might have stored a large amount of cash in your vehicle without your knowledge, then: Don't drive over the speed limit or otherwise break the law and attract attention to yourself.

Also at Organ Pipe National Monument, a vehicle was stopped in the park for speeding and driving in a closed area. The driver, Adam B., age 38 and therefore old enough to know better, could not provide proof of insurance, a license, or registration. Since he was zero for three at that point, a consent search of the vehicle was then conducted. The ranger smelled the odor of marijuana emanating from the luggage rack on the vehicle's roof and discovered seventeen bundles of marijuana weighing 264 pounds. Adam and passenger James S., 26, were arrested. Methamphetamine was found on James during a search of his person. As a bonus, the vehicle was later found to have been stolen.

On the afternoon of June 17, 2002, another driver who should have stayed at home decided that it was okay to drive 70 in a 45-mile-per-hour zone. Ranger Randy Seese was on patrol on Route 209 in the Delaware Water Gap National Recreation Area in Pennsylvania and New Jersey when his radar picked up the speeding black Plymouth

Neon. The driver, Daniel D., compounded his error by trying to outrun the ranger, but only made it as far as a bend in the road, where the report notes "the driver found that his speed of 110 m.p.h. was also in excess of the prevailing laws of physics. The Neon left the road, traveled for several hundred feet, and came to an abrupt halt in thick, viney vegetation along the edge of the forest, completely disappearing into a wall of multiflora rose, blackberry and honeysuckle."

The driver fled into the woods, but his passenger was trapped in the car. After being extricated, he identified the driver to rangers. He also volunteered that his companion had fled because he had no driver's license and "didn't like police," possibly due to the fact that he had just been released from jail in New Jersey. Daniel was soon captured and his escapade added a variety of additional charges to his already lengthy criminal history. Some folks are apparently slow learners!

On the morning of March 29, 2002, rangers at Yellowstone National Park saw and stopped a car on the North Entrance Road that was operating without brake lights and whose occupants were not wearing seatbelts. They found that the driver's license had been suspended due to a failure to appear in court and that none of the three occupants owned the car. A consent search led to the discovery of $8,500 in cash, a loaded nine-millimeter handgun, and drug paraphernalia. Two of the three were arrested and were awaiting trial at the time of the report.

On June 7, 2002, Ranger Brad Headley observed a pickup truck driving over the center line in the Great Smoky Mountains National Park. Headley stopped the truck, which he found to be occupied by three men. A used syringe was in plain sight, and this led to a search and the discovery of 25 grams of methamphetamine, a propane tank containing anhydrous ammonia, a gas generator, and other chemicals and equipment commonly used to manufacture methamphetamine. Vapors were issuing from the generator and tank, so a DEA-approved hazardous material crew was dispatched to clean up the vehicle. The subsequent investigation led to the search of a residence in the Bryson City area and the recovery of additional chemicals and equipment used in the manufacture of methamphetamine. The three men were arrested and have been indicted for manufacture and distribution of the drug. The maximum penalty is life in prison; the minimum penalty is 10 years in jail. It's helpful when some crooks are careless drivers!

Still other people are apparently so determined to get arrested that they go out of their way to ensure success. On September 16, 2003, a ranger was working in his office at the Mammoth Subdistrict Ranger Station in Yellowstone National Park when he heard a loud banging on the front door. When he opened the door, the ranger was confronted by a highly agitated and intoxicated man who was bleeding, screaming, and demanding to be arrested. He then advanced on the ranger with a raised and closed fist.

By the time additional help arrived, the ranger had managed to handcuff the man, who was still combative. Investigation revealed that the man had been in a protracted disturbance of the peace incident in Mammoth Hot Springs and had previously been convicted of disorderly conduct in the park. He was being held pending trial and a psychological evaluation.

If you'd like to meet a ranger in a park, a slightly more subtle way would be to spend a night in a campground, but fail to pay the required fee for the campsite—and just for good measure, be sure to park your vehicles illegally. On September 10, 2003, three young men and a juvenile female made both of those mistakes at the Rock Creek Campground at Chickasaw National Recreation Area in Oklahoma, and in due time they were contacted by Ranger DeDe Mladucky.

During the ensuing conversation, a member of the group asked the ranger to help them jumpstart one of the vehicles, a 1998 Ford Expedition. Ranger Mladucky, being a prudent servant of the public and a diligent law enforcement officer, made a routine check of the vehicle registration, which revealed that the Expedition had been stolen from Oklahoma City. Two of the males, ages 19 and 20, and the female juvenile were arrested on the spot. The third male, another not-so-wise 20-year-old, tried to escape but was captured less than a mile away.

A check of the second illegally parked vehicle revealed that it was also stolen, and a subsequent search found that the car contained several items that had been stolen from as far away as Pennsylvania, including a wallet, credit cards, and a car CD player. I'm sure the prosecutors in at least two towns were glad to wrap up several cases—and happy that this merry little band went out of their way to attract the ranger's attention in the first place. Good thing the owner of that Expedition hadn't bought a new battery recently!

Although it may be tempting to do so, it's definitely better for citizens not to take matters into their own hands in trying to solve a crime, since such efforts can be dangerous and sometimes take an unexpected turn. On March 4, 2002, Bill J., the manager of a sandwich shop in Cherokee, North Carolina, discovered that he had received four expired gift certificates valued at $20 from some female customers. At closing time several hours later, Bill saw a car traveling toward the nearby entrance to the Great Smoky Mountains National Park; inside were women who appeared to him to be the ones who had given him the worthless coupons.

Mr. J. followed the women into the park, recklessly tailgated their car in an attempt to stop them, then passed them and set up a roadblock, which the women avoided by driving onto the grassy road shoulder. Bill pursued them again, rammed the back of their car two times while traveling at high speed, then illegally passed them again and attempted a second roadblock. The women stopped, turned their car around, and fled back to Cherokee at speeds nearing 90 miles per hour. Apparently unable to realize that things were already way out of control, the determined Mr. J. continued pursuit.

The women left the park and stopped at a gas station, where they called 911. Prior to the arrival of police, Bill followed the women into the gas station and demanded money for the expired coupons. The women explained that they had not eaten in Cherokee and had no idea what he was talking about. It was only at this point that Mr. J. realized his mistake and fled before police arrived, apparently concluding that it was a little late for an apology and the old, "Say, haven't we met somewhere before?" line. Based on the information the women supplied, Bill was identified as the suspect, located, and confessed to the incident. Since all of his vigilante efforts had occurred in the park, rangers were consulting with the U.S. Attorney concerning appropriate charges.

Fortunately, some crooks apparently can't resist the temptation to put their ill-gotten gains to immediate use. On an April morning, several windsurfers at Cape Hatteras National Seashore in North Carolina reported thefts of their equipment. That same afternoon one of the victims saw a man windsurfing on items that had been stolen from him earlier in the day and notified rangers. This would be somewhat akin to stealing a car and then driving it up and down the street in front of the owner's house.

Based on the description provided by this witness, Ranger Mark White tracked down the 20-year-old suspect and by 4:30 p.m. had him in custody. The arrest led to the recovery of about $3,000 worth of stolen equipment and a variety of felony charges, including breaking and entering, possession of stolen property, and possession of drug paraphernalia and a controlled substance.

The official report didn't mention it, but I suspect that there was an unusual odor in the air when this guy was caught. No, I'm not talking about the drugs—I think it was the distinctive smell of bozone.

32

You've Got Questions, We've Got Answers

Those friendly park rangers you meet all over the country are human, after all, and occasionally one will slip up and say what's really on his or her mind! When you've just been asked the same question for the 716th time that day, or if the question is really outlandish, it's sometimes hard to keep up your enthusiasm. More often than not, however, those folks in the green and gray uniforms manage to bite their tongues and keep on smiling. The following are just a few examples of answers some of my fellow rangers would like to have given at one time or the other, along with some that were actually used with mixed results.

I was assigned to the Big Thicket National Preserve in southeast Texas at the time that it was still a new part of the national park system. As is true in most rural areas, the local grapevine was both active and effective, so a trip down a country road by the rangers en route to the park didn't go unnoticed. As a result, we sometimes ventured out in unmarked vehicles and civilian clothes to get a better idea about what was really happening out there in the woods. We even had fun making up some magnetic signs with the names of bogus companies that we'd sometimes slap on the side of a pickup truck that had regular state license plates instead of government tags.

On one such trip, two of my fellow rangers, dressed in their blue jeans and flannel shirts, were driving a pickup with regular state license plates. Just as they were leaving the park on a muddy, backwoods road, they met a pair of good ol' boys in their four-wheel-drive truck, who were headed into the park. As was common practice, both vehicles slowed down and eased over to the edge of the road to allow room for both to pass, then stopped as they came alongside to exchange greetings. The driver of the four-wheel-drive truck leaned out the truck window and gave the strangers a quick once-over. Their disguise as fellow woodsmen apparently passed muster. The driver leaned out the truck window, shot a quick stream of chewing tobacco onto the ground between the two trucks, gave the rangers a friendly grin, and greeted them in a slow drawl.

"How-dy! You boys kill anything yet today?"

The ranger driving the pickup grinned back and replied, "Nope, didn't see anything worth messing with." However, he admitted later that what he really wanted to say was, "Nope, didn't kill anything, but we think we winged a couple of poachers!"

At the Grand Canyon, we got more than our share of visitors who were clearly attempting to "see" as many parks as possible during the shortest period of time. As a result, one of the more common questions was, "We've only got about fifteen minutes. What can we see here in that much time?"

I never heard anyone actually do so, but one of my co-workers said she was always tempted to answer such questions with something like, "Gosh, sir, you really can't see much of anything in a park this big in that period of time, but you could buy some nice postcards of the canyon right over there."

Occasionally, a ranger giving a perfectly correct answer still gets into hot water. I heard about a young lady on duty at a visitor center who was approached by a visitor with one of the dreaded "bird questions." I say dreaded because rangers are automatically expected by some visitors to be able to instantly identify every variety of bird, tree, flower, mammal, fish, insect, reptile and rock, along with every other object, living or dead, that was rumored to have been found in the park sometime in the past, now occurs in the park, or might possibly turn up in that park sometime in the future, or that exists anywhere else on the face of the globe. Furthermore, the descriptions of the item to be identified provided by some visitors are frequently more than a little vague. While most rangers do their best to study the birds and beasts in their area, being an expert on everything is obviously an impossible task.

In this case, the visitor had a pretty accurate description of the bird in question. The lady told the ranger that they had seen a flock of black birds with bright red patches on their wings, and she wanted to know what kind of bird that was. The ranger must have given a silent sigh of

One of the best parts of the job—a ranger at Colonial National Historical Park in Virginia shares a special "Hey, Ranger" moment with a young visitor to Jamestown. (National Park Service)

relief, because this was an easy one. After confirming that these birds were all black except for the red area visible on their wings, the ranger confidently replied, "Yes, ma'am, that's a Red-Wing, sometimes called a Red-Winged Blackbird."

The visitor was immediately incensed at what she perceived to be a flippant reply, and before the ranger could produce a copy of the bird guide to confirm her answer, the lady stormed out of the building. She later wrote a letter to her congressman complaining about the "smart-alecky" park ranger! I hope her boss included a copy of the page from the guidebook in the reply to the congressman, and I've always wondered how the congressman's staff handled their reply back to the constituent.

On the flip side, we sometimes encounter visitors who have a sense of humor. A man once approached me and remarked that he could identify "any bird in the world." I had to admit that this was a very impressive feat, and asked him how long he had been studying birds in order to be able to do that.

"Not long," he replied. "It's either a robin, or it's not a robin."

Unfortunately, we couldn't get by with that level of knowledge in the ranger ranks!

I used my intuition about what questions are likely to be commonly asked to have a little fun one afternoon with a fellow ranger at the Washington Monument. It was a warm, early summer day, and the line of people waiting to board the elevator was already pretty long. A ranger was stationed on the walkway leading to the monument to provide initial information for visitors. Since my family and I were there on vacation, I looked pretty much like any other tourist.

As I walked up to the ranger, I said, "I'll save both of us a little time, so just give me the answers to your three most common questions."

The young woman gave me a startled expression, then grinned and promptly said, "Okay, the wait for the elevator ride to the top is about forty-five minutes, it costs ten cents a person, and the rest rooms are right down that walkway about 200 yards."

I gave her a smile back and said, "Thanks! You were three for three!"

She took one more look at me, laughed and said, "You're Park Service, aren't you?"

"Yes," I admitted. After quick introductions, I remarked that when visitors came up to me in certain locations, I was sometimes tempted to just go ahead and answer the questions before they had a chance to ask them. I didn't ever do that, but this was too good a chance to pass up. She agreed and thanked me for helping make her day.

Occasionally, we just can't resist an opportunity for a little fun with a visitor, especially when it looks like they'll take it in stride. Big Thicket National Preserve in Texas is one of the more recent additions to the NPS and is an area that allows hunting, with certain conditions, under its enabling legislation. I was working there during the park's early years in the 1980s.

Hunting in the park required a free permit from the park, and there were a specific number of permits available for various parts of the park on a lottery basis (a drawing).The first year of the hunting program, those interested in a permit came to one of several locations to sign up prior to the start of the season. This gave us a chance to explain the program in person to potential hunters and provided some other interaction as well.

Since this was a new park in deep East Texas, there was still more than a little suspicion on the part of many of the locals about this new federal presence in their neck of the woods. Like just about anywhere else, the Thicket and surrounding area had lots of really nice people, but it also took some pride in having a tad more than its fair share of renegades and outlaws. This second group of people and the rangers were engaged in an ongoing game of sorts, sizing each other up. Much of this game resulted from some pretty radical concepts that the park introduced—such as limits on the number of deer a hunter was allowed to take in a year, and even more revolutionary, the idea that hunting wasn't allowed for anything that moved, 24 hours a day, 365 days a year.

As at almost every park, our staff was woefully inadequate for the size of the area and the job at hand, but we did our best to keep the local outlaws guessing about our schedules, day-to-day activities, and even the number of rangers we had available. The hunting permit sign-up gave us a chance to have a little fun one day and tip the odds in our favor just a bit.

It's common for a lot of outdoorsmen to use military surplus ammunition boxes to carry various items of gear in their boats or vehicles. The metal boxes are inexpensive, watertight, and almost indestructible. The park had a chance to get some of these boxes through military surplus channels at a nearby army base. As sometimes happens, there was a little mix-up in the paperwork and instead of a dozen or so of the boxes, we end up with a *dozen* dozen boxes. We didn't really need 144 of the containers right away but figured we'd use them eventually. Storage space was at a premium in our new, rented office space, so we just stacked the extra 120 or so boxes about four high along the outside wall of a building inside our fenced parking area.

As it worked out, the people coming in to apply for a hunting permit all walked right past that stack of empty ammo boxes. A couple of us were walking across the parking area when we encountered several of the hunters and stopped to chat. Several minutes into the conversation, one of the locals figured it was worth a try to fish for a little useful information and asked casually, "How many rangers you boys got working here anyway?" The opportunity was just too good for us to pass up.

"Well," one of us replied, "we've brought in quite a bit of extra help for hunting season, and with so many new people it's a little hard to keep up. However, when we go out on patrol, we each take an ammo box for some of our gear, and when we come back off our shift, we just put our box back on the stack over there." Gesturing toward the small mountain of olive drab containers, the ranger continued, "That'll give you a general idea, anyway."

The hunters' eyes all swung in unison over to the pile of boxes, then back in our direction. I'll have to say that for at least that brief moment, we'd have made a professional poker player proud with our deadpan expressions. After a short silence the conversation moved on to other matters. Our "customers" suspected their legs were being pulled, but they weren't quite sure just how hard!

For the record, we *had* brought in some extra help that fall, and our four seasonal rangers who would work for the next six months or so doubled our staff in that district of the park, so our comment about bringing in "quite a bit of extra help" wasn't untrue. We also frequently took an ammo box for our camera, lunch, or other items when we went on patrol—this little conversation just didn't say how many extra boxes we had!

Rangers aren't the only ones with a quick comeback, but they don't always work out as hoped. An ongoing problem at Lake Mead National Recreation Area involved a state law that required boats pulling water skiers to have both a boat operator and an observer above a specified age on board. The requirement was a good one for safety's sake: if the skier fell or had other problems, the observer could immediately tell the operator to stop the boat. That allowed the boat operator to presumably pay full attention to driving the boat, rather than spending time looking back over his shoulder at the water skier. So far, so good.

One summer day a state game warden stopped a boat towing a skier. The occupants of the boat included the operator and a large dog, but no separate observer. The boat operator protested that he did have an observer, as the law required. He claimed that the dog was trained to watch the skier and bark if the skier fell down. The current law does specify that the observer be a person, but the warden was intrigued and consented to a demonstration.

The boat and skier got underway and a short time later the skier intentionally fell down into the water. Sure enough, the dog immediately went absolutely berserk, barking and running around in the boat.

This same drill was repeated three times, with identical results. The warden agreed that the dog was probably more attentive to its task than a lot of human observers, but there was one other small detail: the law also requires the observer to immediately hold up an international orange flag at least twelve inches square when the person being towed is in the water but not actually underway. Standard practice is to attach this flag to a short stick, which makes it easy for observers hold the flag up over their heads when needed. This was a smart dog, but he had the standard canine equipment of paws instead of hands, which made it pretty well impossible for him to comply with the orange banner routine. As alibis go, however, this boater gets five points for a nice try.

So, if you have a question during a visit to a park, by all means ask a ranger. Just try to show a little mercy and make your inquiry as reasonable as possible. He or she will do their best to help you out, because as public servants rangers don't have the luxury of following the advice of a French philosopher and scientist named Fontenelle, who suggested in 1686, "It isn't very intelligent to find answers to questions which are unanswerable." Maybe you could help out by trying not to ask too many unanswerable questions.

33

Tales from the Wild Side

The NPS publishes an electronic newsletter called the *Morning Report* that is distributed most weekdays via the Internet to parks all across the country. In addition to passing on information of general interest to park employees, it also includes a summary of newsworthy incidents that occurred recently in national park sites. For a number of years a ranger named Bill Halainen has, in addition to his other duties, compiled information received from parks near and far into concise and readable summaries in those newsletters.

This chapter and the following one entitled "Don't Be a Victim of Your Vacation" include a few excerpts from those *Morning Reports*. I've added to Bill's text at times to provide some explanatory information or editorial commentary and have also edited out a few names to protect the innocent (or guilty) parties. I hope you will find these accounts both interesting and informative and trust that you will be so amazed at some of the following misadventures that you will never consider getting yourself into a similar fix!

One of those reports included the following account, simply titled, "Rescue." On May 25, 2000, a 61-year-old man named John failed to return from a day hike in the Grand Canyon. His cousin notified rangers and told them about John's planned route. Despite the fact that temperatures down in the canyon that day ranged from a high of 111°

to a nighttime "low" of 102°, he had set out on his jaunt with only two small bottles of water, no food, no flashlight, and no map.

Rangers established containment points on several trails and began a sweep of trails along the man's expected route. When no sign of the hiker was found, the mission was expanded to include an aerial search. During a second flight, rangers familiar with the history of lost persons in this same area spotted John, who had been hiding from the searchers, believing they were "bad guys." Hallucinating from severe dehydration, he still had water in one of his bottles, but told rangers he hadn't drunk it "because a man sitting next to him said it was bad water." (This was not a promising sign, since John was alone on his hike). He was flown out and treated at a local medical facility. Doctors said he would not have survived another day if he hadn't been found at that time.

The only good news about John's situation was that he had at least informed a family member about his plans and his intended route. Without that information, it is unlikely he could have been rescued, given the vast area included in the Grand Canyon.

A report from 1998 had the unusual subject, "Search; disorderly horse." That title was actually a pretty succinct summary of the situation. It seems that on the afternoon of May 17, rangers at Great Sand Dunes National Monument in Colorado received a 911 call about a saddled but riderless horse not far from the park's entrance station. When last seen, the horse had been headed south through the brush. A ranger and park maintenance employee responded and spotted the rider, who appeared to be uninjured, chasing the horse. She managed to catch her steed and began to lead it off to the north.

A few minutes later, the ranger was flagged down by a member of a group of four riders, one of whom proved to be the recently unseated rider. It turns out that the group had purchased four horses from the Adopt-A-Wild-Horse program, and they were using the park as the starting point for a cross-country ride to Montana. Just in case a little refresher in geography would come in handy, it's quite a ride from central Colorado to even the closest point in Montana. Unfortunately, there seemed to be a minor detail that was creating a little problem—none of the horses had been quite "broken in" for riding. (Maybe there's a reason it is called the Adopt-a-*Wild*-Horse program?)

Later that afternoon the group resumed its attempted ride, with three riders following one route and the fourth following a second route. It may or may not have been significant that the single horse following a separate route was the same one that had caused the earlier problem. The *Morning Report* entry was silent on the obvious question—was rider number four or horse number four choosing to follow a different route? Then again, maybe riders number one, two, and three wanted to keep their distance for a while, lest their horses get any ideas from steed number four. All four riders planned to meet at a previously established campsite in the nearby Rio Grande National Forest.

Within the hour, the ranger received another call, reporting that horse number four had once again dumped its rider, who had chased her mount for half an hour in the dark. She had then walked to park headquarters and was there now, seeking assistance. Efforts to find the horse proved fruitless, so the ranger and hapless rider headed for the camp, arriving only to find it empty.

A few minutes later, one of the remaining three horsemen arrived in camp. He reported that the trio had lost the trail in the dark, and since they had no flashlights, they had decided to build a fire and sit tight. After a while, he had decided to try to find the camp and the fourth member of the group, retrieve the flashlights from the campsite, and return to the riders waiting beside the fire. Unfortunately, there was one small detail—there seemed to be some question about the exact location of the remaining pair and their campfire.

A search was begun, and the last two riders were finally located around 11:30 p.m. Flashlights at the ready, the party made its way back to the trail and followed it toward camp. As they had feared, however, the horses refused to cross the high water in a creek, and more time was lost searching for a place to ford the stream. Finally, four undoubtedly weary riders all made it into camp. Well, actually it was three weary riders, one weary would-be rider and three horses—whose reactions were not included in the report.

Efforts to recapture the missing horse resumed the next day, but were abandoned after five hours of chasing it along the park's south and west boundaries. It's unknown if the group ever made it to Montana—or even out of Colorado.

Another entry from June 2000 might be entitled, "With friends like these . . ." On the previous afternoon, a man named William from Sanaford, West Virginia, was swimming in the New River in West Virginia, at a spot known as Terry Beach. William, who was 47 years old (and therefore old enough to know better) had apparently consumed an unknown quantity of alcoholic beverages before or during his swim. He eventually became exhausted, yelled for help, and then slipped under water. He did not resurface.

Luckily for William, a public-spirited local resident commandeered an inner tube, swam out to the point where the missing man had last been seen, found him under the water, and pulled him to shore. When they reached dry land, the victim was blue, unresponsive, and not breathing.

It looked like William's good luck was going to continue because two of his friends, who'd also been drinking, began to administer CPR. The man's good fortune continued and a third person, who was not part of his group (and therefore at least had the potential of being sober) attempted to help in the resuscitation effort. Unfortunately for William, his friends took offense for some reason at this assistance, and a fistfight ensued over the question of who would revive the unconscious man. This turn of events presumably made it difficult to keep up the proper rhythm for CPR. Under the circumstances, William would have probably been glad to say he really didn't mind who was giving CPR, but he wasn't much help at this point.

This is, of course, actually a very serious situation, and I am making light of it somewhat only because at this point rangers arrived on the scene, reestablished order, and continued treatment of the victim. Fortunately, CPR was effective, and William resumed breathing. He was taken to a hospital for further treatment.

On the serious side, I want to make a definite point that alcohol or drugs figure heavily in far too many serious incidents, both in parks and throughout the country. Many other situations have a much less favorable outcome than this one at New River, so I trust that all of my readers will act more responsibly than this little band.

The following account may help you understand why I believe that the limited dollars spent on emergency services in your national parks represent one of the best investments made by American taxpayers. This report from Grand Canyon National Park, entitled "Multiple Rescues," also illustrates how thinly stretched those emergency services can be on a lot of days. I'll add a few explanatory comments in (parentheses) throughout the narrative to clarify a few points.

"On July 10th, park SAR (Search and Rescue) personnel had to respond to and manage several life-threatening incidents throughout the park":

- "A 51-year-old man with an altered level of consciousness was reported below Indian Gardens on the Bright Angel Trail. (This is roughly half-way between the top of the canyon's South Rim and the bottom of the Grand Canyon.) Two park medics were flown there by the park's helicopter to check on the possibility of heat stroke. The patient was flown to the park clinic for treatment."

- Just as the above mission was being completed, the park received a report of a 25-year-old woman who had fallen thirty feet from the North Kaibab trail at a location known as "The Box," while stepping back to take a photo. (This steep and narrow trail leads from the North Rim of the canyon to the river. It is on the opposite side of the Grand Canyon from the previous incident. The closest help was at the Ranger Station at Phantom Ranch, located in the very bottom of the Canyon.)

  "Phantom Ranch rangers ran four miles to the scene with emergency medical equipment and were joined by other personnel who were flown to the site. (Note: Those four miles are uphill, and I mean seriously uphill from Phantom Ranch!) A portable radio repeater was brought to the area by helicopter. (A repeater allows transmissions from handheld radios to be picked up and relayed a greater distance. In steep terrain like the interior of the Grand Canyon, there are many places that are normally out of range for two-way-radio messages.) Monsoonal rains complicated the response. (This is a polite way of saying this took place during a serious downpour!) The woman was stabilized, transported by wheeled litter to the helispot, then flown to the South Rim. Her injuries included fractures of her wrist, leg and vertebrae in her lower back."

- "During the North Kaibab incident described immediately above, a ground-to-air radio transmission came in from the Colorado River near Quartermaster Canyon reporting severe anaphylaxis in a 46-year-old woman. (Translation: Due to the terrain, the only communications from many places in the bottom of the canyon is via a radio that can contact aircraft which happen to be passing directly overhead. The woman in this case was on a commercial river trip, and was having a severe, life-threatening allergic reaction, perhaps due to an insect sting or similar injury. This location was many miles away from the rescue that was underway along the North Kaibab Trail.) Due to the distance, response time, and other ongoing incidents, the park asked the Arizona Dept. of Public Safety's air rescue unit to respond. A helicopter was dispatched from Kingman. The woman, who was in severe distress, was evacuated to a hospital in Kingman."

- "While these incidents were underway, a report was received of a 20-year-old male with severe heat exhaustion at Bright Angel Campground at Phantom Ranch (in the bottom of the canyon). He was treated by park medics and flown by helicopter to the park clinic."
- "Park dispatch received a satellite telephone call (the only other way to communicate from many places along the river) from Hatch River Expeditions on the Colorado River at nine p.m. reporting that a 25-year-old woman was bleeding heavily, was suffering from an altered state of consciousness, and had a systolic blood pressure of fifty. (Translation: This lady was barely alive!) An NPS paramedic interviewed the river guide to obtain detailed information. The ability to communicate via satellite telephone was critical in a decision to initiate a night, inner-canyon rescue operation. (Flying a helicopter into the depths of the Grand Canyon is risky business under the best of conditions, no matter what the operators of air tours over the canyon would have you believe. Unpredictable air currents can quickly throw the aircraft off course, and flying within the rocky walls of the narrow inner canyon in the dark is an extremely dangerous trip.)"

  "Due to the monsoonal rainstorms, the park sought assistance from the 66th Air Rescue Squadron at Nellis Air Force Base, but they were unable to respond due to lack of personnel. (Military rescue flight crews and some law enforcement aircraft have specialized equipment that at least helps when flying in the dark, but this still requires long hours of training). The state DPS air rescue unit again responded, this time from Flagstaff. The crew employed night-vision goggles during the operation. The woman was treated and taken to the Flagstaff Medical Center, where she underwent surgery for a fibroid tumor."

  "The park's SAR coordinator attributes the successful completion of these complex and urgent missions to the preparedness and efficient response of NPS and volunteer rescue personnel, as well as outstanding support from the state Department of Public Safety."

Just "another day at the office" for the guys and gals at places like the Grand Canyon. If you'd like to read more about these real heroes, find a copy of the July 2000 edition of *Reader's Digest* at your local library and enjoy the story entitled "Search & Rescue at Grand Canyon."

The weather often plays a big factor in outdoor misadventures. By mid-March each year many people are ready to head back to the out-of-doors, and in some parts of the country it can feel like spring has arrived. March of 1993 provides a good example of the need to pay attention to weather forecasts before starting a trip, as well as being prepared in case the weather takes an unexpected turn for the worst.

In this case, weather had been the big news for days as forecasters warned that a huge storm was taking aim at the eastern United States. They were right! The media and even the National Weather Service later dubbed the Blizzard of 1993 the "Storm of the Century." Before it was all over, every major airport on the East Coast was closed at one time or another, almost every interstate highway north of Atlanta was closed, and travel came to a virtual standstill in parts of twenty-six states.

As predicted, snow started falling in places like Asheville, North Carolina on Friday, March 12. So, how did visitors to parks in the area respond to all the highly publicized warnings of an impending major weather event? On the day before the storm hit, a group of two adults and six eighth-graders from a school in Connecticut headed out on an overnight hike in Virginia's Shenandoah National Park.

In the Great Smoky Mountains National Park, ten groups of seven students and a counselor (a total of eighty people) from a school in Cranbrook, Michigan, set out on their annual trip in the park for an Outward Bound-type experience, in which students hike with counselors through the park for several days. I can only presume that they were bound and determined to make their annual trek, weather forecast notwithstanding. Further to the west, at the Big South Fork National River and Recreation Area along the Tennessee–Kentucky border, a troop of twenty-four Boy Scouts from Nashville and a group of four high school boys were camped in the park's backcountry.

The storm lived up to and then exceeded its billing, with snow drifts at Shenandoah up to twenty feet deep. Mt. Mitchell, North Carolina, had drifts of fourteen feet, and a weather station at Flattop Mountain in that same state recorded a wind gust of 101 miles per hour. Travel became virtually impossible—even snowplows were unable to force their way through the deep drifts.

Across the United States at least 270 people died as a result of the storm—but miraculously, everyone was eventually rescued from the parks. Their survival in most cases was the result of adequate equipment and supplies and extraordinary efforts by rescuers from the parks and the military, which provided critical helicopter support. In some cases, hikers had to be hoisted out of the woods by helicopter; in others, military medics were lowered into the backcountry to treat people suffering from hypothermia. Even though everyone survived, many were suffering from hypothermia and frostbite by the time they were brought to safety.

Some were especially fortunate, because they were *not* well prepared. Part of the group at the Big South Fork National River had ventured into the backcountry wearing tennis-style shoes and windbreakers; one had lost his shoes and was wearing only his socks when the group was found by rangers, who had to battle their way through drifts over eight feet deep to reach them. Hopefully those near-misses illustrate an important point—take the weather forecast seriously, be properly equipped, and plan for the possibility that conditions will be even worse than expected.

I'll close this chapter with an entry from the October 29, 1998, *Morning Report* that was again entitled simply, "Rescue," but one which makes me a firm believer in divine intervention. This guy was simply too "lucky" to be lucky!

Tom, a resident of Logan, Utah, drove to Grand Teton National Park on the night of October 10 to go climbing. He planned to solo climb (mistake number one) on the eleventh and return home that evening. He left no information about which peak he intended to climb, which route he intended to take, or where he planned to leave his vehicle (BIG mistake number two, because the Tetons cover a lot of real estate).

On the afternoon of October 12, a day after he was due to return home, Tom's wife telephoned the park and reported that her husband was overdue. Rangers located Tom's vehicle at the String Lake trailhead just before 5 p.m. That at least narrowed the most likely search area down to the central portion of the Teton Range—still a lot of territory. (We'll call this "Good Fortune Number One.")

Shortly thereafter, two rangers began an aerial search in the park's contract helicopter, flying primary trails and travel routes often used in that area by climbers. Most parks don't have the funds for their own helicopter and pilot. Instead, if one is available at all, it's on a contract basis from a private company and usually available only part of the year. The rangers in this helicopter were looking for obvious attempts to attract their attention, such as smoke or a flash from a signal mirror. Only ten minutes into their flight, they spotted a white t-shirt hanging in a tree near the base of Summetry couloir. (For you non-mountaineers a couloir is a "mountainside gorge, esp. in the Swiss Alps." Lots of climbing techniques and terms originated in Europe.) This would prove to be critical to the outcome, because it focused the aerial search in this general area. (I've dubbed this "Exceptionally Good Fortune Number Two" because it turned out later that the shirt had absolutely nothing to do with the missing climber!)

Less than two minutes after spotting the t-shirt, the rangers saw a solo climber in the upper reaches of a couloir. ("Amazing Fortune Number Three," considering the size of the search area.) I also attribute this quick work primarily to great knowledge of their area by the rangers, along with exceptional eyesight! The individual appeared to match the description of the missing climber, and more significantly, he appeared to be injured and unable to move.

Keep in mind that Tom's car wasn't found until about 5 p.m. and this situation occurred in October. Daylight was waning rapidly as the helicopter returned to its base and was configured for what is called a short-haul rescue. In simple terms, one ranger would act as a spotter while a second was flown to the scene, hanging beneath the helicopter at the end of a long line or rope. This is not nearly as easy as it looks on TV, and requires skill, stamina, and very steady nerves on the part of both the rangers and the pilot! Winds along the faces of mountains are often very unpredictable, and a sudden gust or change in wind direction could spell disaster for everybody involved.

Shorthauls are often used in situations such as this, where the victim is located on the face of a steep (or vertical) slope and there is simply no place to land a helicopter. A friend of mine was formerly a Navy helicopter pilot who flew rescue missions in Yosemite National Park. He once described to me several such flights, where the only way to get the rescuer to the victim was to swing him like a pendulum on the end of the rope until the arc got him to a point where the rescuer could make contact with the face of the mountain and then secure himself to the rock while he tended the victim. While this was going on, the rotor blades of the helicopter were *much* too close to the mountain itself. The true heroes in this world aren't the ones you see in Hollywood!

Back at Grand Teton, the climber spotted on the mountain was, in fact, Tom, who was stabilized and then evacuated via a short-haul extraction, which means that both Tom and a ranger took a ride on the end of that 150-foot rope. This was necessary because it was impossible to land the helicopter at Tom's location and bring him onboard. The pilot then flew to a nearby safe landing zone and gently lowered the ranger and victim to waiting hands on solid ground.

Tom was safely plucked from the mountain less than three hours after the initial report was received. (This is "Amazing Good Fortune Number Four" when you consider that the search was begun with only the knowledge that the climber was probably "somewhere" in tens of thousands of acres of some of the most rugged mountains in the lower 48 states.) Rangers estimated that a conventional ground rescue and evacuation to the nearest landing zone would have required, at a minimum, a team of twelve to fifteen people, and would have extended well into the following day. At the time of the report, Tom was hospitalized with a fractured collarbone, fractured arm, multiple fractures of the pelvis, and multiple scrapes and bruises. He had fallen an undetermined distance on the previous day. The fact that he survived at all seems to be nothing short of amazing.

My one hesitation in relating these amazing stories is that some people hear such accounts, and expect instant rescue from any place on the planet. Any number of factors could have resulted in a much different outcome: the availability of the helicopter, along with a pilot and rangers who had the "right stuff"; good weather; adequate daylight. If any of those circumstances had been different, a rescue like Tom's could have taken days, not hours. I hope you'll read on to the final chapter, on ways to avoid being a victim in the first place, and take the tips contained therein to heart.

Don't Be a Victim of Your Vacation

"Let's go to the park!" This year, millions of people will do just that. Whether it's a two-week vacation, a holiday weekend, or just a brief afternoon jaunt, we do love our parks, and for good reason—our experiences there can enrich our lives in many ways.

Unfortunately, not all of those trips will have a happy ending. Before you plan your next outing, take a few moments to consider the following, common-sense tips to help ensure that your next outdoor adventure will be fun, safe, and successful. The rangers and other staff in your parks are great folks, but you don't want to meet them in their capacity as paramedics or rescuers. Furthermore, although most people enjoy seeing themselves on TV, that's not usually the case if they find themselves portrayed on the news as the hapless victims of a needless accident.

Why do some trips end in disaster instead of delightful memories? Park rangers and other emergency personnel can point to several common factors. Avoid these pitfalls, consider the following common-sense tips, and your chances of being a victim of your vacation will be greatly reduced.

1. Start smart! Get current information from on-site staff about the terrain and other local conditions. Are there unexpected hazards in the area? Is the river you plan to canoe unusually high and dangerous due to recent rains? Is the hike you plan to take not really suitable for a family with small children? Check at a visitor center or ranger station for expert advice—local staff can suggest an activity tailored to your interests and abilities.

These rangers at Grand Canyon unfortunately will have plenty of chances to put their rescue training to use. Just be sure you aren't their next customer! (Grand Canyon National Park)

Clay Jordan, Deputy Chief Ranger at Virginia's Shenandoah National Park notes, "All too often hikers find themselves in trouble because they have underestimated the conditions in the backcountry and are unprepared for what they actually turn out to be. The conditions may be hotter, colder, steeper, longer, or slicker than expected. Hiking in the park is a wonderful experience, but it is not just a 'walk in the park.'"

Be sure you get information from park staff or other reliable sources, rather than relying on friends or other visitors in the area. Their well-intentioned advice may not always be accurate or up-to-date.

At 8 p.m. on a July evening a couple from Huntington, West Virginia, began a rafting trip at the New River Gorge National River. They borrowed a raft from a friend who told them that their planned trip would take only an hour or so and would be easy because the river was flowing at a low rate. Both of these considerations were important, because the woman was seven months pregnant!

Unfortunately, their friend was wrong on both counts. The distance for this trip is actually about ten miles, and the low river flow meant

"Hey, I thought this was supposed to be an easy trip!" Be sure you get good information before you start on any activity in the Great Outdoors. (Bureau of Land Management/ Photo by Louise Austermuchle)

that the trip would take more than five hours and would be extremely hazardous. I'd rate those as important factors, especially if you are inexperienced and start a river trip just before dark! When the couple failed to return by 10 a.m. the following morning, friends notified the park. Rangers began an immediate search and the pair was found about two miles downstream from their starting point. They had spent a restless night on the river bank under their raft. Although frightened and hungry, they were otherwise uninjured—and incredibly fortunate.

Investigation revealed that they had not been wearing their life jackets and that they'd initially intended to take their seven-year-old son on the trip. According to the woman, they had decided to get off the river when they had almost flipped the raft in a major rapid. At least they made one good decision by ending their trip at that point and waiting for help.

2. Take stock! Make a realistic assessment of your skills and equipment. Are you really ready to canoe those rapids or climb that peak? Is every member of your group up to the trip or are they simply going along with the crowd? Beware of peer pressure and the "macho factor," which isn't limited to teenagers and males under the age of thirty! Do you have the specialized equipment for an activity such as caving or climbing—and do you really know how to use it? Don't rely on information gained from simply reading a book or watching a video or from a quick lesson from the guy in the next campsite. (Maybe he's only seen the video, too.)

If you're new to the activity or aren't experienced in the out-of-doors, get adequate training and information before starting out. Many tragedies and near misses occur because visitors simply fail to use basic, common-sense equipment, such as life jackets while boating and helmets while biking or climbing.

Patty Shafer is a ranger at Colorado's Rocky Mountain National Park, which has more than 200 search-and-rescue incidents a year. She notes that while some of these are purely accidents or medical emergencies, others occur when visitors are ill-prepared for the high altitude environment or overextend themselves in the backcountry. She stresses the importance of being prepared both physically and mentally for a trip into the backcountry, taking the proper equipment—and knowing how to use it—and being self-reliant.

On August 14, 1998, Michael, age thirty-four, his five-year-old son Matt, and another couple were canoeing on the Jack's Fork River in the Ozark National Scenic Riverways in Missouri. Their canoe capsized and all four suddenly found themselves in the river. Michael, who was not wearing a life jacket, grabbed his son, who fortunately was wearing a life jacket, and pushed the child toward shallow water. Michael then disappeared under the water for two or three minutes and resurfaced, unconscious, about 150 feet downstream. He was pulled to shore and CPR was begun. Michael was flown to a hospital in Springfield, Missouri, where he was later reported to be in stable condition. Many similar situations occur in parks every year, and the outcome is often not as successful. A life jacket can help save your life only if you are wearing it!

On April 13, 2002, rangers at Yosemite National Park in California responded to reports of cries for help coming from the vicinity of a climbing area known as Five Open Books. They found that climbers in two different groups had sustained injuries when the lead climber of the upper team dislodged a rock the size of his head. The falling rock struck a glancing blow to the helmet and shoulder of a climber below him, then glanced off the helmet of the leader of the second group before striking and breaking that climber's forearm. The incident commander on the rescue noted that two lives were saved because the climbers were wearing proper helmets. Know what equipment you need for your planned activity—and use it!

The proper equipment isn't limited to an expedition into the wilderness. At Fire Island National Seashore near New York City, the first-aid station often receives requests to remove splinters from visitors who were walking on boardwalks in bare feet. Just keep in mind that flip-flops are not suitable footgear for a hike on anything but perhaps a paved sidewalk—or that boardwalk near the beach.

3. Be weather-wise! Check the local weather forecast for the area of your activity and be prepared for both predicted conditions and unexpected changes. Remember that conditions can vary dramatically between the valley floor and higher elevations. Many outdoor calamities occur simply because people are not prepared for unfamiliar conditions or for a sudden weather change. Extremes of heat, cold, or precipitation can dramatically affect your ability to enjoy or even survive an activity. Hypothermia (depressed body temperature) is a major killer in the outdoors. It can occur quickly if you get wet and cold, even at temperatures as high as fifty degrees. One source states that a surprising number of hypothermia cases occur in Florida!

Heat can be just as dangerous as the cold. On May 25, 2001, a group of forty college students and professors from Pennsylvania went on a hike in a rugged backcountry section of Arches National Park in Utah. Summer comes early to the Utah desert, and weather there in May is certainly different than it is in Pennsylvania. A check of the forecast might, therefore, lead a prudent person to be prepared for the heat by taking plenty of water and considering whether an activity is simply too risky in very hot weather.

Following a climb out of the steep, 800-foot-deep Colorado River canyon, several members of this group began exhibiting symptoms of heat exhaustion. The trip leader decided that the group could not descend back into the canyon because the route was too steep and exposed, so he led them cross-county to another canyon where descent was easier.

Not surprisingly, more members of the group became ill from heat and lack of fluids, and even worse, two became lost. By then it was mid-day and the temperature was still rising. Proving that "better late than never" still holds true, the leader finally made a 911 cell phone call and reported the group's situation. A multi-agency search-and-rescue mission was launched that eventually involved thirty-seven people from Arches and Canyonlands National Parks, St. Mary's Hospital Air Care, and several Grand County agencies.

Although a number of the students were suffering from various degrees of heat exhaustion, after receiving treatment they were able to walk out under their own power. Three, however, required rescue from the canyon, including one in serious condition who had to be flown out by helicopter. All three were hospitalized, but were released later that evening. Searchers found the two missing people just as the last heat victim was evacuated from the canyon. The high temperature for the day was 99°—measured in the shade. Everything considered, this group was very fortunate. Check the weather, be prepared, and most important, consider whether your planned activity is prudent in view of the conditions.

4. Watch your watch! Do you have enough time and energy to enjoy the activity and complete it safely? Many incident reports begin with the words, "The victims were caught by darkness and unable to make it safely back to their starting point." Allow more than half your available time for the return trip, especially if the second half is uphill. Rangers at Grand Canyon have a good rule of thumb for hikers in that park: Determine how long you have to complete your trip, and when you've used one-third of that time, turn around and head back.

When I worked at the Grand Canyon, fellow rangers sometimes warned hikers heading into the canyon on one trail that it's "seven miles down but seventy-seven back!" If you live in the "lowlands" and are visiting an area above 5,000 feet in elevation, allow several days for your body to adjust to the altitude before you tackle a strenuous activity. Otherwise, you'll probably be wondering who stole the oxygen from all that nice, clean mountain air!

In February 2001, two visitors to Haleakala National Park in Hawaii decided to take a four-mile hike to a waterfall before catching their flight home. Unfortunately, they seriously underestimated the time required for their walk and found themselves still on the trail without a flashlight when darkness fell. They did use some ingenuity—the man tried to use the flash on their camera to illuminate the trail, but when the flash would no longer work, they were afraid they would walk off one of the cliffs in the area in the dark and had the wisdom to stop.

By then it was about 8 p.m. and since they were a two-and-a-half hour drive from the airport and had a 9 p.m. departure, it was pretty obvious they were going to miss their flight! Their one piece of good news: They had a cell phone, were able to make a call to 911 for help, and were found unharmed by rangers. They were lucky they were in an area where the cell phone worked—in many parks that's not the case.

5. "Don't leave home without it!" Carry emergency essentials. Be prepared for the unexpected! The amount of equipment you take will vary widely based on the activity, season and location, but a small day pack can carry the items needed to avert disaster and should be taken even on a short hike. A sudden weather change, an injury, or taking the wrong fork of the trail can suddenly turn a brief stroll into an unexpected overnight campout. There are many suggested lists of ten essentials to carry even on a short day trip—you can find an example on the Internet at www.nps.gov/romo/visit/park/hike/essentials.html.

As a minimum, a pair of large plastic trash bags for each person in your group can become a rain suit or shelter; matches in a waterproof container can provide an emergency warming fire; a small flashlight can light the trail if daylight runs out sooner than you expect. High-energy snacks are useful even for a short hike. Unless you're in the tropics or the desert in the summer, consider some extra layers of clothing and a warm cap. Extra water or non-alcoholic beverages are especially important in hot weather. Most important, know what to do in an emergency.

Oh, one last word about those waterproof matches—if you decide to start a fire to stay warm or attract the attention of rescuers, be sure you clear the surrounding area of flammable materials before you start a fire. In June 2002, the mountains of northern Arizona were ravaged by a series of huge wildfires and a number of homes were destroyed. Sadly, one of those fires started when a signal fire by a lost hiker got out of control. Don't make a bad situation worse!

A man from Knoxville, Tennessee, was training for a marathon and decided to go for a twelve-mile trail run in the Great Smoky Mountains National Park. The afternoon of February 19, 2004, was unseasonably warm, with a high of about 60°, so he left home wearing only a t-shirt, shorts, and running shoes. He drove to the Tremont area of the park, parked his car, and started running on what he planned to be a loop route that would bring him back to his vehicle. Unfortunately, he started on the wrong trail and immediately got diverted onto an unmarked route, then ended up off-trail, where he was caught by darkness.

Even though he was certainly not equipped for temperatures that would drop to 25° overnight, he had made one excellent decision before leaving home—he had left a note for his wife telling her he was going for a run in the park and would return about 6 p.m. His wife notified rangers about 9 p.m. that he was overdue and a search was begun immediately. Despite an all-night search, he was not found until the next morning. During the night he had bushwhacked down a drainage and eventually reached a road. He had numerous cuts and scrapes and possible broken ribs but was otherwise in good condition. The lesson learned? What you expect to be a short trip on a nice, warm afternoon can easily become a very unpleasant overnight ordeal. Be prepared for the unexpected!

6. Be a groupie—keep your group together! An amazing number of searches result when members of a group lag behind or forge ahead, and then get separated. If you start out as a group, you should stay together and end as a group. Let the slowest person in the group set the pace and determine when it's time for a break; have more experienced members at both the front and the rear of the group. The Three Musketeers had the right idea with their motto, "All for one and one for all."

Many search-and-rescue missions can be traced to the following words: "You guys go on ahead. I'll just rest here for a few minutes and catch up with you at the top." On January 17, 1998, an 11-year-old boy was on a day hike with his parents and uncle on the Appalachian Trail in the Great Smoky Mountains National Park. The boy lagged behind the adults in the group and then panicked when he could no longer see or hear them. Instead of stopping and waiting for them to come back and find him, the boy began to run, to try to catch up. Unfortunately, he became disoriented and ran in the wrong direction. He continued running until he met two backpackers, almost ten miles from his starting point!

Fortunately, the backpackers convinced the boy to stay at their camp, where they fed him and provided warm clothing to keep him from freezing in single-digit temperatures and high winds. Searchers found the boy at the camp at 4 a.m. the next morning in good condition, except for blistered feet. Had he not been found earlier by the hikers, who were well equipped for the cold weather, this incident could have had a tragic ending.

A group of three adults and eight children were on an overnight camping trip in late May at Isle Royale National Park in Michigan. After a day of fishing in the backcountry, they began preparing for the three-mile hike back to their camp. Without the knowledge of the adults, four of the younger boys struck off for camp alone at about 6:30 p.m. But wait, it gets worse! One of the boys, 10-year-old John, stopped to tie his shoe while the other three boys continued ahead. John then strayed from the trail and became lost in the thick forest.

Rangers were notified at about 11 p.m. and five search teams were deployed during the night, covering over twenty-five miles of trail. At about 9:30 the next morning, the boy walked into camp, scared but uninjured. He had spent over three hours wandering around in the woods before he stumbled onto the trail. In addition to staying with his group, the youngster needed to follow rule number seven.

7. Shun shortcuts! Stay on the trail. Shortcutting switchbacks on trails or deciding you know a quicker way and heading cross-country can not only damage the natural scene, it often results in people being hurt or lost.

On an October afternoon, two crew members from a ship went jogging for exercise on a trail in the Bartlett Cove area of Alaska's Glacier Bay National Park. Dave and Ann decided to leave the main trail and follow a game trail, but they eventually lost their route and tried to head cross-country back to the shoreline. They became disoriented and headed in the opposite direction and eventually admitted that they were lost. Their situation then included both good news and bad news.

The good news: Dave was carrying a two-way radio and made contact with their ship, reporting they were lost and giving a general description of their surroundings just before the radio's battery went dead. They had limited supplies, including coffee, water, and an energy bar. The bad news was that they were only marginally dressed for the cold, rainy weather, and temperatures were dropping to near freezing. Searchers found them at 4 a.m. the next morning where they had been smart enough to take shelter under a tree and cover themselves with

"Stay on the trail" is always good advice, but it's essential in places like the South Kaibab Trail at the Grand Canyon. (Grand Canyon National Park)

moss and branches to help conserve their body heat. They were cold, wet, tired and had blistered feet, but were otherwise okay. One moral to this story is: Stay on the trail!

Staying on the trail can take on a different meaning in the wintertime. In late November, three teenage snowboarders were spending the day at Crater Lake National Park in Oregon. They decided to take a "shortcut" back to their car from Rim Village, but went down the wrong side of the ridge, ending up in the park's backcountry. They were poorly dressed for weather conditions, which included seventeen inches of snow on the ground, with more snow falling and temperatures around freezing, and they had no survival gear of any kind. They found themselves wading through knee-deep snow for about five miles before they stumbled across markings for a ski trail. One of the boys decided to try to follow the ski trail and get help. Shortly after midnight, he made it to a telephone and called for help.

Searchers were able to follow his tracks and located the remaining two boys at about 1:30 a.m. They were cold, wet, exhausted, and in the early stages of hypothermia. Given their lack of proper clothing and equipment and the weather conditions, it is unlikely they would have survived much longer if they hadn't been found promptly. A shortcut is not always the fastest way home!

8. Avoid the technology trap! Don't let modern gadgets or gear get you in over your head. If your SUV, mountain bike, snowmobile, or outboard motor suddenly breaks down miles from your starting point, can you make it back to civilization safely? If not, do you have enough essential gear with you to survive until you are rescued?

Don't fall prey to the "911 illusion." Limited park staffs do an amazing job, but visitors often tend to count on the same instant response they get at home. Helicopters may not be available or able to fly due to bad weather and it may take hours or even days for rescuers to reach you. By all means carry your cell phone. It may enable you to summon help quickly—but it may not work everywhere. Ranger Shafer from Rocky Mountain National Park cautions, "Don't count on a cell phone to work in the mountains!" If it doesn't, what's your backup plan in case of trouble?

At the Big Thicket National Preserve in southeast Texas, a local resident decided to take his small boat and go fishing on a nice summer afternoon. As was often his practice, he fished until the last possible minute, leaving just enough daylight to make it back to the launch ramp before dark. This time, however, there was only one problem—the outboard motor on his boat refused to start. He couldn't paddle against the current back to his starting point and drifting downstream in the dark would take him even further from civilization. With no flashlight, food or water, he made a good decision—just wait for help, since he knew his wife would eventually report him overdue. There was only one other problem—as darkness fell, a veritable army of mosquitoes arrived for a tasty snack at his expense.

The fisherman's wife did in fact report her missing husband and by 2 a.m. he had been located. We would have missed him in the dark, however, if he hadn't wisely stayed on board his boat, because the only part of his body that was visible was literally the whites of his eyes. In a desperate defense against the attacking insects, he had covered every square inch of his body in thick mud, scooped up from the riverbank! Even so, the mosquitoes apparently got the equivalent of a donation to the blood bank before he finished applying his all-natural armor. All in all he was lucky, and others who have been stranded in remote locations after a mechanical breakdown have not fared nearly as well.

9. Know when to say "when"! Don't let a "once in a lifetime opportunity" be the end of your life. Know when to turn back or ask for help. Too many tragedies occur because people planned a trip for months or years, so they pushed ahead despite bad weather, fatigue, or other dangerous conditions. Take a cue from NASA—if all systems are not "go," then don't go.

Ranger Dan Burgette is the search-and-rescue officer for Wyoming's Grand Teton National Park and has more than 25 years' experience in that park. He notes, "Leaders need to accept leadership responsibilities. We see a common problem of the de facto leader (the person who signs out the group, gets permits, and sets goals for the trip) not taking responsibility for decisions to turn back in the face of bad weather, abandoning inexperienced people in precarious situations as they try to go for help, being unrealistic in assessing the abilities of the weakest member of the group, not assuring that everyone is dressed appropriately, or not making good decisions when someone is injured. Leadership can make a huge difference."

Ranger Burgette also notes that "sometimes folks just get stranded. If that happens, they need to be realistic and admit that it is too dangerous to keep pushing their limits until something bad happens. What I try to emphasize is knowing when to call for help. Sometimes people are faced with a problem they can't solve. Call for help!"

The value of this advice is confirmed by the experience of Jeffrey, age 18, and Laura, age 17, who were hiking off-trail on February 2, 1999, at Colorado National Monument. After scrambling up a very steep slope, they reached a sandstone outcrop near the canyon's upper rim from which they could neither go further nor return. Apparently unwilling to admit defeat, Jeffrey jumped twenty-five feet to a rock below—and fractured both ankles. Laura may have been younger but she was certainly wiser. She declined to follow his example, stayed put, and began calling for help.

Another hiker heard her cries and summoned assistance. Jeffrey was taken to a hospital for surgery; his smarter companion was assisted safely down by rescuers and able to hike out under her own power.

Don't take unnecessary chances, know your limits, and know when to call for help. One of twenty-three Ohio hikers who became stranded on a mountain in Alaska is helped to a U.S. Coast Guard helicopter. (U.S. Coast Guard/Photo by Petty Officer Christopher S. Grisafe)

On an early spring weekend, a church youth group from Louisiana made a spring break trip to the Buffalo River in the Arkansas Ozarks. Most had never been in a canoe, and they had anticipated the trip for many months. After camping overnight, they planned to make an eleven-mile canoe trip, even though the river was high due to recent rains. To make matters worse, the forecast called for a cold front, with thunderstorms and falling temperatures. Despite advice from the rangers and signs warning that the "river is high and dangerous—experienced canoeists only," the group decided to go ahead with their float trip. Their reasoning was that "we may never have another chance." They were almost right, but for the wrong reasons!

Fortunately, rangers learned from the canoe rental company that the group was on the river and decided to begin a search before they got word of trouble. When the group was located, all of them were soaked, exhausted, and in early stages of hypothermia from repeated capsizing into the cold water. Everyone survived, but it was an unnecessarily close call. This story had a happy ending only because a couple of rangers weren't too swamped with other incidents and were able to be proactive in averting a tragedy.

In a similar situation, Steve, 39, and Richard, 45, decided to canoe the St. Croix River (Minnesota and Wisconsin). You would think they were old enough to know better, because in early April the river was at flood stage and about six feet above the recommended level for canoeing. The water temperature was about 40°, the air temperature in the mid-30s and dropping, and heavy snow was falling periodically. Sounds like a great time for a canoe trip, doesn't it? It apparently did to Steve and Richard, who launched their canoe and headed downstream. Given the conditions, you might expect that they would at least take some basic precautions.

Their boat soon took on water and sank in three-to-five-foot-high waves. Steve was at least wearing a life jacket and was able to swim to a nearby island, where he was able to use a cigarette lighter and build a warming fire. Richard, the older but clearly not the wiser, was incredibly not wearing a life jacket, despite the very hazardous conditions on the river. His only smart move of the day was to at least hang on to the swamped canoe, which carried him about a dozen miles downstream before he was rescued. Fortunately, he had been observed by a local resident, who saw him being swept downstream and called for help. Both men were taken to a hospital, where they were treated and released.

Many similar incidents don't have a happy ending. "Know when to say when" and be willing to call off an activity when conditions aren't right for your trip. Each year rangers at the Grand Canyon respond to an average of 400 medical emergencies, and more than 250 people have to be rescued from the canyon. The majority of these victims aren't middle-aged couch potatoes who forgot they weren't in shape; they are young, healthy males between the ages of 18 and 40. Their common mistake: Attempting to hike to the bottom of the canyon and back in one day. For some excellent tips on hiking safety, especially in hot weather, see the website for Grand Canyon National Park at www.nps.gov/grca/grandcanyon/dayhike/smart.htm.

10. Don't "go for the gusto"! Beware of alcohol and drugs. While this is good advice in any situation, using either one during an outdoor activity can tip the scales against you by clouding judgment and coordination. Unfortunately, this is a key—and very avoidable—factor in a significant number of injuries and deaths in parks every year.

At 3 a.m. on an October morning, rangers were called out of their park residences at the Golden Gate National Recreation Area in California to respond to a report that several people had fallen off a cliff. Later investigation would determine that a group of five people in their late teens or early twenties had gone to the Fort Funston area of the park that night and had evidently consumed both drugs and alcohol.

Someone in the group then came up with the idea that it would be "cool" to roll down a 200-foot-high sandstone cliff that ends at a beach. What they failed to realize in their less than sober condition was that the last fifty feet of the cliff is nearly vertical. As a result, the final part of their "roll" was more like a free-fall. All five were successfully rescued with the help of city paramedics, just before the incoming tide cut off vehicle access to the beach. Some of them suffered serious injuries, confirming that something that seems like a good idea when you're "under the influence" often looks a lot different when your brain is functioning properly!

11. "Here's your sign!" Don't take unnecessary chances—obey warning signs, guardrails, and special advisories; they are there for a reason. Every year, people are hurt or killed when they climb over fences, safety rails, or disregard "area closed" signs.

A 12-year-old and his family were visiting the Upper Geyser Basin in Yellowstone National Park. Signs throughout the area warn visitors to stay on the boardwalk and trail, both for their safety and to avoid disturbing the fragile thermal pools. As this group approached a pool that is surrounded by a fence, the youngster left the trail, went around the fence, and stuck his hand into the thermal pool!

Fortunately, this was a cooler part of the pool, and the boy wasn't burned. Not content with that escape, he then kicked a rock into the hotter section of the pool, and the hot water splashed onto his leg. He was treated for burns at the Old Faithful Clinic. Hopefully, he and his parents learned that their tax dollars were spent on that fence for a good reason. This boy was lucky, since other visitors in similar situations have suffered extensive, serious burns. Perhaps you had the same question I did when I first read this account: What were the parents doing all this time? A corollary to tip number eleven is: maintain control of your children, no matter what their ages may be.

Just before dawn on an early summer day, a visitor to the Grand Canyon fell forty feet while trying to retrieve his camera, which had fallen over the edge of the canyon. Rangers were able to rappel to his location, secure him to keep him from falling further, and provide advanced life support treatment. While he was very lucky that he hadn't fallen a lot further, the man ended up paying for a very expensive private air ambulance ride to a hospital, where he was admitted for treatment of his injuries. I hope if he recovered that roll of film he had some great shots, but I doubt that he'd think in hindsight that the camera was worth it!

At Hawaii Volcanoes National Park, a man was taking pictures from an overlook when his hat blew over the edge of a cliff. It must have been a very valuable hat, because he climbed over the safety railing to try to retrieve it, lost his footing, and disappeared from sight.

Miraculously, he landed in a tree after falling about 100 feet, stopping what would otherwise have been a disastrous 600-foot fall to the floor of the volcano. A technical rescue team was able to retrieve him and he was taken to a hospital for treatment of his injuries. He was very lucky—a number of people die each year under similar circumstances after ignoring warning signs, fences, and other safety measures.

In that same park, rangers post "closed area" signs in hazardous areas near active lava flows. A 19-year-old from New York and four companions entered a dangerous area where molten lava was cascading into the ocean. They later admitted that they had seen but disregarded warning signs. The young woman fell into a 75-foot deep crack and, fortunately, landed on a narrow ledge after falling about 30 feet. Rescuers were able to raise her to safety, and she was taken to a hospital for treatment.

Warning signs are not limited to the backcountry. At Fort Jefferson in the Dry Tortugas National Park in Florida, 32-year-old Mary decided to climb on top of one of the fort walls to take a picture. She must have forgotten about Humpty Dumpty, who came to an untimely end when he fell off a wall. Her sisters later stated that Mary had done so right next to a sign warning visitors to say back away from the edge! Concentrating on framing the photo in the camera viewfinder instead of her surroundings, Mary stepped backwards, walked right off the wall, and fell 42 feet into the waters of the moat that surrounds the fort. Fortunately, she landed in about four-and-a-half feet of water; if she'd fallen to either side, she would have landed on a rubble pile or in very shallow water. Even so, she had to be flown to the nearest hospital, 68 miles away, for treatment of her injuries. Thankfully, modern medicine is more efficient at correcting such problems than all the king's horses and all the king's men.

12. It's not a zoo! Don't feed or get too close to wild animals. "Dancing with wolves" may be a great idea in Hollywood, but not in the real world. Each year people are injured or killed because they ignore warnings to keep their distance from wildlife. How do you determine a safe distance? Yellowstone National Park has some good guidelines—in that park, it's against the law to approach within 100 yards of bears or within 25 yards of all other wildlife. Sometimes, even that's too close. George Minnigh is the backcountry management specialist at Great Smoky Mountains National Park and has seen plenty of wildlife in his twenty-seven years as a ranger. He notes, "If your presence causes a bear or other large animal to change its behavior (stops feeding or changes direction of travel), you're too close!"

Getting too close can definitely be dangerous and you don't have to be in the backcountry. On July 13, 2002, a bison was grazing near the Old Faithful Lodge in Yellowstone National Park. A group of visitors approached to within 15 feet to take pictures of the animal. One man then walked around in front of the bison to see if it would raise its head for a better picture. It did! Responding as bison normally do under such circumstances, it chased the man into the trees, picked him up with its horns, and threw him several feet into the air. He should consider himself fortunate that his injuries were limited to a puncture wound to his leg and many scrapes and bruises.

If you have access to the Internet and want some first-hand proof of the surprising speed and power of large animals, you can see some video footage of wildlife taking on people and vehicles on Yellowstone's website at www.nps.gov/yell/planvisit/todo/viewanim.htm.

13. "Solo" is a four-letter word! Be very reluctant to travel into isolated areas alone. Solo travel can put you at great and unnecessary risk if you should become injured or stranded.

On Monday, August 4, 2003, a 46-year-old woman took a solo hike into a remote and seldom-visited area of Sequoia and Kings Canyon National Park. While descending a steep, unmaintained trail, she slipped and fell about 50 feet, sustaining multiple lower leg fractures, a possible hip fracture, and other injuries. In the only bright spot in her ordeal, she was able to move a few feet to reach a source of water in a nearby creek.

She remained in that location, unable to travel any further, for the next four days. Finally, on August 8, she was discovered by another group of hikers, who left part of their group with the injured woman while others hiked out to get help. In a good reminder that you can't always call 911 and expect instant results in the backcountry, it was necessary for these Good Samaritans to hike several miles to try to call for help. They finally reached a residence in Crown Valley, but because that area is very remote and has no road access, the local resident had to ride on horseback to a nearby peak. From that point, he was finally able to call a friend on a cell phone and report the emergency.

The woman was successfully evacuated just before nightfall, thanks to exceptional work by a California Highway Patrol helicopter that was able to hoist the woman to safety, since there was no place to land a helicopter anywhere nearby. She was then flown to a hospital for treatment of her injuries, but it must have been a very long and lonely four days. Such are the risks of solo travel in the backcountry.

14. Be sensible about security! Use common sense and safeguard valuables (and yourself). Compared to most cities, parks are still relatively safe, but crime doesn't take a vacation and petty theft is one of the most common incidents in many parks. Don't leave items such as cameras, cell phones, purses, and wallets in unattended campsites or in plain view in a vehicle. Oh, guess what—stowing those items out of sight, under the seat of your vehicle, isn't much better. Both professional and amateur "car clouters" know that vehicles left at places like trailhead parking lots are often easy targets and guess where they'll look first when they break into a vehicle?

Lock all valuables in the trunk. If you have a van, SUV, or a recreational vehicle, either keep those items with you, or consider buying a stout, lockable container that can be secured to a fixed object inside such vehicles. Locate your lockbox either in a location which isn't readily visible from outside or at least disguise it with other objects. Most thieves are looking for the easy targets—so don't be one.

15. Don't just do something—stand (or sit) there! If you realize you are lost, stay put and wait for rescuers to find you. Be sure everyone in your group—especially children—knows this basic rule. Ranger

Minnigh stresses, "If you become confused about where you are, do not leave the trail and do not travel at night." More than one person has been seriously injured or killed by walking off a cliff in the dark. While you wait for help, just be sure your efforts to take shelter don't make you invisible to searchers.

Two adult visitors from New Jersey managed to become lost while hiking in the popular Cliff Palace area of Mesa Verde National Park on a January afternoon. Rangers noticed their rental car parked in an area that is closed at dusk and began a search, which expanded to a major effort the following day. Compounding their problem, the two kept moving and had covered about nine miles of rugged canyon terrain before they were found safely three days later! Simply staying put would have saved everyone a lot of time and effort.

In May 2002, a couple in their late twenties planned a three-day backpacking trip in the southern part of Yosemite National Park. Their trip went awry when they lost the trail in snowy conditions. They initially tried to follow a drainage but decided to stop and wait for rescue when they realized that they were lost. Rangers were notified late Monday night by concerned friends and family when the pair did not return to work earlier that day. A search that involved as many as forty people was begun on Tuesday. Helicopter searchers followed the pair's tracks in the snow, which ultimately led them to the lost hikers. Both were hungry and dehydrated, but otherwise in good condition. "This incident had a positive outcome because they had the right gear and clothing, but mainly because they stopped and stayed in one spot once they knew they were lost," said ranger Lulis Cuevas, who served as the incident commander. "Terrain in this area is extremely rugged and the hikers could have easily hurt themselves while looking for the trail," he added.

Perhaps the only possible exception to staying put and waiting for help might be if you are in a very isolated area and are absolutely certain no one knew about your plans and nobody will realize you are missing or where to look. That puts you in a very risky situation and can be easily avoided with this final suggestion in our "Sweet Sixteen" Tips.

16. A little bird won't tell them! Be sure someone knows your plans, and when you expect to be back, so authorities will know where to start looking if you fail to return on time. Be as specific as possible about your destination. This is especially critical for remote or lengthy trips. The fact that you plan to go hiking "somewhere in Yellowstone" is a little better than no information at all—but not much!

On a February morning, 19-year-old Jesse failed to report for work in the park concession at Big Bend National Park. He had told friends the previous day that he was going on a hike. Big Bend covers a huge expanse of rugged mountains, canyons, and desert in West Texas, so a search can quickly become a lengthy and complex operation. Fortunately, Jesse had told his roommate about his planned route and destination. A search was begun at first light, and by 8:30 a.m., ranger and pilot Jim Unruh had spotted the missing man a short distance from the summit of Panther Peak. Jesse had fractured his ankle while hiking back down from the peak. He had crawled to a high spot, where he would be readily visible, and waited for rescuers to find him. Except for the ankle injury, he was in good condition. A quick and efficient rescue was made possible because he made sure someone else knew about his plans and then sounded the alarm promptly when he failed to return.

In the June 4, 2001, edition of *U.S. News and World Report*, Acting National Park Service Director Deny Galvin provided a good piece of advice for anyone planning to visit a park: "Have a good time, don't fall down, and learn something." So, make a trip to a park sometime soon, bring home some wonderful memories, and don't be a victim of your vacation. While you're there, I hope you'll have a chance to say, "Hey, ranger—I'm having a great time!"

Appendix: Sources of Additional Information

Books and Videos

Albright, Horace, and Frank Taylor. *Oh, Ranger*. This classic was published in 1928, with second and third editions in 1929 and 1934 by Dodd, Mead and Co. Long out of print, this is an entertaining and instructive look at life in the early days of the NPS. Try a used book dealer, a library, or online sources such as E-Bay for a copy.

Butcher, Devereux. Revised and edited by Russell Butcher. *Exploring Our National Parks and Monuments*. Roberts Rinehart, 2000, 478 pages. An excellent guidebook that describes in detail all U.S. national parks and natural and archaeological monuments, this work is a great reference source with information about NPS sites.

Butcher, Russell. *Exploring Our National Historic Parks and Sites*. Roberts Rinehart, 2000, 496 pages. The sequel to *Exploring Our National Parks and Monuments*, this is "the essential guide to the land and history of the U.S. national historical parks and sites."

Everts, Truman, and Lee H. Whittlesey. *Lost in the Yellowstone: Truman Everts's "Thirty-Seven Days of Peril."* University of Utah Press, 1995, 62 pages. Editor Lee Whittlesey takes Truman Everts's account of being lost in Yellowstone in 1870 and his 37-day struggle for survival and adds additional information to provide a historical background for the original book. The work is illustrated with historical photographs of Yellowstone that provide a visual account of early-day Yellowstone National Park.

Farabee, Charles "Butch." *Death, Daring, and Disaster: Search and Rescue in the National Parks*. Roberts Rinehart, 1999, 516 pages. A recently retired ranger who was a leader in the field of search and rescue, the author describes 375 exciting tales of heroism and tragedy drawn from the nearly 150,000 search-and-rescue missions carried out by the National Park Service since 1872.

Farabee, Charles R. "Butch." *National Park Ranger: An American Icon*. Roberts Rinehart, 2003, 180 pages. Farabee traces the history of park rangers from the early days of Yellowstone National Park, when the army performed that role, through the establishment of the present-day National Park Service in 1916, and on to the modern era. The book describes some of the duties of early rangers, includes some interesting anecdotes from more contemporary times, and includes plenty of historic photos to illustrate the romance of this unique profession.

Ghiglieri, Michael P., and Thomas M. Myers. *Over the Edge: Death in Grand Canyon*. Puma Press, 2001, 408 pages. A review from *Library Journal* says, "[A]uthors Ghiglieri and Myers . . . have compiled a fascinating chronicle of deaths and dangers in Grand Canyon National Park. The book is arranged by category: falls, dehydration, floods, the Colorado River, air crashes, freak accidents, suicides, and murder. At the end of each chapter is a chronological list with names, descriptions, and causes of the accidents."

"Lost . . . but Found, Safe and Sound." This is a twelve-minute, professionally produced video that is designed to show children, ages four to twelve, what to do if they become lost in remote areas such as parks or forests. It is also available on CD-ROM as a PowerPoint program. For information, contact the Assn. of National Park Rangers, P.O. Box 108, Larned, KS 67550-0108, (620) 285-2107, or e-mail them at anpr@larned.net.

Whittlesey, Lee H. *Death in Yellowstone: Accidents and Foolhardiness in the First National Park*. Roberts Rinehart, 1998, 240 pages. A review from *Booklist* says, "Whittlesey believes that far too many people enter our national parks with 'a false sense of security.' . . . He then goes on to chronicle the deaths in Yellowstone National Park of more than 250 people." In addition to a good history of incidents in Yellowstone, this book provides some excellent tips to help readers avoid encountering a similar fate anywhere in the out-of-doors.

Organizations and Government Agencies

The National Park Service (NPS) has a website (www.nps.gov) with a wealth of information about any park in the system, as well as plenty of other details about the agency, including employment and volunteer opportunities. The site has links to National Park Cooperating

Associations, not-for-profit partner organizations that operate bookstores in many parks and that offer a wide variety of publications, maps, audiovisual programs, and park-related merchandise. For downloadable maps and other information on many NPS sites, see their cartographic division at www.nps.gov/carto. If you don't have access to the Internet, you can obtain information about parks, including mailing addresses and phone numbers, in the guidebooks listed in the previous section.

National Parks Conservation Association is a nonpartisan, nonprofit organization, which since 1919 has been the leading voice of the American people in the fight to safeguard our National Park System. NPCA, its members, and its partners work together to protect the park system and preserve our nation's natural, historical, and cultural heritage for future generations. Members receive the group's excellent magazine, *National Parks*. You can obtain information about the organization and learn about current national park issues at www.npca.org, by writing to NPCA at 1300 19th St., N.W., Suite 300, Washington, DC 20036, or by phoning 800-628-7275. Their website is also a great source of information to help plan your next visit to a national park or to take action to help protect these beloved places.

National Geographic Society, 1145 17th Street N.W. Washington, DC 20036. For general information, write to National Geographic Society, P.O. Box 98199, Washington, DC 20090-8199 (www.nationalgeographic.com) For online store and catalog orders, call (888) 225-5647 or write to P.O. Box 10041, Des Moines, IA 50340. In addition to their famous magazine, maps and books, they publish a variety of trail maps and topographic maps of national parks and similar areas. Some maps are also available on CD-ROM, as printed versions, and as "interactive topographic maps" for GPS users. Their materials are also available at a number of retail outlets around the country and from third-party vendors at many websites.

The Association of National Park Rangers is "an organization created to communicate for, about and with park rangers, and to promote and enhance the park ranger profession and its spirit. Membership of ANPR is comprised of individuals who are entrusted with and committed to the care, study, explanation and/or protection of those natural, cultural and recreational resources included in the National Park System, and persons who support these efforts." The organization publishes a quarterly magazine, *Ranger*. See their website, www.anpr.org or contact them at P.O. Box 108, Larned, KS 67550-0108 or by phone at (620) 285-2107.

National Association for Search and Rescue, 4500 Southgate Place, Suite 100, Chantilly, VA 20151-1714, phone: (703) 222-6277 or (888) 893-7788. Their website (www.nasar.org) notes that "NASAR is a not-for-profit membership association dedicated to advancing professional, literary, and scientific knowledge in fields related to search and rescue. NASAR is comprised of thousands of paid and non-paid professionals interested in all aspects of search and rescue—the humanitarian cause of saving lives—throughout the United States and around the world . . . 'that others may live.'" The website has an online bookstore and is a good source of information about search-and-rescue topics, including training materials. It also provides good links to many other sites relating to search-and-rescue and emergency services. You can also order materials by calling their bookstore at (888) 893-7788.

The Bureau of Land Management (BLM) is an agency within the U.S. Department of the Interior that administers 261 million acres of America's public lands, located primarily in twelve western states. Their areas provide a variety of recreational opportunities. More information is available at www.blm.gov/.

The United States Forest Service is another federal agency that is a major provider of outdoor recreation opportunities. See their website at www.fs.fed.us/ for more information.

The National Weather Service website (www.nws.noaa.gov/) is a good source of weather information for any area of the country. Check the forecast prior to heading out on your next trip to a park—or anywhere else in the United States.

Acknowledgments

Appreciation is gratefully expressed to the following individuals and agencies who provided some of the photographs or information used in this book: Telfair H. Brown, Sr., United States Coast Guard Imagery Branch; Dan Burgette, Grand Teton National Park; John Craig, Bureau of Land Management; Deny Galvin, retired National Park Service employee and former Acting Director of the NPS; Bill Halainen, National Park Service, long-time editor of the NPS "Morning Report;" Antonia Hedrick, Bureau of Land Management; Troy James Hurtubise, Project Troy; Clay Jordan, Shenandoah National Park; Mike Litterst, Colonial National Historical Park; Bob McKeever, retired National Park Service ranger; George Minnigh, Great Smoky Mountains National Park; Jeremy Moore, Bureau of Reclamation; Leslie Paige, Lake Mead National Recreation Area; Mike Quinn, Grand Canyon National Park; National Park Service Office of Public Affairs, Photographic Archives; Patty Shafer, Rocky Mountain National Park; Terry Traywick, Buffalo National River; and, Dick Young, retired National Park Service ranger.

I would like to express my gratitude to the staff at Taylor Trade Publishing who were instrumental in making this book a reality. Special thanks go to Jehanne Schweitzer for her superb work in coordinating the whole project as Production Editor, Mandy Phillips for her help in the editorial and promotion efforts, and Katherine Smith for her work as the Publicist. Patti Miller and Carol Babylon added their skills as copy editor and proofreader, and my local proofreader Edith V. Oates provided a valuable extra set of eyes. Most of all, thanks to Rick Rinehart for seeing potential in the work of a new author, and who went far beyond what was required to offer expert advice and encouragement throughout the entire effort.

It was initially my intention to mention by name colleagues from the National Park Service who were part of the stories in this book or who were instrumental in shaping my career during 30 years with that agency. I quickly realized that space would not allow a complete list, so rather than omit anyone I offer an inadequate but heartfelt thanks to all of you—and your families—who served alongside me as co-workers, supervisors, mentors, and friends. Many of you truly gave meaning to the concept of the National Park Service family.

Finally, neither this book nor my work as a ranger would have been possible without the patience, encouragement, and support of parents, siblings, and other loved ones who often found themselves half a continent away from us due to my job. Most of all, to my wife and best friend Velma, our daughter Kathy, and son David: This book is dedicated to you, with love and gratitude for all those years in remote and sometimes difficult places to live, for the cross-country moves which interrupted your lives, and for all of those times when my roles as dad and husband were interrupted by the demands of rangering. I can only say I couldn't have done it without you!

Sources Quoted

Appreciation is gratefully expressed to the following authors, publishers, and organizations for permission to quote selected passages from copyrighted material:

Introduction, quote from Will Henry, *Chiricahua*, New York: Leisure Books, 1997, page 10. Copyright agent: Golden West Literary Agency. Used by permission.

Chapter 7, "Back It Up Right Here." Royal Navy Corporate Communications, United Kingdom, for the quote from Admiral of the Fleet Sir David Beatty.

Chapter 18, quote describing the Ig Noble Prize from the website for that award, www.improbable.com/ig/what-are.html.

Chapter 18, quote from *A Field Guide to the Mammals*, 3rd ed. Copyright 1952, 1964, 1976 by William Henry Burt and the Estate of Richard Phillip Forssenheider. Reprinted by permission of Houghton Mifflin Company. All Rights Reserved.

Chapter 31, "Crime Still Doesn't Pay." MIStupid.com, The Online Knowledge Magazine, for the definition of the term "bozone" on their web page "Contemporary Vocabulary 2003," posted at www.mistupid.com/people/page063.htm.

Chapter 34, quote by Deny Galvin, former Acting Director of National Park Service, which appeared in the "Quote of the Week" feature, June 4, 2001, issue of *U.S. News and World Report*, Copyright 2001, U.S. News and World Report, L.P. Reprinted with permission.

Appendix, quote describing the mission of the National Association for Search and Rescue from their website, www.nasar.org, used with permission.

How to Contact the Author or Order Additional Copies of *Hey Ranger!*

Perhaps you've experienced or know about an outdoor "misadventure" you'd like to share for possible use in a sequel to this book, on our website or for other educational purposes. Your stories don't have to be limited to national parks—such situations can occur virtually anywhere in the out-of-doors. If so, I'd enjoy hearing from you. Along with your information, just let me know how I can contact you in case I need to clarify any details. If I use your story, you can remain anonymous if you prefer! I'd also welcome your comments or suggestions about this book. You can write or e-mail me at the address shown below.

Need additional copies of this book for yourself or friends? If your local bookstore didn't stock enough copies, they should be able to obtain them for you. If you'd rather order them yourself you'll find all the necessary details on our website (www.heyranger.com), or just request that information from me at the following address:

Jim Burnett
P.O. Box 1519
Athens, TX 75751
e-mail: heyranger@earthlink.net
On the Internet at: www.heyranger.com